RESEARCHING CULTURE

RESEARCHING CULTURE

Qualitative Method and Cultural Studies

PERTTI ALASUUTARI

SAGE Publications
London • Thousand Oaks • New Delhi

© Pertti Alasuutari 1995

This edition first published 1995

An earlier version of this book was published in Finnish as
Laadullinen tutkimus by Vastapaino, Tampere, 1993, ©
Pertti Alasuutari 1993.

SAGE Publications Ltd
6 Bonhill Street
London EC2A 4PU

SAGE Publications Inc
2455 Teller Road
Thousand Oaks, California 91320

SAGE Publications India Pvt Ltd
32, M-Block Market
Greater Kailash – I
New Delhi 110 048

British Library Cataloguing in Publication data

A catalogue record for this book is available from the
British Library.

ISBN 0 8039 7830 8
ISBN 0 8039 7831 6 pbk

Library of Congress catalog card number 95-69791

Typeset by Photoprint, Torquay, Devon
Printed in Great Britain by The Cromwell Press Ltd,
Broughton Gifford, Melksham, Wiltshire

Contents

Acknowledgements

The ideas and thoughts presented in this book have a long history. First, the ideas took their overall shape during the past ten years or so when I have, based on my own and others' research experience, taught qualitative research methods and supervised theses. During that time innumerable people have commented on my ideas and texts I have published, and with their own texts and research examples they have given me new incentives. I couldn't name the individuals, but am very grateful to them all. In the subsequent phases several people have helped and supported me. As I compiled my lectures and notes into a textbook in Finnish (*Laadullinen tutkimus*, Vastapaino 1993), the manuscript, or parts of it, was read and commented on by Merja Kinnunen, Jukka Mäkelä, Anssi Peräkylä, Hannu Ruonavaara and Eero Suoninen. The third stage, preparing the English edition at hand, meant considerable revisions to the Finnish manuscript. Oftentimes, with the sincere objective of translating a chapter or checking the correctness of a translation, I ended up rewriting considerable parts of it. David Kivinen, Hannu Tervaharju and Ilkka Tiitinen translated parts of the Finnish edition and checked the language of the parts I had translated or written anew. Karen Armstrong, Jaber Gubrium and David Silverman went through the whole manuscript and made me clarify my thoughts and language. Thank you all very much. I also want to extend my gratitude to the University of Tampere, which has given me financial support, first for writing the Finnish language 'ancestor', and later for preparing this book.

1

Introduction

Reading methodology textbooks is not always a particularly fun job. A good comparison is trying to learn the rules of a grammar. If you don't know the language, it cannot be learned by just memorizing the grammar and the dictionary. Many grammars are so full of exceptions that the main rule does not get you very far in practical speech situations. Even precisely formulated rules are hard to understand or apply in practice before one has learned some of the language by a natural method. On the other hand, if one has mastered the language, it seems silly to read formulations of the rules one has learned to follow by intuition. What is more, spoken language does not always honour formal rules, so that one's own experience is in contradiction to the grammar.

You may even question why you are reading a methodology book. Some textbooks on qualitative and ethnographic research are little more than collections of anecdotes about the writer's personal experiences. Some of these experiences are enlightening, others just colourful. Many practical pieces of advice are so tied to the researcher's own, often implicit, theoretical framework that they may be misleading for a person with a different theoretical orientation.

Yet methodology textbooks are needed. Although you really learn the art of doing research only through your own experience, it saves a lot of time to use other studies as models and examples. It is even more efficient to read a book of examples, such as the typical textbooks in qualitative research methods. Formulating general rules and their applications is at least a sensible way to organize the research examples into a logical order. And by understanding general rules of methodology, the reader can distance him- or herself from the examples themselves so that applying them becomes easier. A qualitative research process is always to some extent unique; it creatively applies the basic rules and often also creates new ones. In this respect methodology textbooks are useful because they sum up the state of the art in a field of study: by presenting one's own line of reasoning in light of the rules as they are formulated in the textbooks it is easier to argue for its logic and sense.

A Cultural Studies Perspective

In the book at hand I try my best to avoid the impression of a dry grammar by giving concrete research examples. Admittedly this book relies on my own experience with qualitative research and cultural studies. That can be seen for instance in those research examples which are derived from my own and my Finnish colleagues' studies. However, I have tried to avoid the danger of particularism by formulating the lessons I have learned into more general rules of methodology.

Yet, I do not claim a universal status for the way in which stages of qualitative research are defined in this book. The aim of the book is to present the spectrum of qualitative methods as they are informed by the analytic perspective of cultural studies. It is unique in this regard because these methods are usually linked to symbolic interactionism, ethnomethodology or, if a technical survey of the area, to no analytic perspective at all. On the other hand, the view of qualitative research presented in this book could quite as well be called social constructionist. In my view, qualitative analysis always deals with the concept of culture and with explaining meaningful action. To me cultural studies means that one takes culture seriously, without reducing it to a mere effect or reflection of, for instance, economy. On the other hand, cultural studies treats culture and systems of meaning in connection with questions of power and politics. This means that one should not be content with just making new observations about qualitative data with the methods borrowed from the humanities. Such observations must be put to use in explaining or at least problematizing social phenomena. In this sense I see cultural studies – and qualitative methods, as they are approached and developed in this book – as a bridge between the humanities and the social sciences.

What does the cultural studies perspective offer to qualitative research? Theoretically, it does not *oppose* symbolic interactionism or ethnomethodology. Actually they were both, along with other trends such as French structuralism, important ingredients in its development. But the real gist of cultural studies is to *make use* of all useful theories and methods in order to gain insights about the phenomena one studies. By avoiding the accusation of being eclectic, one may end up being theoretically correct but intellectually boring. Instead of that, cultural studies starts from the idea that theories and methods should become not blinders but additional viewpoints on reality. Cultural studies methodology has often been described by the concept of *bricolage* : one is pragmatic and strategic in choosing and applying different methods and practices. The cultural studies perspective emphasizes that the real objective of research should not be to repeat old 'truths', it is to find out about new points that contribute to the scientific and public discourse on social phenomena.

The Aims of the Book

My personal history as a researcher began with participant observation case-studies – much in the way anthropologists are supposed to pass their rite of passage. Although I am still a believer in fieldwork, I have subsequently had experience with analyzing unstructured personal interviews and cultural artefacts, and with applying various kind of methods, including quantitative analysis of qualitative data. The object of study has always been the reason for my search for new methods. Although I believe cultural forms are perhaps best grasped with the means of participant observation, in a complex society many interesting and focal phenomena do not take place in communities where fieldwork methods can be best applied.

In my personal history, moving from traditional fieldwork methods to experimenting with quantitative analysis of qualitative data, I seem to share many others' experiences. In fact the whole division into qualitative and quantitative research is increasingly often challenged – and blurred. The international discussion on qualitative methods and methodology that took place in the 1980s has created a lot of methodological solutions that cannot, without using violence, be classified as belonging to either of the two supposed types of research. For instance, David Silverman (1985, 138–155) presents studies where the counting of cases, percentages and even statistical relations is used alongside qualitative analysis in drawing conclusions from the data. Also Charles Ragin (1989), with his 'method of qualitative comparison' based on Boolean algebra, moves beyond the dichotomy. And in microsociology many researchers have adopted approaches, from, for instance, sociolinguistics, where argumentation is based on statistical relations between 'variables'.

From the perspective of this methodological development the traditional social survey can be seen in a new light; it has to be placed in a larger context. Survey analysis does not have to be subscribed to as a total package, including random sampling from a population, a structured questionnaire, the coding of variables describing an individual person, and statistical analysis of the relations between them. The observation unit can be other than the individual, even when the data are composed of personal interviews. The generalizability of results can be shown in other ways than those based on random sampling. There is a lot of good in the quantitative approach as long as it is not used in the standard fashion. In choosing a method one does not have to buy a whole concept of science.

The same applies to qualitative research. It does not always have to mean either the traditional fieldwork based on ethnograpic participant observation or in-depth interviews of a relatively small number of individuals. Interviewing techniques should be thought of much more in connection with the particular case in mind, and the degree of structure in the interviews can vary according to the particular needs. Material can also be produced in innumerable other ways, or already existing data, such as newspaper articles, books, advertisements and movies, can be analyzed. Whatever is chosen as data, they can of course be analyzed in numerous ways. There is no limit to the possibilities and combinations of the methods of analysis.

The book at hand is particularly aimed at giving an overview of these possibilities. It discusses different perspectives on qualitative material, and ways of conceiving the relation between the researcher and other people

involved. Practical instructions about data management and other tech-
nicalities are given minor weight, and they are always related to the
approach being discussed. Instead, different forms of textual analysis, such
as semiotics, discourse analysis, conversation analysis and rhetoric, are
introduced. In introducing and giving examples of different methodological approaches to qualitative data, usually found only in books and
journals specialized in the respective fields of inquiry, this book serves as a
first aid kit, giving new inspiration, showing where the approaches lead and
how they can be applied in producing new observations about the data. In
that sense it is useful for people planning to do qualitative research, or for
those who already have done their fieldwork but look for new angles on the
material. Those interested in applying a particular method may then
consult further literature on the subject.

I have paid special attention to discussing the *use* of new methods, many
of them derived from the humanist disciplines, to social sciences and
cultural studies; not to treat the observations that can be gained through
them as end-products. Accordingly, chapter 10 is devoted to discussing
how the observations, whatever ways they are produced, are used as clues
in answering the why-(and how)-questions which are at the heart of all
scientific inquiry.

In addition to the methodological side, I have placed emphasis on
writing as an integral part of a qualitative research process. Here, writing is
not a last, separate stage when the researcher 'reports' on the investigation
done. Instead, qualitative research is a textual process through and
through, and a text is all that is left of it for later generations. Therefore,
the last chapter is devoted to the writing process and the rhetorics of social
scientific prose.

As mentioned, I see books on methodology as summaries of the state of
the art in a field of inquiry. This also goes for the book at hand. It attempts
to be a grammar, not a lawbook, of qualitative analysis. I have tried to lay
bare and, by making sense of them, to formulate the rules one follows in
qualitative research. In that sense the book presents a theory of qualitative
methodology. Yet I am sure there are also other ways of speaking the
language of qualitative analysis and new concepts can be created. The case
examples of research designs and qualitative data analysis discussed here
should be understood not as normative rules but rather as food for
thought, to be chewed when working with one's own research design and
material. Certainly, there are also methodological rules of thumb that one
should follow in qualitative research. However, in science there is no
substitute for creative thinking and normatively unbound reasoning.

The Organization of the Book

This book is divided into three parts. Part I, 'Qualitative Research and
Cultural Studies', discusses the main concepts, such as what one means by

qualitative research and qualitative analysis, and how that links up with cultural studies. In chapter 2, I present the theory of the two main stages of qualitative research which explains why part II is called the 'Production of Observations', and part III 'Unriddling'. Namely, part II introduces different ways of actively producing observations of the data; of applying methods whose general task is to enable one to see more than one does with the 'naked eye'. Then, part III, 'Unriddling', discusses various questions related to solving the 'case': how one uses all the observations made about the data in order to say something worthwhile about the phenomenon being studied.

The chapters of part II illustrate two main perspectives on qualitative data. Within the factist perspective, discussed in chapter 5, one considers qualitative data as informants' statements about the reality one studies. However, within the 'specimen' perspective, variants of which are discussed in chapters 6, 7, 8 and 9, one treats the data as specimens, *part of* the reality being studied. One analyzes the nature and structure of that reality, for instance a narrative or a recorded discussion, and maybe makes inferences about other reality on the basis of the specimen. Chapter 10 discusses quantitative analysis of qualitative data as still another observations-producing method, which can be used regardless of whether the data are considered from the factist or specimen perspectives.

Part III discusses the qualitative research process as a whole: how a 'case' is solved and presented. Chapter 11 discusses how one *makes* a case by generating why-questions so that one can then tackle them. Chapter 12 then discusses how one guarantees and argues for the more general relevance of the results of data analysis. Chapter 13 discusses how qualitative research proceeds as a process. Finally, chapter 14 deals with presentational questions: how one makes the points of the research in a convincing and interesting way.

PART I

QUALITATIVE RESEARCH AND CULTURAL STUDIES

2

What is Qualitative Research?

The lay notion of science and scientific research has been largely formed on the basis of natural science. The model for so-called 'survey analysis' (Rosenberg 1968) is often understood as a simulation or application of the classic scientific experiment. This is why it is natural that survey research offers the exemplar for what social research is conceived to be both by the general public and by many of those who have studied in the field. Another reason for the survey's role as the exemplar of social research is the dominant position it has held for so long. All essential elements of survey research – such as sampling technique and the theory of hypothesis-testing – were developed by the 1930s and well-established in American social research in the 1950s. For instance, in Finland right after the Second World War the general public became familiar with the 'Gallup studies' which mainly reported on opinion polls dealing with politics. From the 1950s onwards the social survey was adopted as the prime method of 'modern' empirical sociology.

Can qualitative research be considered as an alternative method in social research, as a set of methods and procedures that are quite comparable with quantitative methods? This is how the issue is often understood and also deliberately marketed by the proponents of qualitative methods. In the methodology section of the university curricula, for instance, there are often two courses, one on 'quantitative' and another on 'qualitative' methods.

This dichotomy and opposition is attractive in its simplicity. Methodology in the social sciences is divided into a two-party system, in which all can choose sides according to their preferences. Yet this division fits badly with reality. All scientific and social scientific research has shared principles, such as an attempt towards logical reasoning and objectivity in the sense that researchers rely on their data rather than on their personal views or value preferences.

Secondly, it is indeed possible to make a distinction between qualitative and quantitative analysis, but both can be quite well applied in the same study and in analyzing the same data. Moreover, as will be shown in this book, in a sense qualitative and quantitative analysis can be seen as a continuum, not as opposites or mutually exclusive models of analysis.

The human sciences cannot be divided into quantitative and qualitative methods. What people mostly refer to when they talk about this dichotomy is research based on social surveys and survey analysis as opposed to 'other' research. 'Qualitative methods' has become a convenient phrase depicting the 'other' procedures and methods. Since that is the origin of the concept, it is understandable that within this grey area surrounding the paradigmatic centre of the social survey one encounters a colourful mix of practices and discourses referred to as 'qualitative methods'. Traditionally, the notion of fieldwork – entering a field, doing participant observation and interviewing informants – has served as the exemplar or key image that has organized and held together those practices and discourses. However, recently different forms of textual analysis and other methods borrowed from neighbouring disciplines have shattered this key image. Moreover, anthropologists and other social scientists have started to question the whole concept of a 'field'.

In light of all this, should we simply condemn the whole concept of qualitative research? Despite the arbitrary origins of the concept, I suggest that it makes sense to talk about qualitative analysis and qualitative research. Qualitative analysis – as opposed to quantitative analysis – is the key concept here, whereas qualitative research refers to the research process as a whole. Let us discuss this in more detail.

By qualitative analysis I mean reasoning and argumentation that is not based simply on statistical relations between 'variables', by which certain objects or observation units are described. In other words, when using qualitative analysis as a means to explain or make sense of a phenomenon we do not use as evidence the frequencies with which something occurs together with another. Instead, riddle-solving provides a good analogy of the type of reasoning employed. Consider the following example: 'What is in the morning on four, in the daytime on two, and in the evening on three legs?' This riddle, describing the human life span, illustrates the basic idea of unriddling. Any single hint or clue could apply to several things, but the more hints there are to the riddle, the smaller the number of possible solutions. Yet each hint or piece of information is of its own kind and equally important; in unriddling – or qualitative analysis – one does not count odds. Every hint is supposed to fit in with the picture offered as the solution.

A riddle as the model for scientific data analysis may seem a bit unorthodox because we are so used to considering the scientific experiment as the textbook example: the experiment where one – often in a laboratory – controls for all irrelevant factors in order to find out about the real causal relations between variables. On the other hand, qualitative analysis cannot be equated with riddle-solving, because the way it is defined here would mean that it is an aspect of all science and logical reasoning. Consider a sociological study solely based on quantitative analysis: at some point the significant relations between variables are supposed to be used as clues in support of a theory about the phenomenon being studied. To talk about qualitative analysis we must assume that there is 'first-level' unriddling involved: that the clues used are not the result of statistical analysis.

With that qualification in mind, we can say that by qualitative research we refer to studies that include qualitative analysis. This means that qualitative research is seen as one sector of the grey area of approaches and methodological solutions surrounding the social survey. The larger area houses a colourful group of answers to methodological problems; solutions where this or that rule of the social survey is followed, without subscribing to the whole set. However, all these methods and practices cannot be called qualitative research without obscuring and losing all sense of the concept. Consider, for instance, the studies where transcribed unstructured interviews, other texts or visual data are afterwards coded to a form that is quite comparable to coded questionnaire data, and where the sole method is statistical analysis. This kind of research cannot be called qualitative simply because of the form in which the data were gathered, not even if occasional excerpts from the raw data are picked out to illustrate the findings. To call a study qualitative research it must be assumed that inferences based on purely qualitative analysis, or other references to excerpts or cases in the data, are used as clues in solving the riddle. However, this definition of qualitative research does not rule out the possibility that quantitative analysis of qualitative data, or even a social survey, is used alongside qualitative analysis.

Because of the familiarity and exemplary role of the social survey, the best way to get an initial picture of qualitative research is by first discussing what the social survey is all about, and what is the particular way in which quantitative analysis attempts to achieve the goal of all scientific research – that is, to make reality answer the questions posed by the researcher. Thereafter, it is easier to see how the same goal is approached in qualitative research. By way of conclusion I will then compare the social survey and qualitative research.

The Principle of Quantitative Analysis

In quantitative analysis argumentation is based on numbers and on systematic, statistical relations between the numbers. Naturally the starting point for this is that the data are transformed – except for the rare cases in which this is already so – into a table format. This means that the observation units are given values in different *variables*. These variables are not always numbers but – when we talk about a nominal variable – may be letter symbols. This is the case when we talk about gender: according to this variable an individual, serving as the observation unit, may be given the value w = woman and m = man. The values could also be numbers, for instance 1 = woman, 2 = man, but they are nevertheless treated as nominal variables in the sense that one cannot compute a mean figure for them or say, for instance, that the average person in this data is 60 per cent female. The observation units are given values in several variables, and the idea of the analysis is to find statistical relations between the variables.

The general principle of quantitative analysis can be compared to the scientific experiment in the natural sciences. In the classic controlled experiment, we start from the hypothesis that an *independent variable* has an effect on a *dependent variable*. If we were to study the effect of sand on the slipperiness of a surface, an experiment could be set up where we measure the distance that a puck, pushed forward with the same force, travels along a surface that is first clean and then sanded. The independent variable would be 'sandiness' (1 = no sand, 2 = sanded), and the dependent variable would be 'slipperiness', measured by the distance the puck slides. The experiment could be organized so that the value of the dependent variable would be measured *before* and *after* the dependent variable (in this case the sand) is allowed to affect the phenomenon being studied. In this case we could conduct 20 tests without sand and another 20 tests with sand added. The effect of the sand would be measured by subtracting the mean value of the dependent variable gained with the clean surface from the mean value of the dependent variable with the sanded surface. Plus or minus would indicate whether or not the sand would make the surface more slippery.

In the social science application of the classic experiment one often also talks about an *experiment group* and a *control group*. In this example it could mean that one wants to exclude the possible effect of changing conditions, such as humidity, on the measurements. Thus the surface would be divided into two areas. We would conduct 20 tests on both areas of the surface, adding sand only to one area, and then repeat the same two times 20 tests.

In addition to this, in a classic controlled experiment there are typically different *test variables* or intervening variables, in this case the fineness of the sand, the mass of the puck and the smoothness of its base, and the qualities of the surface. With the help of the test variables one tries to formulate a general law, mathematical formula or a reason for the action. In the simplest form the test variables help us make sure that the causal relations are real, not only apparently so.

Often the social survey imitates a scientific experiment. To illustrate this, let us take a research example (Rosenberg 1968, 24–26) of a study examining the link between age and listening to religious radio programmes. The data were presented as in table 2.1. The table could be interpreted by saying that age has an effect on listening to religious programmes. However, often variables are associated with other ones in such a way that there only *appears* to be a causal relation between the supposed independent and dependent variable. It may turn out that it can be explained by another intervening variable, associated with the supposed independent variable. This was the case in the research example. Different

Table 2.1   *Age and listening to religious programmes (per cent)*

Listen to religious programmes	Young listeners	Old listeners
Yes	17	26
No	83	74

Source: Rosenberg 1968, 25

Table 2.2   *Age and listening to religious programmes, by education (per cent)*

Listen to religious programmes	High education Young	Old	Low education Young	Old
Yes	9	11	29	32
No	91	89	71	68

Source: Rosenberg 1968, 25

generations also differ from each other in terms of their mean educational level. That is why it made sense to check whether the relation between age and listening to religious programmes would hold in spite of educational level. To do that, another table was computed (table 2.2). This table can be interpreted to mean that when education is held constant, there is no relation between age and listening to religious programmes. Thus educational level is the actual independent variable. In this way, by operationalizing variables and by analyzing the values a variable acquires in different classes of another variable, one can test different hypotheses.

By illustrating the logic of survey analysis with the example discussed above, I do not mean to say that to use the survey method implies that the researcher represents a mechanistic and deterministic theory of social phenomena. The nature of survey analysis as an application of statistics does not by any means force the researcher into conceiving of the relations between variables as causal relationships. The relations studied may also be considered as other types of interrelation, without even assuming that there is a primary causal factor to be found. For instance, the French sociologist Pierre Bourdieu (1984) has applied survey analysis in this less deterministic fashion. As he puts it:

> One has to take the relationship itself as the object of study and scrutinize its sociological significance (*signification*) rather than its statistical 'significantness' (*significativé*); only in this way is it possible to replace the relationship between a supposedly constant variable and different practices by a series of different *effects* – sociologically intelligible constant relationships which are simultaneously revealed and concealed in the statistical relationships between a given indicator and different practices. (1984, 22)

Even if one analyzes the relationships between different variables by the practice known as *elaboration*, described above, this does not imply that one should conceive of the relationship between the independent and the dependent variable as mechanical and deterministic. Consider the finding made in the example above that educational level is the independent variable that explains listening to religious programmes. The researcher could use that finding as one lead pointing toward a theory-of-action interpretation of the phenomenon, for instance by arguing that people doing mental work are less likely to use the radio as a background voice and are, for that reason, less likely to listen to religious radio programmes.

It is also typical of the social survey that the question of generalization is mainly dealt with by using random sampling in gathering the data. In other words, the researcher defines the group of people or other observation units, the *population*, to which the results can be generalized. From this population the researcher takes a *sample* which can be assumed to represent the population.

In quantitative analysis, argumentation is based on average relations, and the starting point for all this is the search for differences between observation units in terms of different variables. The observation units may be individuals or larger groups of people, such as populations in different regions or countries. Just as easily observation units can be time-spans or, say, cultural products, such as newspapers. The principle, however, is always the same: quantitative analysis is based on finding statistical regularities in the way different variables are associated with each other. In quantitative analysis, what is *common* to all observation units does not give any clue whatsoever about the phenomenon to be explained; it is automatically ruled outside the methodological possibilities. What is common to all units in the sample is a characteristic of the *population*, and the limits of the population define the limits to generalizations. It is irrational to ask why, in a social survey based on a random sample of women living in an area, all are actually women. Similarly, if all respondents would have given the same answer to a question, for instance that women have less power than men, the finding could not be explained or interpreted with the help of the data. It would be an interesting finding in itself, but the data would not support argumentation based upon statistical logic that would otherwise support an interpretation about the reasons for this unanimous opinion. Because survey analysis is based on explaining differences between observation units by referring to other variables, the variables have to make a difference.

The Phases of Qualitative Analysis

Qualitative analysis differs in a number of respects. In it, the data are often considered as a totality; they are thought to shed light on the structure of a singular logical whole. Even when the data are comprised of separate observation units, such as individuals or personal interviews, argumentation cannot be based on the differences between individuals in terms of different 'variables'. Qualitative analysis requires an absoluteness that differs from statistical research. One has to be able to explain all reliable pieces of information known to belong to the figure or mystery being solved in such a way that they are not in contradiction with the interpretation presented.[1] As we know, this is not the case in statistical research, where exceptions to the general rule are allowed. When, in the research example discussed in the previous section, it was concluded that a high educational level diminishes an individual's interest in religious programmes, it by no means implies that in the sample there are frequent listeners of religious programmes with a high education, or atheists who have only gone to primary school.

Unlike survey analysis, statistical probabilities are not accepted as clues in qualitative analysis. Often the number of observation units is just too small. Since a single unstructured personal interview easily adds up to 30 pages of transcribed text, it is seldom sensible or possible in terms of research resources to conduct so many interviews that the differences between individuals would be statistically significant.

However, qualitative analysis is not done simply because the resources available are, for one reason or another, too scarce for quantitative analysis. In qualitative analysis a great number of observation units and statistical thinking are neither needed nor possible. Let us consider a historical study of the reasons for the Second World War. There are no historical situations that differ in terms of certain variables, nor is it possible to reconstruct any so that in some of them the war would break out and in others it would not. The analysis and the argumentation of the suggested interpretations have to be based on analyzing this one single case.

Historical research has been characterized as idiographic, as opposed to nomothetic, research. Unlike nomothetic research, in an idiographic study one tries to make sense of a single chain of events or phenomenon, without thinking that the solution should represent a general causal law (for the concepts, see Allport 1937, 1962; Runyan 1984, 166–191). If the pair of concepts has any meaning at all, it could make a difference between research based on the idea of random sampling as a way to achieve empirical generalizations, on the one hand, and research aiming at making sense of observations related to a single case, on the other. That does not mean that an *explanatory model* developed by the latter, idiographic, type of study could not hold also in other cases. If the concepts are defined in this way, it can be said that qualitative research often includes both idiographic and nomothetic elements.

---

[1] Renvall (1965) characterizes the work of the historian in a similar fashion by speaking about formulating structural wholes. By a structural whole he means a group of phenomena that share a rule-bound relation, and there is no exception to the rule. If a researcher meets with an exception, he or she has to reformulate the rule, so that the new case is in concert with it.

Qualitative analysis consists of two phases: the *purification of observations* and *unriddling*. This distinction can only be made analytically; in practice they are always intertwined.

The Purification of Observations

In the purification of observations we can distinguish two phases. First, the material is always only observed from *a particular theoretical and methodological point of view*. To find that particular viewpoint it is often useful to thematize the material from as many angles as possible, but when the choice is made one has to be systematic. When studying the material we only pay attention to what is 'essential' in view of the theoretical framework and the particular questions asked, although even in the same study the material can be perceived from several angles. In any case, in this way the text corpus or the visual material is purified into a more manageable set of separate 'raw observations'. The idea of the second phase of the purification of observations is to further reduce the amount of data by *combining* observations. Separate raw observations are combined into a single observation or at least a smaller number of observations. This is achieved by finding a common denominator or by formulating a rule which, from a particular point of view, applies without exception to all data.

Consider the number series 27, –9, 45, 81 and –36. In order to combine these observations into a single observation we could note that 9 is a common denominator in all of the figures. Similarly, consider material consisting of interviews of people who have moved to the countryside. If some people regard friendly relations with the neighbours as a desirable aspect of country living, while others complain about the lack of privacy, then these statements can be combined by saying that the interviewees share the conception of close neighbour relations.

The starting point for the combining of observations is, in other words, the idea that in the material there are specimens of the same phenomenon. An example of this can be seen when the material consists of news stories from newspapers where the objective is to determine the macrostructure of the news. The same procedure is followed by a student in cultural studies analyzing narratives in order to see if they represent the same narrative structure or how many different structures can be distinguished in the corpus. The construction of a typology of social action is also based on the same idea. The individuals or their separate acts are analyzed as variants of types of social action, defined on a more general level. The data analysis of a historian, trying to puzzle out a unique episode, can also contain similar phases. The data may, for instance, include several slightly disparate accounts in which the episode is described. Using the primary method of the historian, the critical inquiry of sources, the researcher looks for elements that are common to all story variants. On the basis of them, he or she reconstructs a story of what may be assumed to have happened: if several informants independently give the same piece of information, it can usually be regarded as valid.

While qualitative analysis aims at formulating rules or structures of rules that hold throughout the data, in traditional anthropological research these formulations, combining several separate observations, refer to culture as a totality that unites individuals. Differences and 'exceptional cases' are related to the totality, which is the actual object of research. In particular, the conceptions and opinions of informants representing the same speakers' positions are scrutinized from a sufficient distance to see how they, in different ways and variants, illuminate what the researcher is interested in: namely the cosmology and *Weltanschauung* uniting the individuals.[2]

The combining of observations by looking for common features does not, however, mean that the aim of the purification of observations would be to define typical cases or average persons. One does not, for example, add the number series presented previously and then state that the mean is 21.6. Nor does one state that the majority of the figures are positive, or that the mean of the positive figures is larger than that of the negative ones. That is all typical of quantitative analysis, operating on mean figures and statistical relations. Instead, in qualitative analysis a single exception is enough to break the rule, to show that one has to rethink the whole thing. The second-level observation produced by combining several observations has to stand all raw observations without exception; in the data, there cannot be cases contradicting the 'macro-observation', the rule grasping the essence of raw observations. Often this leads to raising the level of abstraction, to a change in the theoretical framework, or at least in the point of view.

Let us return to the example about the ways in which informants speak about their neighbour relations in the countryside. If one of the informants claims to have been surprised at how few neighbours or other residents their family have become acquainted with, it cannot be said that, according to the informants, there are close neighbour relations in the countryside. According to the principles of qualitative analysis, neither can it be said that with only one exception the informants share a conception of close neighbour relations. Such a common conception does not have much weight as proof unless there are so many informants that the conception could be interpreted to represent a 'general opinion'.

---

[2] Bronislaw Malinowski (1961, 23) put this by saying that we have to study 'stereotyped manners of thinking and feeling'. By this he did not mean to suggest that a sociologist (that is the label he uses) draws caricatures of his or her objects, or presents descriptions of average persons. What he meant was that with his or her research material the researcher gives shape to the main dimensions of, and limits imposed by, the view of life of a culture, so that a person with a different cultural background can understand the local manners of thinking and feeling in a culture's own terms. 'Thus, a man who lives in a polyandrous community cannot experience the same feelings of jealousy as a strict monogynist, though he might have the elements of them.'

Should the whole interesting theme now be dropped? Not necessarily. The next steps to be taken in the analysis depend most of all on the research design within which the researcher wants to scrutinize his or her observations.

The forms of discourse we have come across so far still permit us to say that the informants' discourse about country living is structured by the frame whereby country living is perceived from the perspective of close neighbour relations. However, this can be said only on the condition that it is not the interviewer who has introduced the theme of close neighbour relations.

Another option would be to examine whether there are other qualities which set apart the exceptional informant from all others, so that the exception to the rule could be formulated as a qualifier to it. Imagine that the family with a different experience of neighbour relations has a clearly higher social ranking than the others. We would have to gather more such cases to see whether they would form a different type of family who has moved to the countryside. Provided that the lead proves correct, these two groups of families would be analyzed as two ways of family life in the country. Then, to show the relation between the two cases, we could formulate an absolute rule where the migrants with a social ranking roughly similar to that of the older residents have the experience of close neighbour relations, whereas those higher in the social hierarchy lack that experience.

Another conceivable possibility would be to study the interviews as conversations. Are there differences between the contexts in which the interviewees emphasize the closeness of neighbour relations as opposed to scarcity of contacts? In this approach, each reference to neighbour relations would be regarded as the observation unit. The task of qualitative analysis of these cases would be to formulate an absolute rule or set of rules about the interviewees' discourse on neighbour relations.

The requirement of the absoluteness of a formulated rule or rules in qualitative analysis serves two purposes. On the one hand, the requirement partly compensates for the fact that there are often so few cases that average regularities do not prove a thing. On the other hand, in qualitative analysis there is the underlying idea that by formulating a rule that holds throughout the material, the researcher tries to grasp some of the rules that people follow or take into account in their speech or other behaviour. One assumes that the regularities in people's behaviour are due to rule-following, not proof of mechanic causal laws.

Differences between people or observation units are important in qualitative research. Just like in quantitative analysis they often provide clues needed in explaining and making sense of the things being studied. And differences are not that hard to find. In one way or another every individual is unique, just like every leaf on a tree differs from every other leaf at least in some respect. On the other hand, if one concentrates on the endless diversity of life and of the data, in the end it is hard to get a hold on the phenomenon. Everything is covered by the greyness of endless differences. In qualitative analysis it is wise to be careful about making distinctions and constructing typologies: it is clear that if one creates too many divisions and types, it becomes quite difficult to formulate a rule that states how all these differences are linked to each other. Therefore, it is important in qualitative analysis to aim at purifying the raw observations into the smallest possible number of observations.

Unriddling

The second phase in qualitative analysis is *unriddling*. Often, when we talk about the methods of empirical social research, the comparable phase is known as the *interpretation* of findings. That means, for instance, that the statistical relations between variables are given an interpretation by referring to theoretical models, hypotheses and findings derived from previous research. The interpretation of statistical relations as causal relations, and their directions, could also be said to belong to this phase.

In qualitative analysis unriddling means that, on the basis of the clues produced and hints available, we give an interpretative explanation of the phenomenon being studied. Like solving riddles, we should be able to come up with an answer that should not be in contradiction with any of the observations about the case. We can distinguish different kinds of models for unriddling on the basis of the key theoretical concept.

The Weberian (Weber 1978a, 1978b), and later Parsonian (Parsons 1967), theory of social action is an obvious choice for a framework within which to explain social phenomena; particularly when we remember that Parsons meant his theory of social action as an interpretation of a common conceptual scheme that had developed in social sciences, not just of his own or Weber's theory. This overall scheme approaches social phenomena from the viewpoint of action, not from the perspective of natural laws and causality. Although observations about social phenomena, for instance results of survey analysis, are typically formulated in a way that could be given a causal interpretation, within the social action framework they are interpreted as clues about the logic of social action. Likewise, although the social and natural conditions of human existence often present themselves as causal laws, the social action scheme maintains that they do not have a causal impact on action. As Eskola puts it, although there are laws of the type 'if X, then Y' in our environment, in activity the actor '*takes into account* that if X, then Y' (1988, 168–169, emphasis added).

Within this social action umbrella scheme, there are numerous frameworks for explaining social phenomena. For instance, one may try to grasp the particular rule or rules people are supposed to follow in a particular social context, as one did in so-called 'cognitive science', or in the 'ethogenic approach' (Marsh et al. 1978). On the other hand, one may conceptualize the task in such a way that one studies the rules or discourses people take into account in their verbal or non-verbal behaviour. Furthermore, one can study the orderliness of social phenomena by analyzing the structures of meaning inherent in, for instance, myths, institutions or artefacts; and to speak of meaning or to speak of rules is to speak of the same thing, as Lévi-Strauss (1978, 12) says. To take still one more example: one can also conceive of the task of explaining social phenomena in the ethnomethodological fashion as a study of the rules people follow in interpreting each other's behaviour. The common denominator for all these trends is the attempt to find rules in the material. These rules, no matter how they are formulated as observations, are then argued to be proof of, or account for, the regularities of social life.

When the observations produced by the procedures of purification are, in the unriddling phase, weighed as clues, one often makes references to other research and literature. It may be that in a part of the study there is a data set analyzed by quantitative methods, or that the qualitative data have also been quantified so that the statistical relations found between variables are used as clues alongside those obtained by purification.

The observations gained in the purification phase, presented in the form of rules that hold true throughout the data, are not the only kinds of clue used in the unriddling phase. Unlike survey analysis, the empirical data or the 'raw observations' are not forgotten even in this phase. Instead, one studies them in order to find hints useful in suggesting interpretations, and in unriddling the whole case.

Consider again the example of people who have moved to the countryside. If we took as the starting point the 'macro-observation' that the informants conceive of life in the countryside from the point of view of the closeness of neighbour relations, then the idea in unriddling would have to do with the frames within which city life and country life are perceived and discussed in our culture. How can these frames be identified in different phenomena and topics, and how do they, in turn, help us make sense of the frames themselves? This would lead us to pay attention to many different parts, themes and topics in the informants' speech.

On the other hand, if we start unriddling from the observation that the newcomers who are in a roughly equal social position to the other residents regard the neighbour relations as being close, whereas those superior to others do not share this experience, then this could lead, together with other related observations, to an analysis of the social structure and hierarchy of country life. It would be useful to look for differences between the two groups also in terms of other factors. Are there differences in how the informants describe their hobbies, use of time, or their outlook toward social and political issues? What are the typical things that divide the country town residents into different social groupings, and how dense is interaction between the groups? In general, what seem to be the factors that increase or decrease interaction? Would there be statistics or other research available that would give support to the explanatory model constructed on the basis of the case? Could the problematic be operationalized in such a way that we would find an observation unit occurring several times in each of the interviews? By coding such units according to different variables and their values we could make tables and compute statistical relations useful in testing the hypotheses.

Often the new questions coming up during unriddling lead to new operationalizations and purification phases, but an informant's particular, unique expression may also be used as a clue. Additionally, statistics, other research and theoretical texts are referred to. The more the hints related to the mystery being solved, the more the researcher and the reader may trust in the solidity of the interpretation, in that it is not just one of several possibilities. As you know, the same goes for solving a 'case' in detective stories: if there are only a few leads, we can reconstruct several possible stories of what has happened and how the leads are linked to each other. The more clues that fit in with the explanatory model, the higher is the probability that the solution is the right one. Scientific research can never achieve certainty beyond all doubt.

Idiographic and Nomothetic Features

Compared with the purification phase, unriddling may play a larger or smaller part in qualitative research. In a study characterized as idiographic, for example in solving a single chain of events, combining raw observations is not necessarily needed that much. For instance, the source material of a historian studying the reasons for the Japanese attack on Pearl Harbor in 1941 does not consist of variants of a story describing the same event, on the basis of which the researcher would, with the help of source criticism, construct the 'authorized' version. Sources of course partly converge, and present different versions of the same incident, but even then they shed light on it from different sides. It is, however, more common that different sources give different information, bits and pieces that may be more or less reliable, and which may or may not have to do with the phenomenon, process, chain of events or other mystery being unriddled.

The same goes for a physician's diagnosis of an individual's illness, or for a psychoanalytic interpretation about the reasons for an individual's psychic symptoms. Or consider the psychohistorical study which tries to find out why Van Gogh cut off his ear (Runyan 1984). Every available observation or piece of information is of its own kind, and illuminates the mystery being unravelled from its own angle.

Also in ethnographic research, analyzing a culture or subculture, the unriddling phase carries a lot of weight at the expense of combining observations. Even though the source material may include interviews with several informants, they are not treated as variants of each other; they are unlike 'respondents', used to compute a picture of the average person in a social survey. This is also due to the fact that each interview covers slightly different topics, and individual informants are asked different questions. Every society has its own social system, with its division of labour and social hierarchy. Even the most primitive culture is divided into groups –

women and men; chiefs, religious leaders and ordinary subjects. As informants they cannot be treated as similar 'homogeneous' individuals, as observation units to be described by using certain variables. In ethnographic research they are treated as informants holding different speaker's positions, and thus able to shed light on the structural whole being studied from different points of view. Informants are also requested to talk about the history and genealogy of the community. They are asked to tell folk tales, myths and proverbs. They describe their rituals and religious beliefs. Thus the material used in unriddling is many-sided.

In cultural studies interested in modern societies, and even more generally in human science qualitative research, one often collects several versions of text as examples of the same object or theme. For instance, a researcher interested in the structure of the news story is not content with just one exemplary news story; instead, he or she refers to different types of news, to the news as a genre, and perhaps places it in some kind of a space for journalistic discourse (Kunelius 1994). People studying life-stories may take dozens of stories as their data. Qualitative research about the viewing of a television serial or a movie is usually based on several tape-recorded personal interviews or group discussions.

This does not necessarily have to be the case. For instance the study of autobiographies can be based on a single case-study or series of cases analyzed (Gubrium 1993; Hyvärinen 1994 and forthcoming). Yet, usually there are more data used even in a case-study because the researchers want to approach their theme at a more general level than that of a unique case. For example, Gubrium (1993) divides the life-stories he has gathered of nursing home residents into different types, and then discusses each story as an example of the type in question. What is more, by all these unique stories and types, he illustrates the central idea of the study. He points out that what residents say about matters such as the quality of care needs to be understood in relation to the narrative linkages each makes with experiences in and out of nursing homes. Similarly, the structure of a single news story can be analyzed quite well, but by analyzing a relatively small sample of news stories that are as different as possible we can assume that the structure of the news story found by combining the observations in the data also applies to other than just the exemplary news stories in the sample.

Thus, to analyze several 'homogeneous' observation units as examples of the same phenomenon is a means of achieving validity in qualitative research. However, it is approached by raising the level of abstraction, not by looking for an average or a typical case. In this enterprise combining observations becomes important.

The Social Survey and Qualitative Research

To sum up, there are two phases in qualitative research: purification of observations and unriddling. The social survey or quantitative content

Table 2.3   *The phases of research*

Phase	Social survey	Qualitative research
Unriddling	Elaboration; interpretation of statistical relations; references to other research and hypotheses	Interpretative explanation; references to other research and theoretical frameworks
Production of observations	Definition and coding of variables; computing of mean figures and statistical relations	Purification of observations: concentrating on 'essentials'; combination of raw observations

analysis can also be said to include the comparable two phases. The first phase, starting partly already before data collection, includes the definition of variables and codes, the coding of the data, and statistical analysis. In the second phase the findings are interpreted. Some statistical relations may be interpreted as proof of causal relations. Additionally, other information, former research, and hypotheses formed on the basis of them, are used as support in suggesting interpretations.

These two phases of research can be named the *production of observations* and *unriddling*. In what ways do these two phases – which do not necessarily follow each other in a definite temporal order in the research process – differ from each other in the social survey and in qualitative research? Let me clarify this by table 2.3, where these two are compared with each other.

In the production of observations phase both types of research use techniques which enable the reduction of the potential amount of observations into a more manageable number. In this sense a particular characteristic of the social survey is the fact that the reduction of observations is partly taken care of before data collection in designing the questionnaire. It only asks questions that interest the researcher and that are essential from the point of view of the research design, and the alternative answers are predefined. In qualitative research one also has to limit the amount of data to be gathered. For instance, in qualitative interviews or group discussions the researcher only introduces certain topics and themes that are assumed to have a connection with the theme being studied. However, in qualitative research the reduction of data is for the most part taken care of afterwards. The material to be gathered, for instance a mass of text, is rich in terms of its possibilities for analysis, but it is approached only from certain theoretically and methodologically defined points of view.

Both in survey and in qualitative research we can distinguish in the production of observations a phase where raw observations are combined to produce second-level observations. In this regard the two types of research differ from each other most clearly.

The way in which the combination of raw observations is done in qualitative research can be called the actual *qualitative analysis*. The idea is to present the raw observations in the form of rules that hold true throughout the data. The 'exceptions' are essentially important, because they force us to rethink the case, to consider what the first formulation of a rule, thought to be consistent with the data, takes for granted. This helps in reformulating the rule in question.

In the social survey raw observations are combined by applying statistical methods, so that different mean figures, correlations and other statistical test figures are used as clues. In other words, the observations describe averages and typical relations. Unlike qualitative analysis, exceptions are allowed.

There is also a lot in common between the social survey and qualitative research in the unriddling phase. In both types of research one makes references to other research, formerly tested hypotheses and relevant literature in interpreting the observations. There are differences in using the empirical data, however. In the social survey the empirical data appear in this phase only as empirical generalizations, mean figures and as other results of statistical analysis, whereas in qualitative research references to and extracts from the data are used as clues in suggesting interpretations alongside the 'macro-observations' produced by the purification of raw observations. In the references to the data one may discuss a special case in more detail, or, by using quotations as examples, the author may give a hint about a relevant interpretation, or illustrate the interpretation already made.

In the social survey such case examples are usually not used, for the simple reason that the data are too crude for it. There is no knowledge about individual cases; for example individuals only exist as a series of figures describing the values they are assigned in different variables. Sometimes answers to open-ended questions are used as illustrations. Case examples can also be taken from other studies or from novels.

Qualitative research may include quantitative analysis. There may be a separate survey data set designed for this. On the other hand, the qualitative material itself may, from the point of view of an observation unit occurring frequently in the text corpus, be coded and the variables cross-tabulated. Thus, the results of quantitative analysis may also be used as clues in unriddling. Yet an interpretative or 'social action type' explanation is the kernel of qualitative analysis.

Despite the differences between quantitative and qualitative research, as a metaphor unriddling fits, in part to all scientific research. Only the ultra-positivist version of survey analysis does without the phase of suggesting explanatory interpretations. By that I refer to an analysis based on the conviction that with the use of elaboration one finds real causal relations (education affects radio listening and not vice versa), and that such relations are mechanical and lawlike 'forces' of nature. Thus there is no need for an interpretation of the results, to ponder the reason for the statistical relationship. It presents itself as a research result in its own right, not as an observation in need of explanation.

Such a positivist paradigm is, however, a rare exception. Usually there is always the need for unriddling in scientific research. Natural scientists interpreting the results of their experiments and social researchers pondering the correlations between variables are at one point in their research in the same situation: the results of *different* experiments or analyses have to be linked with each other, to construct a whole within which individual results make sense. Often the theoretical framework employed ties the separate findings together in the predicted fashion: the study was, after all, designed to test the hypotheses derived from the theory in question. In such a case there is no problem: the meaning of the results is self-evident. But the situation is not always so problem-free. The findings may contradict the hypotheses derived from the theory, or the theory may itself have holes or anomalies. This can be regarded as a crisis in the scientific work, but science does not develop without them. If the experiments mechanically produce the predicted results, we are no longer talking about science. Rather, we are dealing with pragmatic surveys where the researchers just want to make sure that their presuppositions about this or that detail prove to be right, or where they need to know how common and how wide-spread the already known phenomenon is.

3
What is Cultural Studies?

This chapter discusses the meaning of cultural studies, especially as it is understood in this book. Such a discussion is needed, because cultural studies provides the theoretical frame and the frame of mind for the way in which social research and qualitative method are approached in this book. By being consciously and self-reflexively eclectic in theoretical terms, and pragmatic and strategic in its choice of methods, cultural studies has been important in promoting qualitative research methods. Moreover, it has spread a tolerant attitude towards the use of any methods that may be useful in making sense of what is going on, and in finding new ways of seeing things. Let us therefore discuss the main landmarks of this field called cultural studies.

A New Discipline?

It is difficult to give a simple definition of cultural studies. Initially the term referred to the tradition that was started in Britain by Richard Hoggart, E.P. Thompson and Raymond Williams in the late 1950s, which more recently has been carried on by the Centre for Contemporary Cultural Studies in Birmingham. However, since these early years the concept has evolved into a more generic term referring to a cross-disciplinary field.

Present-day cultural studies is an international intellectual movement in many ways. Since the golden years of the Birmingham Centre, many other institutions and individuals have carried on its tradition. Blundell et al. even argue that Britain no longer serves as the centre for cultural studies: 'With the advent of the Thatcher years cultural studies in England fragmented and was exported to other English-speaking locations, predominantly the United States, Australia and Canada' (1993, 6). On the other hand, present-day cultural studies has many independent roots in several countries. For instance, Janice Radway, whose work *Reading the Romance* (1984) has been considered a landmark in the field, said in a seminar presentation that she had never heard of cultural studies or the Birmingham Centre when writing it. There are also national differences in what is called cultural studies, both due to independent national roots and because of its different places in national paradigmatic fields. What Klaus Bruhn Jensen says of the Danish situation could be applied to many other countries, for instance Finland: '[Cultural studies in Denmark] is not synonymous with the configuration of social and psychoanalytic theories that were, to a degree, imported from the European continent, rearticulated in the UK, and later reexported to the American market, as an alternative to mainstream sociology and literary studies' (cited in Eskola and Vainikkala 1994, 193).

As impossible as it is to define cultural studies, it is more than just a generic term. The studies or researchers who have been, or could be, argued to represent cultural studies share a kind of 'centre position', a distancing from various forms of reductionism. 'Culture' is taken seriously, it is granted some independence, but at the same time it is emphasized that the practices and symbolics of everyday life must not be treated in isolation from questions of power and politics. Moreover, the 'linguistic turn' has played on important role in the development of cultural studies. One could also argue that cultural studies addresses the particular features and problems of present-day development in western societies and in the entire world.

We could toy with the idea that cultural studies is a new discipline, with a birth similar to that of classical sociology (or the 'voluntaristic theory of action') as described by Talcott Parsons in his study *The Structure of Social Action* (1967 [1937]). According to Parsons, the work of several individuals, including Vilfredo Pareto, Émile Durkheim and Max Weber, 'converges upon a single theory' (Parsons 1967, 722), thus forming the ascending discipline known as sociology. Similarly, it could be argued that corners of sociology, anthropology and literary criticism have been cut off or melted away to form and give space to it. The fact that cultural studies is often, and for good reason, said to be cross-disciplinary and even anti-disciplinary fits in with the picture: disciplines are seldom, if ever, carved out of one wood. In the humanities and social sciences disciplines are typically formed around a problematic, a phenomenon thought to be worthy of serious consideration. However, the institutional logic of universities tends to gradually universalize them into 'sciences', which often lose their grip on, or blur, the initial problem they were formed to deal with. The crisis of the old disciplinary field surrounding cultural studies, a crisis which would explain the rise of the new discipline, is also easy to point out. Take literary criticism: today cartoons, films, videos and television are far more important for common people than literature. Similarly, anthropology was born to study foreign cultures and less complex societies in remote places, but time and place have lost much of their meaning in the present world: the 'Other' have moved next door, and 'western' artefacts, television programmes, and economic networks have invaded practically the entire globe. Finally, sociology was born to question how the modern, industrial society should be understood, but many of the post-war, 'post-industrial' developments have evaded the conceptual net provided by established academic sociology, which in many countries became a tool for social engineering and social statistics. In a sense cultural studies could be seen as another generation of sociology; a discipline studying the present social and cultural condition, sometimes called the postmodern condition.

But what is the point in arguing that cultural studies is either cross-disciplinary or a new discipline? Such arguments may be important in science politics and administration. From a nominalist point of view, discipline is a term that is used to legitimate and institutionalize a field of study. Sometimes the rejection of a disciplinary identity, an opposition to the colonizing tendencies of existing disciplines, is, for a new field, strategically good politics. In this instance, all that counts is that getting a grasp of present social and cultural phenomena is more important than theoretical or methodological purity.

On the Concept of Culture

Could the common ground people have found in the crossroads called cultural studies be defined by a shared understanding of the concept of culture? That would make perfect sense, and partly the gist of cultural studies does lie in the way one conceives of culture and society. Yet people suggesting very different definitions of the term 'culture' can be argued to represent cultural studies.

Within the Birmingham School, where the concept of 'cultural studies' originates, the concept of culture has been taken to refer to something like *collective subjectivity* – that is, a way of life or outlook adopted by a community or a social class. This opposes the formerly predominant *hierarchic* notion, which takes culture as referring to the best and most glorious achievements of a people or civilization. However, the roots of the Birmingham School can also be traced back to research on the arts, more specifically literature, whose approaches were imported into Marxist-inspired studies of working-class culture (Thompson 1968; Williams 1961a, 1961b).

The new approach was clearly visible in one of the most significant early works of the Birmingham School that was now known as culturalism: Richard Hoggart's *The Uses of Literacy* (1958), in which the tools formerly reserved for the study of serious literature were now applied to an examination of everyday life and everyday entertainment. This shift in focus allows us to understand that even though family magazines and jukebox music enjoy less social prestige than serious literature, they are nonetheless cultural objects and in that sense comparable to Shakespeare's plays. All cultural products reflect society and everyday life, which was now to become the chief object for Hoggart's studies. Therefore, he also sets out carefully to expand the concept of culture. Culture consists no longer merely in these products and the implicit values they carry, but also 'the wider life they live'. Even though Hoggart has obvious difficulties in hiding his moralistic attitude and élitist contempt for many aspects of the objects he is studying, at least his critique is no longer grounded in abstract and universal criteria of serious art.

In later studies by the Birmingham School on youth and working-class subcultures, which used methods of ethnographic fieldwork (for example,

Clarke et al. 1979; Hall and Jefferson 1975; Willis 1977, 1978), culture referred to each group's or community's way of life and outlook on the world. In this sense the concept of culture is more or less synonymous with the concept of *habitus* as introduced by the French sociologist Pierre Bourdieu. In his study *Distinction*, Bourdieu (1984) uses a statistical data set to identify social groupings which differ from each other in terms of their distinctive life-style – that is, their habitus: they like the same kind of music, they have the same taste in food and clothes, they share the same leisure activities and hobbies. He looks at the statistical relations between the individual's life-style and preferences as an indication of the existence of a habitus that is characteristic of each social class or stratum, of a mode of activity and way of thinking that organizes the individual's everyday life. Culture, for Bourdieu, refers to the resources or to the material, the codes and frames that people use in building and articulating their own world-views, their attitudes to life and social status. This, in a sense, comes quite close to the hierarchic concept of culture: according to Bourdieu, people who occupy higher positions in the social hierarchy have more cultural capital – that is, they are more competent with a wider range of codes and with the criteria of good taste.

In spite of these conceptual differences, Pierre Bourdieu's cultural sociology and the work by the Birmingham scholars both represent cultural studies; indeed the approaches they apply are quite similar to each other. It is not the use of the term 'culture' that counts. Rather, the point is that in both of these approaches one takes a critical stance towards the hierarchic definition of culture, or a 'profane' stance towards art and high culture. Not that art or personal cultural refinement could not be studied, it is just that they are treated as socially and culturally conditioned and defined phenomena, and as such quite comparable to more mundane cultural products or hobbies.

The Meaning of Meaning

Another focal point in cultural studies is the importance it assigns to meaning, and to the mediation of social life through meanings. But what is the meaning of the concept of meaning? Obviously, the 'meaning' of something is what it 'means', but it is surprisingly difficult to move beyond this circular definition. Indeed in the literature the term has been used quite loosely, and with more than one meaning.

In empirical sociological research the concept of meaning often refers to the symbolism that is associated with specific objects or activities. In British research, a subculture is said to be distinguished from others as a 'cultural' group on the basis of the specific objects or activities to which the group has a special relationship (Willis 1978). It is through those objects and activities that the group expresses and realizes its outlook and attitude to life. This approach was also characteristic of cultural studies in Finland during the 1980s. For instance, in our studies of a local tavern (Sulkunen et al. 1985) we looked at how the pub, beer drinking and darts playing represented symbols as well as an actual realization of freedom for the male regulars.

This preoccupation with the symbolism of a certain activity or object tends to draw one's attention to deviations from everyday routine, to morally loaded and controversial questions. The everyday does not really seem to involve anything that would carry real symbolic interest. This is why cultural studies is sometimes seen as a line of work that deals with issues which as such are quite interesting but which all the same are more or less trivial and insignificant in view of the harsh realities of everyday life. This critique might well be relevant, but cultural studies does not probe into the realm of the curious just for the sake of publicity. Rather, the explanation lies in the method it applies: in its analyses of deviance and deviant phenomena cultural studies aims to uncover the way in which the everyday and social life are mediated through meanings. As such the curiosities may not be very important, but they act like a mirror or prism that throws light on the dark centre of normal everyday life. That is, a key aspect of the theoretical perspective represented by cultural studies is the view that 'meaning' is not just a quality of certain specific beings; it is not a stamp that is used for labelling certain objects. Reality is *socially construed* through and through; it is composed of interpretations of meanings and rules of interpretation on the basis of which people orientate themselves in their everyday life.

What has been said above could indeed be regarded as the *theory-of-knowledge* dimension of the concept of meaning, which forms an integral part of cultural studies. From this point of view the emphasis is on the fact that reality only exists to people through meanings. The world does not present itself to us 'as is', but always through the relationship we have to this world.

This, too, can be understood in many different ways. According to one interpretation (which for convenience could be called praxism), reality presents itself to people through the practical relationship we have with the world around us. Practice, here, refers chiefly to the way in which people produce the basic necessities of their life. Social existence determines consciousness; or base determines superstructure, as Marxism would have it. This perspective is advocated among others by materialistic anthropology (for example, Harris 1980; for a critique, see Sahlins 1976) and Marxist psychology (for example, Holzkamp 1976). The underlying assumption here is that objects in reality present themselves to us according to their *end-use*. A hammer, for instance, is seen specifically as a tool that is used for driving nails. In broader terms, this position implies the assumption that in their environment people tend to focus their attention on such beings (and from such a point of view) that have a direct relevance for their practical activity and livelihood. Here, the concept of meaning approximates that of another sociological concept – that is, *function*.

Bronislaw Malinowski, the classical anthropologist and an early representative of functionalism, believed that primitive peoples classified certain
edibles as totems because they were good (or bad) to eat; he claimed that
primitive people's interest in totemic plants and animals was inspired by
nothing but the rumbling of their stomach:

> The road from the wilderness to the savage's belly and consequently to his mind
> is very short, and for him the world is an indiscriminate background against
> which there stand out the useful, primarily the edible, species of animals and
> plants. (Malinowski 1948, 29)

Cultural studies has implied a distanciation from this sort of perspective
which underscores function. In this line of critique cultural studies has been
very much influenced by structuralist anthropology, for example, where
the argument is that the world presents itself to people through an entire
cosmology – that is, through an explanatory system that encompasses the
whole universe. According to this position, people do not only focus their
attention on those objects of reality that have a practical function for their
livelihood, but each culture has its own cosmology, a model which seeks to
explain all aspects of that world. Special attention can be given to animals
or plants that occupy a strategic place in the culture's cosmological system,
although they are of no importance to the tribe's livelihood. This view has
been presented by the French anthropologist Claude Lévi-Strauss, who
suggests this as an explanation for the incredibly detailed knowledge of
many primitive tribes about their environment. This also explains why
snakes, flies, mosquitoes or the shooting star can serve as a clan's totem. In
opposition to Malinowski and other functionalist theories of totemism, he
argues that 'natural species are chosen not because they are "good to eat"
but because they are "good to think"' (Lévi-Strauss 1963, 89). For
instance, the *Hanunóo* of the Philippines classify all forms of the local
avifauna into 75 types of birds, identify more than 60 types of fish and
classify insects into 108 named categories, 13 of which are ants and termites
(Lévi-Strauss 1966, 4).

By emphasizing the independence of culture vis-à-vis 'objective' reality,
that is, independent of the collective consciousness, cultural studies has
wanted to call into question what, in the light of common-sense thinking,
seems to be a plain and straightforward distinction between the concepts of
language and their referents in the reality outside language. In this it has
been very much influenced by semiotics, particularly by the theory
presented at the beginning of the century by the Swiss linguist Ferdinand
de Saussure. Saussure (1966) says that language is composed of signs that
are linked together, and each sign in turn is composed of two analytically
distinct elements – that is, signifier and signified. Signifier refers to the
sequence of phonemes that makes up the word (such as 'tree'), while
signified refers to the meaning of the said sequence of phonemes. When we
hear the word 'tree', we realize that it means tree. Saussure stresses, first,
that the relationship between signifier and signified, between the sound-
image and the concept associated with it, is wholly arbitrary. By this he

means that it is impossible to infer from the word's sound-image what it means. Further, he argues that the relationship between the sign and the reality outside the language is arbitrary: language is not just a list of objects existing in reality. The content of a sign, the meaning of each sequence of phonemes, depends on the other signs with which it appears. Consider the case of a dictionary: the dictionary explains one word by using other words. If we refuse to understand the words that are used in the definition of the entry, we can look for new definitions for all of them. In principle each and every word in the dictionary is involved in defining the other words. In this sense language is a closed system, a 'series of differences of sound combined with a series of differences of ideas', as Saussure (1966, 120) puts it.

Anyone who looks at language and other sign systems from the inside has to admit that language and the process of signification in language is indeed a hermetic system. But is it nonetheless a copy of reality, like a map that culture has spread out on top of 'original' nature? If the meaning of the term 'tree' is in the concept of tree, how is that related to the real tree that grows in nature? The idea of Saussure's linguistics and the semiotic school that grew up on the basis of his theories is to argue that trees only exist to us through the way in which language and culture divides nature into meaningful parts, which are given their own names. Anyone climbing up a mountainside will find it very hard to say exactly where the trees end and the bushes begin. We do have criteria to define the tree line, but no such line actually exists on the mountainside; its place is determined by cultural conventions that people adopt through the medium of language as they are socialized as members of a culture. The same applies to all signification: the environment we perceive around us can be seen as a series of continua that the language system divides into meaningful parts and relationships between the terms used in identifying those parts. It is also important to note that we use a wide range of concepts and conceptual distinctions that actually have no referent in the reality that is independent of language and its concepts. Consider the words *abstract*, *identity* or the *competitiveness of the export industry*. We cannot even think of objects outside language or other sign systems that would depict the content of these concepts. Their meaning consists of all the determinants and definitions that are given to each term. Furthermore, none of these definitions is the actual content or real essence of the concept; rather, that imagined essence is an 'empty centre' surrounded by all the attempts at a definition.

In this sense even the harshest realities of the everyday only exist to us through meanings; they do not exist as such, independently of people's interpretations and understanding. We may bang our head against the realities of practice regardless of how we perceive that obstacle. But we always have some interpretation of the object we encounter. The way in which we react and respond to the boundaries we encounter will always depend on the interpretations we make. This means that life and social activity are grounded in and are dependent on the process of signification. That is why social scientific research, from the point of view of cultural studies, consists in an analysis of meanings; and this applies always, not just when the study is concerned with the meanings embedded in a specific object or an exotic subculture.

Meaning and Norm

What has been said above would make little sense and carry no real information value if social scientists had always agreed on the points made. But this is not the case. Even though meaning has always occupied a place of its own in the sociological conceptual apparatus, sociology has been largely dominated during the past few decades by other traditions, for instance by Parsonian functionalism. Within the prevalent trends, one explains socially organized behaviour by the concept of social norm, not by meaning. Cultural studies can be seen as a critique of the 'norm theory'.

The sociology of norms represents one way of explaining human activity as well as how society is possible in the first place. That is, if we assumed that everyone in society was concerned only with his or her own private interests, then normal, peaceful life in society would not be possible. In norm theory the mystery is resolved by assuming that the social norms assimilated by individuals and controlled by communities regulate the behaviour of individuals. Parsons (1967, 76) compares the concept of norm to the concept of space in classical mechanics.

Émile Durkheim is widely regarded as the founding father of norm theory. In *The Rules of Sociological Method*, Durkheim writes:

> A social fact is identifiable through the power of external coercion which it exerts or is capable of exerting upon individuals. The presence of this power is in turn recognisable because of the existence of some pre-determined sanction, or through the resistance that the fact opposes to any individual action that may threaten it. (1982, 56–57)

In the essay, 'The Determination of Moral Facts', Durkheim (1974, 35–36) talks about 'moral rules', in which he distinguishes two aspects. On the one hand, 'moral rules are invested with a special authority by virtue of which they are obeyed simply because they command'. Obligation is, then, one of the characteristics of the 'moral rule', afterwards referred to as a norm. On the other hand, 'a certain degree of desirability is another characteristic no less important than the first'.

This view of social life is highly individualistic. It is grounded in the juxtaposition of individual with group or society. The consistent behaviour of individuals who are understood as separate from one another is explained by (negative or positive) norm pressure; and if there are no signs of norm pressure, then the consistency of behaviour will be explained by reference to internalized norms (Allardt and Littunen 1972, 21–24). Society is understood as a system of behavioural control operating at different levels. According to Parsons, the cultural system controls the social system, which in turn controls the organism system of behaviour. In other words, the values of the cultural system are institutionalized as structures of the social system, which in turn are internalized in the personalities of individuals, and which regulate their activity through their normative coercion.

The paradox in this individualistic norm theory, in the way it portrays society as an obstacle confronting the individual as rules and prohibitions, is that it actually tells us very little about individuals. The individual, complete with desires and intentions, is taken for granted, while all attention is centred on the normative control that the individual encounters as well as on its impact through socialization (understood as the internalization of norms). The consistent behaviour of different individuals is explained either by reference to the distinctive characteristics of the human race, such as its biological needs, or by the existence of social norms. The analysis leaves out the shared world of meanings that makes possible communication amongst people, the element of language that encounters every individual and the tools it offers for perceiving the world. This is why it is difficult, within the confines of norm theory, to address the question of how an individualistic world-view, the juxtaposition of individual and society, is just one way of perceiving the world. Norm theory is held captive by this modern world-view.

Cultural studies has wanted to draw attention to the fact that not all activity which follows rules and which is meaningful can be explained by norm pressure. There are, namely, two different types of rules that people follow in their activity (Winch 1971). On the one hand, there are *regulative rules* – that is, social norms which force or oblige the individual to behave in accordance with the rules. On the other hand, in their activity people follow *constitutive rules* when they communicate with each other. These rules help to explain to others what the person concerned means. All rules can of course be studied from both perspectives. From the point of view of constitutive rules, for instance, the rules of chess define the game specifically as one of chess; but the person who is plotting to cheat his or her opponent will look at the rules as regulative. Similarly, in language-use following the rules makes speech understandable, but the schoolteacher will look at language from the vantage point of grammar, as 'correct' or 'incorrect' language.

In spite of what has been said above, it is important to note that the social norms applied by social groups and society at large to control the activities of individuals are nonetheless an important object of study for critical social research. It could be suggested that by focusing its attention on social norms, sociology is in effect examining power and power structures.

However, this sort of view of power is a very narrow and restrictive one, even though sociology has tended to define power in the manner described above, as an opportunity for getting others to act in a specific way in spite of the opposition. According to Michel Foucault (1980), power has been understood as a negative force, as something that imposes limits, prohibitions, orders. Power, thus defined, is anti-energy: all it can do is make its subjects incapable of doing anything and everything it prohibits. The model is borrowed from the juridical exercise of power. According to Foucault, there is a tactical explanation for the adoption of this concept of power: 'power is tolerable only on condition that it mask a substantial part of itself' (1980, 86). Its success depends on the extent to which it is capable of hiding its own mechanisms. As Foucault says:

> Would power be accepted if it were entirely cynical? For it, secrecy is not in the nature of an abuse; it is indispensable to its operation. Not only because power imposes secrecy on those whom it dominates, but perhaps it is just as indispensable to the latter: would they accept it if they did not see it as a mere limit placed on their desire, leaving a measure of freedom – however slight – intact? Power as a pure limit set on freedom is, at least in our society, the general form of its acceptability. (Foucault 1980, 86)

Consider the study by Paul Willis (1977), *Learning to Labour*, which sets out to address the question of how working-class kids, in spite of the comprehensive school system in England, get working-class jobs. The study disproved the common theory that this is due to normative coercion or to a latent ideology that suppresses working-class youths and thus reproduces the prevailing class structure. The reason, as it turned out, lay elsewhere, namely in the way that the lads thought about things, a way they had created all by themselves; in their interpretations of the school system's ideology of mental work which they thought profoundly offended their masculine identity. So through their resistance against the ideology prevailing at school and in society at large, they were themselves involved in reproducing the power structure or the strategic situation in which the working class voluntarily submits to its position. Here, too, the view of power simply as a set of coercions and norms would be too narrow and misleading; the analysis must also take in the cultural forms that have evolved historically and through which the individuals with their desires and intentions are produced.

However, although the concept of meaning is central to the cultural studies perspective on social life, this is not to say that the concept of social norm should simply be dropped. Normative control is of course an integral part of social reality, but the point is that in each case it is necessary to interpret the social meaning of the norm or the internalized norm that appears as self-control.

Take, for instance, the rise of the temperance ideology and the Finnish temperance movement at the turn of the century. What was it that appealed to people in the notion of abstinence, or in the norm of moderation in drinking, and caused such a mass movement to grow? It would be much too facile to argue that people started to drink less because abstinence had become the social norm and that the temperance movement made sure it was observed. The question we need to ask is: what was the social meaning of the norm of temperance? The argument I made in my own study on this subject (Alasuutari 1992a, 9–20) is that this was essentially a way of legitimizing a new and changing attitude to drinking. As far as I can see, this change in attitudes had to do with a process of individualization, with liquor becoming increasingly a commodity, and with the legislative changes that were taking place. The traditional way of drinking in connection with major occasions, such as harvest festivals where the folk on the farm decided together to spend a certain amount of the harvest in liquor, was confounded by the fact that you had to go to town to get the booze and that you needed money to buy it; and money is private property. An individual is inclined to think of the use of money within the perspective of individualist calculus: shall I spend my money on booze or buy something else? Large numbers seemed to opt for the latter alternative, but in making this choice they also needed an ideological justification for their new habits. That is, the notion of individual benefits had never before been applied to drinking habits. According to the prevailing values, drinking was not controlled by individual people but by custom and by community rules related to drinking situations. There was also a similar system of community regulation for dating manners between young men and women. The popularity of the temperance ideology had to do with the fact that it represented the difference between old and new habits from a new perspective; a perspective where the rejection of traditions is seen as acceptable and desirable. In this new perspective it was stressed that it requires considerable self-discipline to resist the desire for drink. The concept of self-discipline and the related thought-model served to turn everything upside down: old traditional habits were regarded, from this point of view, as 'natural', wild, immoral, short-sighted activity that was aimed purely at self-enjoyment. The ideology of temperance, stressing the principle of self-discipline, represented the new modes of activity that were useful to the individual and useful to society as well, as a model that served the common good.

One of the key concerns of cultural studies has indeed been to study the social construction of desires and the cultural background of normative rules. For instance, recent research on the consumption of cultural products has been drawing attention to such questions as how to draw a dividing line between 'high' and 'low' culture; what makes high culture so valuable and mass culture normatively condemnable. In other words, activity is not explained by reference to the social norm which encourages that activity; the question now is: what is it that makes us want certain things and denounce others?

The Social Construction of Classifications

One of the scholars who has drawn attention to the tastes and styles that find expression in the consumption of cultural products is the French sociologist Pierre Bourdieu. However, his main research theme is not the social construction of desires but cultural class theory, which seeks to distance itself from Marxist class theory. Bourdieu (1984) has elaborated a theory of the role of cultural systems of distinction in social practices. For Bourdieu, the hobbies of an individual and his or her artistic taste, for instance, serve as an indication of cultural capital which can be exchanged, by means of various strategies, into economic capital and social status. In this line of thinking social classes are not deduced from people's different, antagonistic positions in production, but the production of commodities and wage labour are regarded as just one of the spheres in which social statuses and class distinctions are produced and reproduced. Apart from an analysis of positions in production, Bourdieu considers education as well as upbringing and the consumption of cultural products to be important spheres in which individuals accumulate cultural capital.

Bourdieu's cultural class theory is an attempt to analyze the post-industrial society of the present day. In that society, the majority of the population, including top managers of major corporations, are wage employees; and the lower-level management, white-collar employees and blue-collar workers are all to a lesser or greater extent, through their job, representatives of an abstract 'owner'. This means that the dichotomous criterion of traditional Marxist class theory – that is, the ownership of the means of production – has become a very abstract phenomenon. At the same time, with the continuing advances of technology and automation, the numbers involved in physical labour have continued to decline. The 'middle class', as defined on the basis of involvement in 'mental work', has emerged to become the biggest single, albeit internally heterogeneous, class. It has become increasingly difficult to make straightforward and unambiguous distinctions between the 'middle class' and the 'working class', which is increasingly using modern computer technology in its jobs. In this situation the traditional signs of class difference, such as differences in life-styles and artistic taste, appear as increasingly arbitrary signs you can toy with and even exchange in order to upgrade your status. Struggles between different professional groups for prestige and wages are increasingly becoming semiotic struggles of classification, in which the key issues of contention concern job labels and the rights of different groups to use them.

The shift towards post-industrial (or post modern) society has served to lay bare many of the mechanisms that are based on the cultural logic of capitalist society and that keep that society intact. One of these mechanisms is the impact of the principle of equality among individuals, or abstract citizenship, on class differences. Bryan S. Turner argues that bureaucratic individuation, brought about by the growth of universalistic citizenship, undermines the relevance of particularistic features of indi-viduals: 'One effect of the spread of universalistic standards of citizenship has been the erosion of ascriptive categorisations of persons. Gender, age and ethnicity become increasingly irrelevant for the continuity of capitalist production' (1986, 13). It is this that leads to notions of social class becoming more and more abstract and at the same time more and more problematic. As soon as a feature is identified that characterizes a group of people, such as the 'working class', that characteristic is interpreted as an indication of injustice and people try to get rid of it. The paradox is that it is precisely the characteristics that are shared by a group of people that make it possible for them to organize themselves as a 'class,' to develop a sense of solidarity, a cohesive feeling of 'us'. The more successful the class is in its struggle for equality, the less useful this notion of class, originally defined on the basis of certain traits and characteristics, will be as a determinant in identity formation. That is why the modern notion of class is mainly an abstract, statistical phenomenon. Indeed rather than *specific* classes, reference is now typically made in a figurative manner of speech to the 'class dimension', a complex, or a void centre of a sign system where signs of 'class' are also used as evidence. In this sense it is possible to find 'class differences' on the basis of virtually any criteria. But, on the other hand, at the level of individuals they only appear as *individual* differences.

The Concept of Meaning and Cultural Studies

In thematic terms cultural studies is a broad field of study that takes in a wide range of different theoretical traditions. The themes covered in the examples above provide far from an exhaustive account. Even the very concept of culture is understood in many different ways within the field. At the end of the day perhaps the only feature that cultural studies really shares in common is the position that reality and social life are always and essentially mediated through meanings.

This is not to say that the concept of meaning is a novel one; on the contrary, it has occupied a central place in many social science traditions well before the beginning of 'cultural studies'. In Max Weber's *Verstehen* sociology, for instance, meaning is one of the key concepts; and the same goes for Lévi-Strauss's structuralism as well as the phenomenological tradition. These different lines of inquiry differ from each other in terms of their theoretical orientation. Whereas structuralism underscores the point that the deep structures of culture are primary in relation to the subjects they produce, the chief concern in phenomenology is to look at how the individual tries to interpret the world and to make sense of it.

The specificity of cultural studies lies in its 'eclectic' intention of integrating different lines of inquiry and orientations. It is stressed in the field of cultural studies that in their extreme forms the exclusive focus on subject and structure are both equally impossible caricatures. Even the seemingly most individualistic interpretations of the world are never truly and thoroughly individual and unique. On the other hand, the 'deep structures' of culture only exist as people act and behave in accordance with those structures or make use of them in their activity. Indeed the line of inquiry that is known as cultural studies is perhaps best described as a crossroads, the arrival, through the application of concepts from various disciplines, at a shared view that it is useful to study cultural distinctions and meaning systems from the point of view of both actors and structures. Within cultural studies it is stressed that meaning structures do not use people, but that in making sense of the world and in acting within that world people use and apply 'meaning systems', 'cultural distinctions', 'models', 'schemes' or 'interpretation repertoires'. On the other hand it is stressed that the models or distinctions commonly used in society consti-tute – that is, produce and reproduce – social reality (including the subjects themselves), and are an integral part of that reality. It is no doubt precisely because of this emphasis on the dual nature of meaning systems that the concept of discourse – particularly as it has been used by Michel Foucault – has become so popular. This concept seeks to unravel the juxtaposition between reality and conceptions of reality: it refers both to meaning systems and to practices or entire institutions organized by those systems or perceived within their framework.

Cultural studies has explored the concept of meaning from various angles and studied the mediation of social reality through meanings in different ways. The ethnomethodological emphasis on cultural studies, for instance, stresses that the researcher should not try to suggest interpre-tations of people's world of meanings, to try to move into their minds. The interpretation of meaning is regarded as an activity that is characteristic of everyday situations of interaction: we look at what other people do, and infer on that basis what they 'mean' or 'think', and then respond on the basis of the interpretation we have made. It is one of the key tenets of ethnomethodology that the researcher should not compete with laypeople over such interpretations of meaning; the researcher should not try to offer the ultimate interpretation as to what things 'really' mean. Rather, the ethnomethodologist is concerned to study the *methods* or the rules of interpretation that people follow in their everyday lives. Ethnomethod-ology, as the name implies, is concerned with studying the 'ethno-methods' of popular interpretation. Its object of study consists of observable, concrete, incarnated social activities through which actors produce every-day situations and practices and are capable of acting in those situations (Garfinkel 1984).

To take the ethnomethodological point into account in cultural studies is to stress that one must refrain from guesswork, from interpreting the symbolic meaning of disconnected objects or practices. Instead, one is studying observable clues, such as practices or modes of speech, used in making interpretations about, and later arguing for the existence of, discourses or *structures* of meaning. The identification of such discourses – serving as 'methods of common understanding' (Garfinkel 1984, 31) – then makes the phenomenon understandable, and in that sense explains it.

However, even when the concerns of cultural studies are defined in these terms, it still remains preoccupied with the mediation of social life through meanings or *semiosis*. In a sense this may be seen as a reaction to earlier mainstream sociology where the treatment of this theme has received much less attention. No doubt cultural studies also reflects the post-war era of ours, which has been called 'post-industrial' and even 'postmodern'. Because of migration and the world economy, for instance, different cultures interact and mix with each another, not least through the mass media. The continuing movement towards internationalization will certainly make it more and more difficult to retain one's faith in naïvely self-evident meanings, interpretations and identities.

4

Theoretical Framework and Method

Scientific Research and Pragmatic Survey

I'm sure you have sometimes experienced the pleasantly tantalizing feeling that is aroused by the beginning of an affair. How can you know if the other party's behaviour is natural friendship, or would he or she be interested in closer interaction or a romance? You can make sure by taking the initiative openly, but to err would be embarrassing, and a clumsy pass would break the sensitive situation. You just have to be content with interpreting signs, making interpretations, but on the other hand you must be careful not to betray yourself, to interpret the signs according to your own wishes. On the other hand, your own interpretation can be tested in a careful manner by finding out how the other party reacts to this or that seemingly innocent advance.

Scientific research is a similar enterprise; you interpret signs and actively produce new clues.[1] By using hints and clues we try to infer something that could not be noticed from observations with the 'naked eye'. The pragmatic survey, on the other hand, is a type of information-gathering, however systematic and reliable, where you never try to go 'behind' the apparent facts. Consider a newspaper reporting on an opinion poll conducted by a market research company. The results, based on a representative sample of the total population, predict what proportion of votes each candidate in a presidential election would receive, and how the figures have changed since the last opinion poll. In such a case we are definitely dealing with a pragmatic survey. It would be a scientific study if it contained a *problem*, a 'why' that the research design is set up to answer. In such a case it would

---

[1] Keller (1985) points out that the love affair is far from a new metaphor used for scientific research. Plato used the same metaphor, and the later seventeenth century conflict between the alchemists and the Baconians was first and foremost a battle between two gender-related metaphors: Bacon drew a parallel between natural science and a prudent marriage between spirit and nature, a marriage that subjugates nature, whereas the alchemists, who lost the battle, used the trope of sexual intercourse, the uniting of spirit and *materia*, the female and the male.

present interpretations about the meaning of the figures, for instance to use the findings as evidence for suggested explanations about the changes in the popularity of the candidates.

Observations and Clues

In scientific and in social scientific research the *observations* (or findings as they are often called in social surveys) made in empirical research are never treated as 'results' as such; they are not taken at their face value. Observations are treated only as *clues*, which we try to interpret in one way or another in order to get 'behind' the observations. Of course the information that a certain percentage of the population is going to vote for a candidate is somewhat interesting in itself. The general interest of empirical observations does not, however, make the enterprise of collecting them scientific research and, vice versa, the low interest value or small societal significance of observations does not make research based on them poor. Empirical observations and research results are two different things; 'interesting' data can be used poorly in research, and normally irrelevant things may lead to important and scientifically interesting research results. Just consider Sigmund Freud, whose theories about the psyche were partly based on the analysis of slips of the tongue and jokes.

In natural science, for instance in atomic physics, empirical measurements do not usually mean anything to a person unfamiliar with the field. In social research, instead, it is sometimes hard to differentiate between the research results and the empirical observations, because they are often of intrinsic interest. They 'mean' something – that is, they can be interpreted in different ways by just using common sense, without the need for guidance provided by the researcher's interpretative models. If it is reported that the sitting president has lost support, for instance, the public and the press draw their own conclusions from these observations – that is, they consider the observations as clues. Unlike in natural science, the observations can also change the phenomenon being studied, because the objects of research also draw their conclusions. To complicate matters even further, let me remind you that the conclusion to be drawn and measures to be taken by those involved may be an object of speculation in the press. It may be thought that the presidential policy has been seen as unsuccessful by the public, and that is why the president is expected to 'improve his image' in the near future.

Theoretical Framework

In social research it is sometimes hard to see the difference between empirical observations and clues, which is the form in which the researcher treats them. However, that does not mean that the difference should be forgotten, or that it can be regarded only as a relative one. It is even more important to make a clear analytical distinction between observations and clues. In scientific research, observations are always treated as clues in the sense that they are considered from a particular, explicitly defined point of view. Such a point of view is called the *theoretical framework*. Consider the following extract from a qualitative interview dealing with family viewing of television (see Alasuutari 1992b; Alasuutari et al. 1991):

Q: Well, what kind of TV-movies do you like?
A: . . . Usually these that have action . . . and older ones, these new ones are not that interesting very often . . . comedies [unclear] I watch.
Q: Okay. Have there lately been any of those on TV that you have watched?
A: Movies?
Q: Yeah.
A: I wonder what I've seen the last time . . . I don't remember . . . we were just on a trip, and that's why it's been a while since I've seen a movie.
Q: Well . . .
A: [interrupts] Frankly I don't remember what film I saw the last time.
Q: Yeah. Well then, how often do you usually watch movies?
A: Maybe once a week . . . I see a movie.
Q: Okay. How carefully do you choose the ones you watch?
A: It is . . . quite carefully usually . . . on the basis of the name, and then I have to know about the movie, to have a hunch that it may be a good movie.
Q: Okay, do you have any favourite directors or actors so that if they appear in it you will watch the movie?
A: Yeah, it's the famous directors and actors who are [unclear] then that's the ones I watch.
Q: Do you have some favourites?
A: Not actual favourites, it's just the most well-known names . . . there are . . .
Q: Would you give me examples?
A: Examples? . . . Well, Fonda is one . . . very famous, then, of the directors . . . it's hard to remember them . . . Coppola is a famous director whom I watch, whenever his films are shown, they haven't shown that many on TV.

This kind of interview can be studied from many perspectives. One could estimate the number of films each interviewee watches per week, and see how this correlates with the individual's educational level and occupational status. Following the example of Pierre Bourdieu (1984), one could count the directors and actors each informant mentions, and regard this as an indicator of the individual's 'cultural capital'. According to Bourdieu's results (1984, 585, 530), it is typical of the working class to be more interested in actors than in directors, whereas the middle and upper classes are able to identify more directors. We could also pay attention to the image that the informants want to convey of themselves: does the individual convey his choice of films according to their directors (because he thinks that this is seen as more 'cultivated'), but cannot, when asked, name that many directors? One could, moreover, analyze the interaction between the interviewer and the informant by using methods of conversation analysis: how does the interviewer, for instance, communicate that she is moving from one theme to the next? etc.

In the previous section it was mentioned that in research one always tries to get 'behind' the observations, that they are not taken at their face value. This does not necessarily imply that one does not believe that the informants tell the truth. We may regard the informants' estimates of the number of films they have seen during the past week as quite truthful or generally valid enough. In this case going 'behind' the observations would simply mean that each respondent would be given a variable value according to their answer, and the statistical relation of the values of this variable to other variables would be regarded as an indicator of the phenomenon being studied. An observation is regarded as a clue that leads the researcher to the conclusions presented as results, or – to say the same seen from the other side – it is considered as proof of the hypotheses.

Although in studies based on interviews – whether they be structured or unstructured – one sometimes asks the interviewees roughly the same questions as those that are addressed in the study as a whole, the answers as such cannot and must not be regarded as research results. Imagine a study trying to find out why people watch television. When individuals are asked about it, we may very well assume that by making a typology of the answers we can at least identify habitual viewing, informative viewing and recreational viewing. Even though the researcher may, on the basis of the answers, argue that television has certain functions that serve basic human needs, we still have to bear in mind that the answers themselves do not prove the theory right. It is required that the researcher presents an argument that shows how such a typology of needs makes sense, and that the typology in question provides a good interpretative framework for the observations. One could try to redeem the right to use the notion of 'habitual viewing', for example, by showing that people watch more television during prime time regardless of programme contents.

Method

To be able to differentiate between the observations and the research results, we need an explicit *research method*. The method consists of all the practices and operations which the researcher uses to make observations, and of the rules by which these observations can be modified and interpreted in order to assess their meaning as clues. For instance in statistical research the researcher points out the rules by which he or she has formed certain variables and coded their values. Additionally, there are rules which say when one is allowed to regard a relation between two variables as statistically significant. Similarly, in qualitative research one discusses the ways in which the material was gathered and, for instance, the criteria used in classifying the cases.

Without an explicitly defined method, without clear rules which tell what conclusions one is allowed to draw from different kinds of observations, research easily turns into an activity where you try to prove your prejudices right. A poorly defined method and an analysis built on vague intuition does not enable the data to prove the researcher's hypotheses wrong or his or her research design impaired. The method is without doubt poor if it does not enable the data to surprise, if the empirical analysis cannot even in theory give the researcher feedback that shows the need for improvements in the hypotheses or the design.

The method has to be in harmony with the theoretical framework of the study. If the data consist of a small number of personal interviews, you cannot even consider trying to find out what are the attitudes of a nation towards foreigners and what are the factors that affect these attitudes. In order to answer such a question we need a representative sample. A social survey cannot answer the question of what work means to individuals, or how their relation to work can be seen in the way they organize their everyday life. If you study structures of meaning, the way in which people conceive of and classify things, the material has to consist of texts where they speak about things in their own words, not of questionnaires where they have to answer predefined questions by choosing predetermined alternatives. Conversation analysis, which concentrates on the formal features of conversations, is not a good choice of method if you want to know what people think about nuclear power. In this case the method has to pay attention to the contents, not the formal features, of speech. It can of course be said of all these examples that as additional information an analysis based on any method can give new clues or bring out interesting viewpoints.

The Idiosyncrasy of Qualitative Material

The theoretical framework determines what kind of data to collect and what method to use in analyzing them. Or to state it the other way around, the nature of the material places limits on the possible theoretical frameworks and research methods. Therefore, the theoretical framework and the relevant method is an important, long-range solution. In qualitative research this solution is particularly problematic because it is typical to observe and ponder the object of study from many sides, to problematize every self-evident viewpoint. How, then, is it possible to choose a theoretical framework, to apply a method that produces only a certain kind of observations and to consider them as clues only from a particular, explicitly defined point of view?

Because of the utmost importance of the theory and method chosen, it is characteristic of qualitative research to collect materials which make many kinds of questions and problematics possible. One has to be able to change the viewpoint, lens and focal distance as freely as possible, not to gather data that consist of observations made through a single methodological lens. This is the case in survey analysis: the researcher only knows what predetermined options each individual, described by predefined variables, has chosen as answers to predetermined questions.

One could think that an ideal data set would, from this point of view, consist of material that exists in spite of the study and the researcher. They are often called *naturally occurring data*, and the gathering of such data is carried out by means of *unobtrusive measures* (Webb et al. 1966). The term refers, for instance, to non-participant observation, and generally to forms of data collection in which the object of study is in no way obtruded upon by doing the research. On the other hand, the tradition of qualitative research knows the method of participant observation well. In it the researcher takes part in the activities of the community being studied, and interviews the people, so that the research process is far from an unobtrusive one. What, then, is the idiosyncrasy of qualitative data?

It is characteristic of qualitative material that it is rich, multi-dimensional and complex, like life itself; but this does not necessarily mean that it consists of authentic situations or documents – that is, objects that would have existed or events that would have taken place despite the study. The situations in which the observations are made may be organized just for the study, but the material consists of reports that document the situations as carefully and accurately as possible. Thus, one is not *collecting material in certain situations*; the material, rather, *consists of documented situations*. In qualitative interviews, for instance, one does not only make notes of the answers to predetermined questions. Rather, one also makes detailed notes of the form in which the interviewer presents his or her questions. The object of future analyses is a literal transcription of the whole situation.

The accuracy and minute detail of the documentation is of course a relative thing, and it also depends on the documentation technique available. Compared to detailed notes made by the interviewer, a tape-recorder is a superior and exact device, even though it only records the verbal side of the situation. To record non-verbal communication one needs a movie or video camera, and in a group discussion situation there should probably be several of them.

On the other hand, the analysis is seldom made by listening to the original tapes or viewing the films. It is simply impossible to handle a large data set without reducing it to a smaller and a more manageable form. It depends on the transcription technique as to how much of the richness and many-sidedness of the qualitative interview or observational data can be preserved, and what sides are ruled out in a more detailed analysis. Just how much hesitation, staggering or repetition one is allowed to edit, or how much vernacular or spoken language expressions are changed into a written language format, depends on the aspects the researcher is going to concentrate on in his or her analysis. In conversation analysis people are very strict in this sense. Unfinished sentences are not completed, hesitation and staggering are transcribed as exactly as possible. The lengths of the

44 The production of observations

pauses and the louder and softer tones are marked, as are the points at which participants speak at the same time. Accordingly, in conversation analysis there have been studies about the rules followed in turn-taking, and about the functions of pauses and staggerings in conversations. If the researcher is not intending to study any of these aspects of conversation, a detailed notation does not pay.

Even such notation is quite standardized and incomplete compared to the richness and fineness of all the information any competent speaker of the language gets by listening to the tape. And this only applies to the tape; notation of non-verbal information on a video-tape is seldom used, and it is very crude compared to the notation of verbal information. On the other hand, making such observations is already part of natural language, and it has always been a part of fieldwork methods in the sense that the researcher has made notes in the notebook of his or her observations about the atmosphere of a situation, the friendliness or aloofness of the informants, and so on. It is, true however, that in such notes people do not usually adequately record the actual observations on which the inferences are based.

No matter in how crude or detailed a fashion the data are recorded and documented, they are almost inexhaustible when compared to the degree to which they are eventually utilized. The point I mean to make here is not that qualitative material is always underemployed although this is no doubt also true; but instead I wish to note the idiosyncrasy of qualitative material as compared to survey data.

Imagine two expeditions sent to a foreign planet to examine a substance that exists there but is unknown on the planet earth. One expedition runs different kinds of tests and makes measurements out of one thousand samples of the substance in question, whereas the other expedition takes a dozen specimens to be brought back to earth for analysis. The specimens of the substance can be scrutinized, studied from every angle, and consideration can be given as to what kinds of analyses to do and what qualities to measure. The scrutiny of the substance may lead to the development of totally new test methods and to new dimensions disclosed by these methods; it may be that even the present conception of the known substances and elements changes. The situation of the expedition that brought with it only the results of all the tests and measurements is different. If the unknown substance has nothing that cannot be found with the old methods, no unknown elements or strange dimensions, the test results can reliably serve as means by which to locate the substance in its place in the classification system of the known substances. Moreover, the results of the measurements give a good conception of the homogeneity of the substance, or whether we are in fact dealing with several materials that only look similar. This expedition may for instance show that the research results of the expedition that gathered only a few samples actually deal with a certain variant of the substance.

If it turns out that the unknown substance is impossible to describe with the old qualities, however, if the known measurements are irrelevant in studying them, the whole data set, consisting of the results of tests and measurements only, is very unsatisfactory. It will give a conception about the surprising qualities only if and to the extent that the traditional measurements give second-hand information about them. It may well be that the peculiarities of the analyzed substance go unnoticed by this team of researchers.

The difference between survey data and qualitative data is similar: survey data consist of measurements that have to do with the phenomenon, whereas qualitative material consists of specimens; they are a piece of the world being studied. That piece can never be brought to the desk of the researcher with all its edges, but even in a somewhat condensed form it is open to a range of approaches.

By arguing that qualitative material is more like a piece of the world being studied than just a set of measurements of that world I do not mean to say that we could simply study that piece, measure its dimensions, 'generalize' the results to the totality (population), and in that way find out what the world being studied is like. Scrutinizing, measuring and analyzing that piece is of course needed, but the results are useless as long as we do not know from what corner of the world the piece has been broken off.

Qualitative material is a piece of the world being studied in the sense that it is a specimen of the language and culture under study. What can be said about the phenomenon being studied, or how it can be made to answer the researcher's questions, is a totally different matter. The material may consist of writings or speeches recorded in different contexts and made for different purposes, or it may consist of interactive situations linked with the phenomenon under scrutiny in a number of ways. Observational data about a football game sheds light on some sides of the phenomenon, player interviews or group discussions on other sides, and newspaper coverage of football matches discloses yet other viewpoints about it. When drawing conclusions from the data set or parts of it, the researcher always has to be able to define the 'cultural position' of the data (Mäkelä 1990): when this material talks about this topic in this way, what can be concluded from it? The cultural position of the data must not simply be stated by way of giving a definition of it before starting the 'actual analysis'. Instead, it is a part of it: the interpretation of the meaning of the observations must be proven right or at least sensible and plausible by making references to other research and relevant literature, and by showing how the interpretation works in organizing and 'decoding' the data.

But no matter what the cultural position of the data is, the possibilities for the analysis and interpretation of qualitative data are not restricted to one or even two viewpoints of what the data tell about or reflect. The position of the data in the whole of the phenomenon only gives general guidelines as to the possibilities of analysis. The natural language itself includes a vast amount of information even when compared to an extensive survey data set.[2] When all the information contained in the speech heard on the tapes is added to it, it can be said that the researcher's creativity and imagination are the only limits to the possibilities of analysis.

In the following six chapters I will discuss some of the viewpoints from which qualitative data can be approached in order to actively produce observations, to find things that cannot be seen with the 'naked eye'. The list of these viewpoints is not meant to be exhaustive, but I hope that it gives some idea of the possibilities.

---

[2] For instance a data set dealing with television viewing (see Alasuutari 1992b), consisting of 89 personal interviews, and lasting from a half hour to an hour, amounts to 3.56 megabytes of transcribed text. The main data set in a study surveying the class structure of Finnish society (Blom et al. 1992), containing 1435 respondents and 124 variables, is 3.36 megabytes.

5

The Factist Perspective

Structured interview data, and also 'open-ended' interviews, are often approached from what is here called the *factist* perspective. It is a variant of empiricism, but it has a more specific meaning, because it makes sense to speak about the factist perspective only when we are dealing with questionnaires, interviews and speech.

The central characteristic of the factist perspective is that it makes a clear-cut division between the world or reality 'out there', on the one hand, and the claims made about it, on the other. This means that the act of putting things into words, or the interactive situation in which words are uttered and all kinds of signs are produced, are not considered as useful material because they are not facts about the world 'out there'. Similarly, many genres of folklore, such as jokes or proverbs, are primarily irrelevant as data. The characteristics of language and of the situation are only taken into account as possible noise in the channel through which information about the world is conveyed, or as distortions in the lens through which the reality is observed (see figure 5.1).

A second characteristic of the factist perspective is that it makes sense to reflect on the truthfulness of the given information or honesty of the informant. The information may concern the informants themselves, or they may be used as observers of other reality, but a measure of trustworthiness is expected as a qualification for useful data.

A third characteristic of the factist perspective is a pragmatic or common-sense notion of the truth and reality the researcher is after when conducting the interviews or studying other sources. One wants to find out about the actual behaviour, attitudes or real motives of the people being studied, or to detect what has happened. The factist perspective is, in fact, easy to recognize: we are dealing with it if it is possible to suspect that the informant or other source may lie, mislead or be dishonest.

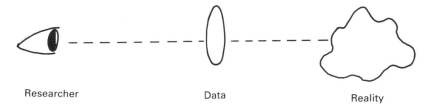

Researcher   Data   Reality

Figure 5.1   *Conception of data in the factist perspective*

The factist perspective should not be confused with the common aim that all research be objective, in the sense of being based on empirical evidence and not relying on the personal views of the researcher. The factist perspective does not hold a monopoly in respecting this criterion; it also applies to the work of other perspectives considered in other chapters of this book. The particularity of the factist perspective is in its narrow conception of worthwhile 'facts' or data: it only makes use of those subjects' statements that are believed to reflect truth 'out there'. The concept of fact can of course be seen more broadly.[1] If, say, a person claims to be the one and only real Santa Claus, the statement is obviously not truthful in the 'out there' sense, but, on the other hand, it is true that the person has made such a claim, the kind of truth which we take up in later chapters.

As already implied, the factist perspective is by no means the only possible viewpoint for qualitative data. It considers qualitative material, such as life-stories or newspaper articles, as sources whereby people inform (or disinform) us about an object of study. However, the same materials can also be seen as objects of study in their own right. Thus, one can study a life-story as an example, a specimen, of a 'story' or 'life-story', not as a source that informs us about the life or the personality of the story-teller. Similarly, a newspaper article can be studied as a specimen of a 'newspaper article', as the object of study, not as a source possibly giving us 'facts' about an event. This viewpoint – let us call it the *specimen perspective* – will be dealt with in more detail in the following chapters. Let us now concentrate on the factist perspective.

Making Typologies

Consider this fragment of an interview dealing with radio listening:

Q: What are the usual situations in which you listen to the radio?
A: At work for instance. You turn it on in the morning and off when you
       leave. That is, I have a radio on the desk, and I listen to it all day long.
       That's one thing, and then I have the radio on almost from dawn to dusk
       at home, I listen . . . I don't necessarily listen to any particular
       programme that I would go and look up in the newspaper, it's rather
       that I almost always have a particular channel on, a channel that just
       happens to have good programmes. But I almost always have it on,
       unless I really listen to the music.

From the factist perspective, this kind of interview would be conceived of as speech in which the respondent gives the interviewer information

---

[1] The word 'fact' comes from the Latin word *factum*, which means something done, or a deed, which in turn comes from the verb *facere*, to do. Thus, to say that something is a fact is roughly the same as to say it is a deed. Or more generally, every sign or trace is a fact: made, recorded or pointed out by someone. In this sense the word 'fact' can be equated with the words 'observation', 'clue', 'lead' or 'evidence'.

about her behaviour, in this case about radio listening, or about her constant properties, such as age, sex or occupation. These pieces of information are often used so that when a large enough number of individuals are asked the same questions, the answers amount to an overview of the behaviour of the population. Additionally, when one analyzes the way in which different variables are linked with each other, for instance how age is associated with how and how much radio is listened to, one can try to explain human behaviour.

From the factist perspective, people's particular ways of telling about themselves or their lives is irrelevant except for the manner in which it may affect the reliability of the information given. The kind of interviewing technique exemplified above would be bad for this purpose in that, with open questions, one would probably not be able to collect the same data from all respondents. Therefore, when only applying the factist perspective it is more common that the questions and answer options are preformulated. Thus, instead of an interview the respondent chooses the most proper alternatives to questions in a questionnaire.

In a qualitative approach the factist perspective is applied in a somewhat different manner, because the argumentation cannot be based on statistical relations between variables. To organize the data by constructing various types is quite typical. Consider applying the factist perspective to the data from which the quotation presented above is taken. In the data, there are 48 individuals who were asked about their radio listening. According to the grounded theory approach developed by Glaser and Strauss (1967; Strauss 1990), the researcher would first find two extreme cases in terms of radio listening: interviews that would differ from each other as much as possible. Then he or she would ponder what makes them different. The next step would be to see if all the data could be divided into two in terms of this dimension or criterion. If not, other dimensions, within which cases differ from each other, would be sought. Finally he or she would come up with a typology in which every case fits in a box. This of course presupposes an appropriate level of abstraction. A rough classification forces one to bundle up noticeably differing cases into representatives of a single type. By paying attention to small differences or too many dimensions, the researcher ends up with a typology where each class is housed by only a few cases. In an extreme case all interviewees represent their own class.

This kind of typology should not be a result as such, but only a starting point for analysis and interpretation. It is quite common to conceive of the types of this kind as different ways of life, which also makes it understandable why people behave, in the issue being studied, in different ways. In the radio research example we would, for instance, end up with radio user types. Often the analysis shows that the representatives of such types also differ from each other in terms of traditional sociological background variables, such as age, sex or type of residential area. Yet we are not dealing with preliminary research searching for promising hypotheses, or with quantitative social research operating with a 'mini-sample', because at

its best this kind of analysis makes sense of the relations between variables
– that is, why different people live in different ways.

The construction of types of way of life on the basis of qualitative data is
possible because the data are in fact perceived from two viewpoints. On
the one hand, one looks for information about individuals' backgrounds
and their real behaviour. On the other hand, in order to grasp the
'subjective sense' of a way of life, the data are considered as material in
which people tell how they conceive of their action; what their motives for
action are, and what meanings they give to different things. J.P. Roos's
article, 'Life Stories of Social Changes: Four Generations in Finland'
(1985) is a good example of this approach. In the article Roos divides the
autobiographies he has read into four types, which represent four ways of
life and four generations. As he puts it: 'The material used . . . gives us a
direct glimpse into the experience of generations as understood by Karl
Mannheim – i.e., people whose lives are based on roughly similar historical
sequences and who tend to hold certain values in common' (1985, 182).
The 'generation of wars and depression' was born between 1900 and 1920.
The 'generation of reconstruction and growth' was born between 1920 and
1935. The 'generation of the great transformation' was born during or soon
after the war. Finally, the 'suburban generation' consists of those who were
born and presently live in suburban high-rise areas of large and medium-
sized cities. Because of the shared experiences that differ from generation
to generation, each of these four generations represents, Roos argues, a
characteristic way and view of life, evidenced by the autobiographies they
have written. He argues that from the third generation onwards we can
speak of 'non-experiences':

> Sudden changes, if they occur, are induced by people themselves, as part of an
> attempt to change and control their lives. But still their lives are, compared with
> previous generations, much 'emptier', lacking dramatic events, great experi-
> ences, and achievements. (Roos 1985, 185)

As can be seen above, Roos is actually looking into *lives* through the lens
provided by the autobiographies. When studying qualitative material from
the factist perspective, researchers ignore the fact that they are actually
reading texts or accounts. This is of course far from the only possible
perspective to life-stories – or to any texts for that matter. In chapter 7 we
will discuss narrative analysis of life-stories among other stories, and in
chapter 8 there is a discussion of a rhetorical analysis of life-stories.

Indicators and Testimonies

How can we assume or make sure that what we get from the stories,
accounts or descriptions is truthful? What if the interviewees or informants
lie, or the observed subjects pretend to be other than their normal selves?
When applying the factist perspective one always has to, in one way or
another, solve the problem of how trustworthy the given facts are. A
critical inquiry of the sources is an essential part of data analysis. To put it

more blatantly, as a methodological approach the factist perspective can be equated with different methods by which the truthfulness of given information is ascertained or assessed.

The criteria by which the validity of the sources is assessed depend on the type of sources or, rather, the viewpoint from which the information in a source is approached. In broad terms, we can distinguish two types of sources or variants of the factist perspective in qualitative data. Let us call them the *indicator* and *testimony* approaches.

When a piece of information is used as an indicator, it means that one considers it as indirect evidence about the question one is trying to solve. Naturally occurring data are actually ideal material to be used as 'indicators'. Consider for instance a declaration of war as a source in studying the chain of events related to a war. In such a case the information obtained is not affected by the act of gathering it. However, data gathered by obtrusive measures and perceived from the factist perspective is often considered also as indicator data. Although respondents or 'study subjects' are bothered by questions, they are not told what the questions or the whole interview aims at, and that is why it is assumed that the answers can be used as fairly reliable indicators.

Within the testimony viewpoint one considers a source as a testimony about the things one is studying, for instance the habits or belief systems of a community. Within it, a source or an extract of a source – for instance an interview – is considered as a more or less honest, objective and accurate description of the aspect of reality the researcher is studying. The source is assessed in the same way we conceive of a testimony in court: if we think that the witness is lying, the testimony has no value, unless we think we can see 'through' it to the truth of the matter. For example newspapers, when used as sources that report the chain of events one is trying to unravel, represent testimony as a source type.[2]

The same source may be used as both an indicator and a testimony. Even a declaration of war may be used as a testimony, if the account for declaring the war is considered as evidence about the reasons for it. Likewise, the memoirs of Otto von Bismarck may be used as evidence about the historical events they tell about – that is, as testimony – but they can also be used as indicators that, for instance, reflect the personality of the author or the 'spirit' of the time.

These two source types coincide with two methods used to check or improve the truthfulness of the information people give. Let us call them the *mechanistic* and the *humanistic* method.

The idea of the mechanistic method is to attempt to avoid the 'reactivity of measurement' (Bernard 1988, 150; Dooley 1990, 106) – that is, the fact that the act of gathering information by bothering people with questions or

---

[2] The distinction between indicator and testimony approaches resembles the distinction between *relic* (*Überrest*) and *tradition* sources made in German historiography (Kirn 1952, 8–31; Rüsen 1986, 85, 106). The distinction was first introduced by Droysen (1960).

other requests affects the information actually received. There are many ways reactivity is avoided or restricted. The interviewees or study subjects are often given limited information about the purpose of the study. The subjects may not be told why the particular questions are asked, or how people are observed. Sometimes the subjects are misled or even cheated.

The humanistic method is in a way the opposite of the mechanistic one. The key concept of this method is 'rapport' (Berg 1989, 29–30; Bogdan and Taylor 1975, 45–48; Georges and Jones 1980, 63–64). It is thought that if the researcher makes friends with the informants, and if the informants trust the researcher, they will also be honest with the researcher.

The mechanistic and humanistic methods are not mutually exclusive. For instance, in anthropological fieldwork they are both used. Researchers want to stay in the field long enough to become 'invisible', part of the human environment they observe. On the other hand, they also want to develop 'rapport' with the informants. Abundant field experience, confidential relationships with several informants and cross-comparisons of data make pretension, lying or play-acting both unsuccessful and unlikely.

On the other hand, such cross-comparison is not always possible. Accounts concerning habits or beliefs shared by a community can be validated by cross-comparisons and triangulation. Likewise, one can at least try to control for an overall validity of personal background information or accounts concerning individual behavioural patterns by using other sources, or one can make an estimate about the accuracy of the given information by comparisons with other studies. However, when we are trying to find out about people's subjective experience and motives for action, the situation is different. It is almost impossible to assess whether the picture an individual gives about his or her personality and mental life is reliable. We cannot even know the 'real' motives behind our own deeds. Why did I actually want to have children? Whatever motive I present, I can always doubt that it is an excuse, a retrospective rationalization, or that it does not really hit the point. To solve this problem, it is often suggested that one should use the so-called 'in-depth interview', in which interviewee and interviewer become 'peers' or 'companions' (Reason and Rowan 1981, 205).[3] By conversing with the interviewees several times, by establishing a confidential relationship with them, one wants to get to the internal truth, to break the 'happiness barrier' (Roos 1985, 188).

Both methods used in improving, ascertaining and assessing validity can be sharply and justly criticized. The problem with the mechanistic method is its tendency to reduce language into a transparent lens, or answering questions into reflex-like activity. This inclination can be seen in the idea that by standardizing the questions and other characteristics of the

---

[3] Some feminist writers, such as Stanley and Wise (1983), have suggested the same approach also for ethical reasons. They claim that feminist researchers should attempt to achieve a non-hierarchic 'subject–subject relationship' with the interviewees, and that a qualitative 'depth interview' is good for these purposes. For a discussion of this, see Silverman (1993, 94–99) and chapter 8 in this book.

Table 5.1   *The indicator and testimony approaches*

Approach	Method of improving validity	Relation to facts studied
Indicator	Mechanistic: avoidance of 'reactivity of measurement'	Information used as indirect evidence of the facts studied
Testimony	Humanistic: attempt to develop 'rapport'	Information used as testimonies of the facts studied

interview situation one tries to surpass the fact that the data consist of answers to particular questions, probably interpreted in various ways. Paradoxically, the human elements of the research design, namely language and reflexivity, are considered as sources of error which one attempts to get rid of. The weak spot of the humanistic method is the underlying idea that the interviewees possess the truth, that the problem is to make them tell it. Human relations and interviewing techniques are seen as the main research method. In this perspective, honest, confidential, 'heart-pouring' talk is equated with important information and in-depth analysis and, vice versa, superficial talk, small talk or dishonesty is equated with less important, less 'penetrating' and insightful research results. Here the humanistic version of the factist perspective misses the point that dishonesty or pretension is itself interesting data. For instance, if the interviewees pretend to be somehow 'better' than they are, it tells a lot about shared values.

The characteristic weaknesses embedded in the indicator and testimony approaches, and the related mechanistic and humanistic methods of improving validity, show that there is no guaranteed method that ensures we get the truth. For instance, take the indicator approach and mechanistic method: although words do not always mean the same thing to different individuals, and answers cannot be equated with reality 'out there', in many cases it makes sense to phrase the questions in neutral terms and identically to all interviewees. Likewise, although honesty is not sufficient proof of a testimony that tells the truth, it is always useful to distinguish it. One cannot, for instance, use 'irony' or 'pretension' as a lead if one cannot distinguish it from serious or honest talk.

The two variants of the factist perspective, the indicator and testimony approaches, should be seen as resources in assessing the possible uses of the data. Similarly, the mechanistic and humanistic methods of appraising and improving validity should be seen as tools that are applied according to the situation. Table 5.1 presents the basic characteristics of the two variants of the factist perspective.

The Survey as an Indicator Approach

In a sense the indicator approach, when employed within the factist perspective, is a paradox. On the one hand, the mechanistic method used in trying to improve validity cherishes data seen as part of, or as a specimen of, the reality being studied: it is a good starting point for a non-existent or low 'reactivity of measurement'. On the other hand, the factist perspective makes a clear difference between the data and the reality it gives information about. The dilemma is that social scientists are interested in phenomena that only exist through language and can often be studied only by asking questions or making requests of 'respondents' or 'subjects'. If one is, for instance, interested in people's daydreams and fantasies, it is hard to think of anything other than interview data or psychological test batteries. The indicator approach tries to solve the dilemma by keeping the subjects in the dark. It is reasoned that if the people do not know what the researcher is actually studying, they are less able to manipulate the results. For instance, a typical survey can be characterized as an indicator approach, because the respondents are not directly asked about the question the researcher is trying to answer. The respondents' answers to separate questions are treated as indicators. The respondents may be asked about their age and hobbies, and the statistical relations between them are regarded as evidence which may verify or falsify a theory.

To be able to treat the respondents' answers as indicators, as indirect evidence of a hypothesis, survey researchers usually try to prevent the respondents from finding out what they are really after. In this instance, the survey methodology would speak about attempts to eliminate or restrict the reactivity of measurement. Consider McIlwraith and Schallow's (1983) study of the link between individuals' media use and fantasy lives. To assess how people used the media, they designed a Media-Use Checklist for the study and administered it to classes of students in the summer sessions of two universities. 'Several days after completing the checklist . . ., students from these classes were recruited by different researchers to participate in an ostensibly unrelated experiment in which they completed 23 subscales of the Imaginal Processes Inventory, a lengthy measure of daydream and fantasy processes and contents' (McIlwraith and Schallow 1983, 81). At both times of testing, the students were asked to provide background information, which enabled accurate matching of the same individual's questionnaires from both sessions.[4]

The mechanistic method of aiming at validity can be justly criticized. No matter how naïvely respondents answer the questions, they cannot be equated with a reality 'out there'. On the other hand, not all information gained through interviews must be condemned right away. A critical inquiry of sources requires the use of common sense. By analyzing the

---

[4] McIlwraith and Schallow's study is a good example of how requirements of the research design set by methodological thinking may lead to obvious ethical problems. It would however, be overreacting to draw the conclusion that surveys must be dismissed because of ethical problems. On closer scrutiny, no method is guaranteed against ethical problems. Moreover, even 'fooled' subjects may approve of the objectives of a study and, vice versa, the results of ethically impeccable research may be used against the interests of the subjects studied.

source and its function one can attempt to estimate how reliable the received information is. In terms of interview data this means that there is reason to be more sceptical about data concerning issues that are in some way delicate or morally charged than about answers to more neutral questions. In a normal situation there is hardly reason to suspect that the interviewees would lie about things like marital status or occupation, but the situation may already be different when people are asked about the kinds of television programmes they watch. Men, for example, do not often admit to watching soap operas:

> There's lots of programmes like, what was it now they used to show . . . there are these Dallases and Falcon Crests and . . . I can't watch them at all.

In a case like this there is every reason to be sceptical about the interview data because one can assume that watching romantic series is not in accordance with the predominant male role, so that some men may attempt to hide their real behaviour. The same phenomenon can be seen in alcohol research. In a survey of Finnish drinking habits held in 1984, respondents were so prone to forget or hide their drinking that overall alcohol consumption estimates based on the interviews amounted to no more than a rough third of national sales records. All over the world, consumption estimates based on interviews and questionnaires rarely account for more than half of the amount of alcohol actually sold and consumed (Simpura 1987, 15).

If the critical inquiry of sources raises doubts about the reliability of the gathered data, attempts are usually made to check and possibly correct them by comparing them to other sources. If we think about data consisting of personal interviews, it is possible to verify some of the source information, but in most cases it is practically impossible. When it was mentioned above, for example, that, according to the research, only a third of the actual consumption is revealed by questionnaires, it does not mean that it would simply be possible to multiply by three the consumption a person has reported. This would presuppose that all respondents forget or cover up drinking to the same extent. This is certainly not the case. Instead, it must be said that there is cause to be sceptical about the results of social surveys measuring alcohol use, at least in terms of the amounts consumed. The validity of the results – that the variables really measure what they are supposed to measure – is never merely a technical question or a problem to be estimated by a simple computation pattern. Instead, the reliability of the data must be assessed one question at a time.

It must be kept in mind that even if certain source data in a given problem setting seem to lack validity or appear useless, they are by no means useless in general. While we may, for instance, assume that the respondents typically underestimate the amount of alcohol they consume and the frequency of their drinking occasions, this does not imply that the same answers would not be valid if we were to study the temporal changes of alcohol use within various population groups, when the research is carried out year after year with a sample representing similar population groups.

Fieldwork as a Combination of Indicator and Testimony Approaches

The key concept of the indicator approach, avoidance of reactivity of measurement, also permeates the methodological thinking of traditional methods of anthropological fieldwork. Participant observation can be seen as a solution to this and related problems. From Bronislaw Malinowski (1961[1922]) onward it has been stressed that a researcher has to stay in the 'field' long enough to become 'invisible' (Berg 1989, 61–64), a 'fly on the ceiling'. Malinowski puts it this way:

> It must be remembered that as the natives saw me constantly every day, they ceased to be interested or alarmed, or made self-conscious by my presence, and I ceased to be a disturbing element in the tribal life I was to study, altering it by my very approach, as always happens with a new-comer to every savage community. In fact, as they knew that I would thrust my nose into everything, even where a well-mannered native would not dream of intruding, they finished by regarding me as part and parcel of their life, a necessary evil or nuisance, mitigated by donations of tobacco. (1961, 7–8)

It is thought that a long duration in the field enables the researcher to observe people in their 'natural habitat' or 'authentic' situations, even though the researcher is one of the people present. Even information gathered by asking questions is perceived this way. For instance, Malinowski seemed to think that the endless silly questions he posed made answering them a mechanistic, somehow reflex-like behaviour. This has been problematized and disavowed by the new ethnography, for instance by Paul Rabinow (1977). However, Malinowski had the idea of the humanistic method of ascertaining validity, and the idea of rapport linked to it. When the people studied create rapport with the researcher, they do not need to fool or lie, even if they can get away with it.

It is the distinctive combination of the indicator and testimony approaches to data that constitutes the method of anthropological field-work. In it, the researcher – in addition to doing participant observation – uses informants to collect information about local traditions, customs, beliefs and notions. A long duration in the field enables the use of several informants, cross-comparisons of observational and interview data, and it contributes to establishing rapport with the key informants. Fooling the researcher will then be difficult and unlikely for two reasons. First, the researcher has observational data from so many different situations that he or she can recognize play-acting or a lie. Secondly, rapport makes cheating on the part of the informants both needless and morally difficult.

Since the days of Malinowski, the role of the people studied in ethnographies has gradually changed, and this can be seen in the way they are called and how they are present in the text. In traditional anthropology the 'informants' inform the researcher about the community or local culture being studied. The actual contents of the interviews, the statements made by the informants, are, with the exception of key indigenous concepts, rarely quoted. The knowledge possessed by the author very much relies on the information given by the informants, but the truthfulness of the facts presented and interpretations made are only discussed in the section where fieldwork and data-gathering are described. The position of the narrator of the text is quite comparable to the position of the narrator of realist literature: it is ever-present and omniscient. It is as if the truth itself were the narrator. If the narrator gives voice to someone else, it is probably a historical source or another researcher describing the same phenomenon. Let us take an example from Mac Marshall's study *Weekend Warriors*:

> Trukese seek to personify the attributes of a good person and avoid those of a bad person, and each individual's reputation for personal character is based primarily on performance. The judgments of others derive from one's actions in what are considered to be relevant test situations.
> The word *pwara* is used generally to refer to courage and power in all sorts of social situations, and in this sense it describes a person of competence. . . . According to Caughey,
>
> > The classic test of *pwara* is a challenge to fight. The person of pwara shows no fear in such a situation, he acts ready, willing, and eager to fight to the death. [1970, 17]

(Marshall 1979, 56)

In contrast with traditional anthropological ethnography, in sociological and cultural studies ethnographies as well as present-day anthropology the people being studied are increasingly often given voice in direct quotations. That is mainly because in the social sciences and cultural studies one does not think it is possible to use informants who speak *for* other individuals, who describe the way 'we', as a community, think and act. Since one is often studying one's own 'complex' society and culture, there is no difference between the researcher and the 'Other', or it is minimal. Even if one is studying a community, such as a subculture, one assumes that there are disagreements and different points of view. That is why the people, called 'interviewees', are mainly asked to speak for themselves as individuals. The way of life and typical attitudes claimed to be shared by the subculture are pointed out and constructed by the researcher on the basis of individual statements and other pieces of information. That is why claims made about the truth are often authenticated by using quotations from the interviewees describing their personal life and experience.

Another reason for the use of direct quotations is an increased interest in the textual aspects of qualitative data, for instance in interviews or tape-recorded discussions. Many of these perspectives on qualitative material represent variants of another perspective, where the material is treated as a reality in its own right, not as a set of sources that tell about the reality 'out there'. That perspective will be discussed in the following chapters, but the particular ways things are said may also be treated as indicators.

The Life-Story Method as a Testimony Approach

When studied within the factist perspective, life-stories are often approached as testimonies. When the stories are collected with the means of 'humanistic' (Silverman 1993, 95) qualitative interviews, the interviewees are more or less fully informed about the objectives of the study. This is often regarded as an ethical norm. In that sense they are treated less as 'respondents' and more as 'informants' of their own life. The viewpoint on the data could be characterized as 'testimony', even though the 'informants' are not asked to describe a 'typical' life-history. Instead, the 'typical case' is compiled and constructed by the researcher on the basis of the individual examples which the data consist of.

How, then, does one try to get to the truth of the matter? In this instance, life-story researchers (Bertaux and Bertaux-Wiame 1981; Bertaux and Kohli 1984) talk about a process of *saturation*: the collecting of new stories by new informants can be stopped at the point where nothing new comes out; when the new cases repeat already familiar patterns.

Bertaux and Bertaux-Wiame's (1981) study of life-stories in the Parisian bakers' trade is a case in point. On the basis of the life-stories and other data they gathered, Bertaux and Bertaux-Wiame constructed a picture of the set of socio-structural relationships that form the institution of the artisanal bakery in France. By drawing primarily upon life-stories as evidence, they could explain why in France more than 90 per cent of the bread is still produced by small bakers, while in most other industrial countries artisanal bakering has disappeared long ago, bread being manufactured in large factories and delivered by trucks all over the land. The answer lay in a continuous flow of bakery workers from the countryside. The researchers realized that the Paris bakers disliked taking in young apprentices. Instead, they preferred to hire young workers already trained in some small provincial bakery and who moved to Paris looking for better salaries; workers who are trained to work very hard for small wages. When an old baker and his wife want to retire, they sell the bakery to such a young bakery worker and his wife by lending the money to the young couple. The young lady has to keep the bakery shop open five and a half days a week, including Sunday morning. Her husband, in turn, works nights baking the bread. Such a life is too hard to be tolerated by Parisian kids. Most bakers also orient their own sons away from the trade. This is what Bertaux and Bertaux-Wiame learned, but how can we be sure of the information based on the life-stories? It would seem reasonable to assume that at least there are great personal or situational differences. Instead of basing their claims about validity on the (lacking) representativity of their 'sample', Bertaux and Bertaux-Wiame base it on a process of saturation.

> While we were conducting our fieldwork, however, we came to realize that a process was taking shape, which seemed to indicate that we had moved in another realm than the one of testimonial sample representativity. This new process could be summarized by saying that every new life story was confirming what the preceding ones had shown. Again and again we were collecting the same story about poor, usually rural backgrounds, about very hard exploitation and training during apprenticeship; about moving from village to town, from town to city, from city to Paris (of course this last feature was to be expected). Again and again we heard about some specific health problems – which many workers, especially the young ones, related to their own physical constitution instead of to their working conditions. And despite our efforts, we still could not find a single adult bakery worker born in Paris or even in its suburbs. What was taking place was a process of *saturation*: on it rests the validity of our sociological assumptions. (1981, 187)

The saturation point reached in the research process is a distinctive experience. At a certain point the interviewees begin to repeat each other. One starts to guess what the interviewee's answer to a question is going to be before hearing it. And yet the interviewees may seem to come up with the answer at that very instant, often delighted by realizing a fitting interpretation of something they had never thought about before. It is a strange experience, and indeed a good indication that there is enough of this kind of data.

Does the saturation point in data collection indicate that the individuals are, after all, very much alike? There is certainly some truth in that, but there are also other aspects to it. The saturation process is produced by the repeated orchestrated form the interviews begin to take as an interaction process. Although the interviews are not 'structured' in the sense that all interviewees are not asked the same questions, the interviewer will develop a certain routine in going through more or less the same themes with the interviewee. A qualitative interview session, covering the particular themes the researcher is interested in, is like a familiar play where one actor has rehearsed her leading lady's role so well that she is able to adjust to any improvisation on the part of her opposite if he happens to forget his lines. This does not mean that all the observed similarities between the interviewees were just due to the same role they are allotted in the interview. The 'impact' of the interaction situation depends on the questions. People do not usually invent the facts of their life-history in an attempt to please the interviewer, but the view of their life may be very much guided by the themes covered in the interview. Individuals cannot be reduced to the contents of an interview session, no matter how 'unstructured' it is.

When written autobiographies are used as the data set, it is not even possible to develop 'rapport' and a confidential relationship with the subjects. How does one know whether the stories are 'real' or 'honest' –

that is, how does one go about applying the factist perspective in such cases? Even without the possibility of using other data for checking purposes, in studying the life-stories of four generations of Finns, Roos seems to be able to tell a 'true' story from a 'false' one. According to him the younger generations especially are engaged in 'façade-building':

> People know very well how one's life should look, but they don't know how one should really live. The façades may be anything from elaborate setups meant to hide the absolute misery of one's personal life, to a simple emptiness of life: nothing is revealed even if there is nothing to hide. (Roos 1985, 188)

In other words, even though Roos is naturally unable to draw conclusions about the life behind the scenes, he takes the need or lack of need to build façades, the 'real' or the 'insincere', as a classification criterion for ways of life. The solution is interesting, but we must bear in mind that even an open and sincere account of one's own life in an autobiography cannot be equated with life itself; the relation between life and story is much more complicated.

The Testimonial Use of the Social Survey

As has already been said, the social survey is a textbook example of the indicator approach. Social surveys seldom stray from the principle that the respondents are to answer only questions which directly concern themselves. Thus we are dealing with first-hand information. Moreover, since the respondents are not told the meaning and function of particular questions, it is thought that information stemming from a single source – in this case the individual informant – is considered reliable if there are no particular reasons to suspect that the data might be unreliable.

Even on those occasions when the social survey is used to question the informant about other people, for instance members of the same group, the answers are considered as 'indicators', as the attitudes or views of the respondent. When this method is applied to forming a picture of typical attitudes, modes of thought or behavioural patterns of a given group, society or people sharing a certain social position, it is done in a particular way. First each respondent is asked about his or her personal attitudes and views, after which one analyzes how attitudinal variables and the variables describing position or membership in a group correlate with each other.

So, survey is used as a source type and a form of gathering facts in a rather limited manner. Nothing would actually prevent the kind of survey usage in which the informants would be asked to provide eyewitness reports about an event the researcher takes an interest in, or to use their sociological imagination and local knowledge and ask them to tell about the life-styles of their own society or other groups they are familiar with. The general principles of source criticism used in the study of history could then be applied to such answers: if several informants say the same things and there is no special reason to doubt the picture they yield, the information can be considered relatively reliable.

We were faced with these kinds of questions some years ago in a sociological research practice course. Our objective was to study who goes to see ice-hockey matches, and how going to see them relates to people's way of life. In addition to participant observation, information was gathered from a few secondary school classes, since the observation had shown that young boys and girls also went to see the matches. Our idea while devising the questionnaire was to study how going to ice-hockey matches related to the musical preferences of the youth. This question setting was partly due to the fact that the sociology majors themselves took a rather negative attitude towards the whole topic of the practice course, as it was so far removed from their own life-styles and leisure activities.

We decided to include two types of questions in the questionnaire. On the one hand, the informant was asked about his or her hobbies, musical preferences and interest in going to see ice-hockey matches. On the other hand, there were questions about what kinds of youth groups there were in school and which kind of youth go to watch ice-hockey matches. These open-ended questions brought out some very interesting answers. For example, as an answer to the question of which youth groups there were in school and how they could be told apart, one of the respondents drew a map of the schoolyard showing where the various groups, punk rockers among others, hung out during breaks. Some answers stated that the only people to go to ice-hockey matches were the 'disco kids'.

In principle such haphazard information can be put to good use by applying the principles of source criticism. Thus, if several schoolchildren describe the same youth groups or think that ice-hockey matches are attended by the very people who have taken a liking to disco music, the information may be seen as relatively valid. Of course one may suspect that a school class has made a joint decision to cheat the researcher.

Combining Factist and Specimen Perspectives

As a text or corpus of texts, qualitative data always have their own structure or structures. As such, the data can always be studied as a reality in themselves, as a specimen, regardless of their relation to the outside reality they are supposed to tell about or reflect. On the other hand, language is the medium by which we convey information, so it is only natural to consider textual data from that perspective. Regardless of the main perspective on the material, the factist perspective is usually also applied to it. For instance, in studies based on qualitative interviews, whatever the perspective on them, the data can be described by telling what kinds of people at which age have been interviewed. Similarly, it is not uncommon that a study analyzing news items as texts uses the same news items also as background sources, as in the following: 'When the National Health Act was passed in Parliament, *Helsingin Sanomat* wrote . . .'. The supposed facts thus stem from the material being analyzed, even if their validity may possibly have been verified using other sources.

On the other hand, to study the inherent structure of qualitative data, for instance a text or a text corpus, it often helps to make better inferences about the status of the source, when perceived from the factist perspective. Take, for instance, Steven Feierman's study *The Shambaa Kingdom* (1974). It is a history of Shambaa mainly based on oral tradition, such as the myth of Mbegha. In order to use the myth as a historical source he first treats it as it is, as a myth with all its characteristics. By comparing the Mbegha myth to the older Sheuta myth and to similar myths that existed long before the founding of the Shambaa kingdom, Feierman reasons that the transformation of Shambaa society by the heroic figure Mbegha led to a transformation of the myth. In other words, he argues that descriptions of historical events were integrated into the myth. To assign the stories told about Mbegha the status of a myth does not deprive it of all value as a historical record. Instead, sound historical analysis of oral tradition is a matter of careful comparison of different versions of the myth so that the historical and timeless symbolic elements can be distinguished. No matter what kind of data we are talking about, in most cases they also have value from the factist perspective.

It can nevertheless be said that to apply only the factist perspective to qualitative data is to underutilize it. In the richness of language the qualitative data include a lot of information, which also reveals things beyond the material itself. A great deal of it remains unused if language is thematized as a mere (and inaccurate) means of describing reality, as a mere lens. Even when historical research attempts to find out what has really happened by studying different texts, there is every reason to apply other methods of studying texts in addition to the factist perspective. They improve the scholar's chances of drawing well-founded conclusions about the validity of the facts.

6
Cultural Distinctions

In the previous chapter we discussed the *factist perspective,* in which the texts used as the research material are assessed as more or less honest and truthful statements about outside reality. Narrativity, interaction and cultural distinctions (to be discussed in this chapter) represent another, contrasting counterpart to the factist perspective. Here, truthfulness and honesty are not relevant notions within which to approach the material, because it is scrutinized in its own right. We will call it the *specimen perspective.* The concept is an important one, because the factist perspective and the specimen perspective divide the field into two parts.

What is meant by the specimen perspective? Unlike data seen from the factist pespective, a specimen as a form of research material is not treated as either a *statement about* or *a reflection of* reality; instead, a specimen is seen as *part of* the reality being studied. Therefore, honesty is an irrelevant concept to be used in assessing the material. A specimen may be badly representative of the whole, or it may be technically bad, but it cannot lie. If we, for instance, try to find out what makes us laugh at jokes by analyzing a sample of them, we do not think that the people who told the jokes are lying. The difference between the two perspectives is defined in table 6.1.

Table 6.1   *Factist and specimen perspectives*

Perspective	Data and reality	Truthfulness and honesty
Factist	Separate	Required
Specimen	Reality of data	Not a relevant question

When we look at cultural distinctions in qualitative material, we are not concerned with the truthfulness of the information gained from, for example, an interviewee. The study of cultural distinctions is, instead, one way of analyzing how an individual or a text under scrutiny is conveying the story, whether it be true, honest talk or mere fabrication. When analyzing cultural distinctions and their interrelations we study what classifications and distinctions a text contains, and how it thus constructs reality. Consider as an example the following excerpt from an interview:

1   – How much does your family generally watch TV?
2   – Well, the grown-ups watch the news, and now that we have the cable we watch the French news broadcasts from the cable. My husband's a French teacher, see.
3   – I see.

4 – Or then he records them. They're on at eleven, you know. Those are the ones we regularly watch, but of course there's some programmes, movies or other interesting programmes, that we do watch. But we don't actually have the TV on all the time, us grown-ups. Our youngest kid is an exception though.

5 – So the TV would be on at what time in the evening?

6 – When the news begins.

7 – Oh.

8 – Half-past eight.

9 – And not earlier?

10 – Not, unless of course there's something we like to watch. What is there? Well, the pop songs review comes after the news, that we watch. Movies are usually also on after the news. Or if there are some, like, documentaries, the nature programmes we aren't that keen on. But things relating to our jobs, I teach history and my husband does too. So we usually watch the programmes that deal with history. Of course we also like to record them.

11 – Yes.

12 – Not nearly all of them though. But in general you could say around half-past eight. That's about it.

13 – Uh-huh. What kind of programmes do you personally prefer, aside from the news, are there any series that you regularly watch?

14 – No, it's been years since I, well, now I'm forty-two, maybe ten years ago I must've. Nowadays not, well, hardly ever. Programmes like *Dallas* and the like, for example, I may have watched an odd episode or two.

15 – Yes.

16 – And then there's the kinda detective series. The ones on Saturday or is it Friday.

17 – *Hill Street Blues* and stuff?

18 – Nah.

19 – On Saturdays then? *Miami Vice*?

20 – No, well sometimes. I wonder how many episodes I've watched . . . It has to do with the other things that are going on on a Saturday night, like, the telly is on more. But I really can't say it would be on all the time. But these things before the news, the ones that last about an hour, they are the only ones we happen to watch.

In statement 2 a difference is (implicitly) made between adults and children; the interviewer is given to understand that they watch different programmes or that their viewing habits are different. Statements 6–8 reveal that the half-past eight news organizes the evening. In statement 10 'movies', 'nature programmes' and 'documentaries' are separated and described as different programme types, and through them the family's programme preferences are characterized. In statement 14 another programme class, '*Dallas* and the like' is added. Furthermore, statement 16 mentions 'detective series', the content of which is further specified in statements 17–20, to the effect that *Hill Street Blues* and *Miami Vice* do not exactly belong to 'detective series'.

Distinctions between the various categories of things and objects always link up as well, like in statement 2, in which the adults and children distinction links up with a distinction between 'habitual watching' and selective watching. This linking of one distinction to the other is called *articulation*. In Latin, *articulus* means a member, part or subdivision of a sequence. When applied to language and speech, articulation depicts, for instance, the subdivision of the chain of meanings into significant units (Saussure 1966, 10). Often, the concept is used to refer to articulation on a 'higher' level: to the way in which differences in terms of one class of meanings are linked up with differences in another.

In fact, a great deal of current research in sociology or cultural studies is engaged in studying the way in which elements of discourse are associated with other ones to then present our cultural world as given. For instance, race, gender, sexual orientation and class have been addressed from this perspective. Consider a semiotic approach to race. The Africans who were brought to the United States, and who identified themselves as the Ibo, Yoruba, Fulani, etc., were rendered 'black' by an ideology of exploitation based on racial logic – the establishment and maintenance of a 'colour line', which then produces the category of 'white' as its contrasting counterpart (Omi and Winant 1986, 64). This distinction is then associated with other distinctions, such as individual differences and the nature/culture opposition, to legitimize institutional arrangements and inequalities (see also Donald and Rattansi 1992; Gilroy 1987).

Semiotics as a Theoretical Basis

As a methodological approach the study of cultural distinctions is quite simple. The only premise is that the researchers distance themselves from what is concretely stated in the texts. The attention is fixed on how it is stated and how the views or ideas expressed are being produced through different distinctions and classifications. We may find several theoretical backgrounds for such an approach. One of the most common is semiotics.

In the theory of semiotics we start with the notion that language is full of different distinctions and articulations. Even though it would seem natural in an everyday mode of thought to see language as a list of names for real objects, the reality is in actual fact not as simple as that. The way we perceive an object and distinguish it as a separate entity depends on the concepts we use. Besides, language includes a lot of words which do not have a referent outside language. These facts lead to the main idea of semiotics, according to which language is 'a system of distinct signs corresponding to distinct ideas' (Saussure 1966, 10).

Due to the systematic nature of language the meaning of an individual word is defined partly by all the other possible words it excludes. Therefore the previous statement 'well the grown-ups watch the news' includes an implicit distinction between adults and children. It is true that it also excludes several other sentences which are possible in principle, such as 'well the horses watch the news'.

Within some of the trends of traditional structuralism, represented particularly by Lévi-Strauss (1969, 1976), the assumption is that culture consists of certain objective structures or binary oppositions, which different texts reflect and which can be found in them. The assumption of some essential or original binary oppositions, however, stems from a rather metaphysical and speculative basis. It is safer to start from the assumption that we must employ our cultural competence in order to locate the 'essential' and often – implicitly or explicitly – recurring dimensions of distinction in a text. Therefore there is absolutely no reason to think that the semiotically and discourse-theoretically oriented way of analysis presented here would be a mechanical method; that one could simply pick up a text and chart its articulation structure on the spot. One must be careful with claims that the cultural distinctions arising out of a text are somehow essential or central structuring units of the text. The only thing a researcher may say, using the text as evidence, is that it contains at least these articulations and dimensions of distinction. Which aspects of distinction the scholar pays attention to always depends on his or her points of interest or research setting. The study of distinctions provides an angle from which to study the material, not a ready-made method.

The Membership Categorization Device

One example of a method of studying cultural distinctions from a different theoretical basis is called membership categorization device (MCD) analysis,[1] which Harvey Sacks originally devised in the 1960s. The theoretical background of the approach Sacks developed resembles phenomenology, the social constructionism of Berger and Luckmann (1967) and some other approaches later developed within cognitive psychology. These include among others the schema theory (Mandler 1984) and cultural models (Holland and Quinn 1989).

According to Sacks, the information we require in everyday life is organized into membership categories: people, perhaps other objects as well, are recognized by placing them into certain categories. For example, a person may be classified into the category 'child'. Each individual category is a member of at least two groups of categories: a child can also belong to the category 'girl' or 'boy'.

Actions also define categories – that is, actions are category-bound. For example the action 'to cry' suggests the identity 'child'. Various qualitative adjuncts can also be understood as category-bound.

Different categories have a hierarchical relation to each other. Crying is associated with the category 'child', which denotes a life phase. If a child does not cry, he may be said to act like a 'man'.

Pairs formed by two logically connected parties are called standardized relational pairs by Sacks. Social reality may be analyzed through them. Such pairs include men and women, mothers and children or pupils and

---

[1] For a more detailed description see Potter and Wetherell (1987, 126–137); Sacks (1992a, 40–48); Silverman (1993, 80–86).

teachers. The parties of such standardized relational pairs are often designated qualitative adjuncts: for example, we talk about indifferent mothers and neglected children.

It is easy to discern certain similarities between semiotics and MCD analysis. When Sacks notes that reality is often conceived through standardized relational pairs, he points to the fact, already pointed out in semiotics, that texts divide social reality into parts that are meaningful for the members of a culture. When those who have analyzed the categorization devices 'members' use have additionally stated that the parties of such standardized relational pairs are often given qualitative adjuncts, we are dealing with approximately the same thing that has been called articulation in semiotics.

Emic and Etic

The analysis of cultural distinctions within a text differs from the way in which one normally 'codes' the data by organizing them into a typology of cases. Instead of forcing one's own categories on the data, the researcher analyzes the constructs that people use or that exist in the material.

Admittedly, such coding often aims at using as little force as possible, so that the types would 'rise from the material' rather than the scholar forcing the cases into a predefined grid. It may even be that the categories used in coding 'are derived directly from the language of the substantive field'. In this instance Strauss (1987, 33–34) speaks about *in vivo* codes as opposed to *sociological constructs*, which are codes formulated by the sociologist. This comes close to the gist of the analysis of cultural distinctions, but analyzing cultural distinctions cannot be equated with using *in vivo* codes.

The difference between *in vivo* terms and sociological constructs is in the way codes are formulated, but in either case one is struck by the idea of *coding*, of marking and organizing the material according to some criteria. Certainly, going systematically through the research material to identify particular instances is often a phase in doing qualitative analysis, but that is not the point here. When studying cultural distinctions within texts we are not dividing the material, for example texts by different authors or interviews with different individuals, into different classes using some criteria. The objective is to study what distinctions the texts themselves contain, how, for example, interviewees conceive of and construct a phenomenon in their speech. Using the terminology of Kenneth Pike (1954), the American anthropologist, we can say that while analyzing cultural distinction systems we are not making *etic* classifications created by the scholar; instead, we are analyzing *emic* classifications found within the text itself. Here, 'analyzing' is not the same thing as 'coding': one is instead engaged in analyzing how emic distinctions on one level are linked up with those on another one to form discourses as structures of meaning.

Let us return once more to the interview excerpt above, especially to statement 4. In it the interviewee says: 'But we don't actually have the TV

on all the time, us grown-ups. Our youngest kid is an exception though.'
My interpretation above was that the previous distinction between adults
and children articulates with the distinction of 'habitual watching' and
'selective watching': the adults represent selective watching, children for
their part habitual watching. Yet am I not at this very moment in my role as
a researcher creating classes, 'habitual watching' or 'selective watching'?
The interviewee certainly never used such terms.

The study of emic *concepts* does not mean that we can only use the very
terms which appear in the texts themselves. When a researcher detects a
distinction that appears repeatedly in the text, he or she gives it a name as
an empirical generalization, as a characterization which describes the
distinction in question as closely as possible. Of course in the research
report the scholar has to mention as many diverse examples as possible, so
that the reader may decide whether the name given to the notion in
question gives a true picture of what the texts are all about.

In other words, in the study of cultural distinctions we are studying how
people – or texts – themselves classify and construct things. It is not a
matter of dividing the texts into different classes; instead, it is a matter of
studying the meaning structures of the texts.

Distinction Systems and Other Reality

It is of course possible to combine etic-type coding with an emic approach.
Let us imagine that the previous distinction between habitual watching and
selective watching would only appear in part of the interviews or that only
a certain group of interviewees would emphasize that they watch television
selectively. If other special features back this up or if one considers the said
distinction in some sense essential in terms of the question setting, then
one could separate these interview texts into a type of their own – as
opposed to the others where the emphasis on selective watching does not
exist.

In fact, a researcher can never do without 'etic' constructs. To do
research always entails concepts used as tools in making sense of the object
of research, no matter which way it is approached in the first place. The
emic approach means that one is trying to get a grasp of the members'
conception in order to make sense of practices and phenomena, but even in
saying that one resorts to many analytic or 'etic' constructs.

What about the truth of the matter, then? Are we not being rather
gullible in the example described above? Should we attempt to infer, from
a standpoint based on critical data analysis, whether the adults ever
habitually watch television just to pass time?

Such inference has actually not been made here. The result of the
analysis so far is only that the interviewee makes a distinction between
habitual watching and selective watching, and that she herself states she
only watches television selectively. What conclusions will later be drawn
from this observation is a completely open question. From a factist

perspective this observation would be studied in terms of whether it might be true or not, but that is only one of the possibilities. From the point of view of cultural studies interested in meaning structures and discourses the observation would be interesting in itself. What does such a distinction reveal about the culture in which it is made? And what is revealed by the fact that the interviewee identifies herself as a selective watcher? The inherent doubt in the factist perspective standpoint that the interviewee 'pads' reality is symptomatic. We could infer that selective watching is regarded as the more acceptable and desirable behavioural pattern. Thus the question of whether the interviewee is telling the truth, whether she is honest, is not relevant in this type of analysis.

What is the actual difference between the analysis of cultural distinctions and the factist approach to the subjective experiences of the interviewees, as it was discussed in the previous chapter? It goes without saying that analysis of cultural distinctions can be utilized if the attempt is to find out the individuals' inner conceptual world or the motives for their actions. This kind of question, however, is not a necessity. To state that the texts contain a distinction between habitual and selective watching does not imply that one has looked inside people's heads. In the first phase one only proves, relying on the material, that such an articulation really exists. It is another question what further conclusions will eventually be drawn from it.

It is possible to infer and attempt to prove that the said distinction, brought up in the interview, is important for a certain segment of the television audience, and makes their action understandable. One may test such an interpretation, for instance, by studying viewer statistics.

It is also possible to examine the appearance of this distinction as proof of the fact that it is included in our cultural models, or interpretative repertoires (Potter and Wetherell 1987, 146–157) which each and every one of us would use if we were required to answer questions on our TV watching habits. Regardless of the terms used, this is what is always at issue in texts and talks; as members of a culture and a language community we have no option but to use and apply those articulations which are part of the culture and thus also understood by others. Studying which interpretative repertoires people actually use could mean that one analyzes the way in which interpretative repertoires are connected to the speech context; watching television is talked about differently to an interviewer than to a workmate or a good friend, and even a certain character of a TV series can be talked about in different terms depending on the situation.

However, even if we emphasize the situation-bound nature of discourse and submit it to analysis, then this does not exclude the possibility that at some point in the study one attempts to draw conclusions about the individuals' thoughts and actions by analyzing their discourse or interpretative repertoires. When we are studying the articulations that appear in the material, we are analyzing the text exactly as text. However, this does not limit the scope of possible interpretations made from the produced observations or the application of other avenues of analysis.

7

Narrativity

Let us look at an excerpt from an interview in which a woman is asked to describe the plot of a TV show she has recently seen.

1   –Okay, could you tell me about the plot of the last episode of one of the two shows you saw?

2   –Well this Colb . . . *Bill Cosby Show* was of course easier 'cause they are always like . . . they're not really episodes, they're more like one night . . .

3   So there was this father and mother who had fallen ill or it was the mother first . . .

4   and then the father came home, he was very sick as well and they were both in bed

5   and the mother said to the father that you can't be sick now because I am, and you know we have to sort of take turns . . .

6   but . . . but both of them were so sick that their son was given the authority to be, to take care of the daughters, two of them were still at home and . . . to keep the house going and to take responsibility for everything

7   and then he started giving these . . . he just did the thinking and planned how to organize things and give orders . . . delegated the jobs to one or the other of the girls, and . . . so he was like the boss and . . .

8   then the girls realized that this is not going to work, that they're just being bossed around and so they went to mum and dad to say that he's taking advantage of them

9   and it ended up in mother saying that she cannot be sick, she has to get up . . .

10 It was like. . . . It has quite funny, funny incidents . . . there's always something funny going on, and they are very nice the father and mother, a funny couple, and the mother is, I think, a lawyer and the father he's a doctor, he is a pediatrician and . . .

11 – Yeah.

12 – And children are of course . . . they understand their parents the parents understand their children [laughs] and . . . all these niceties are shown of course . . .

13 that is, it's quite, erm . . . nice . . . nice cosy series, where you don't have to think that hard, I mean when you watch it it is sort of fun and such that I kind of like that . . . it sort of comes easy . . .

14 – You can relax. Yeah, is it really that it's an ideal family?

15 – Well, I don't know if it's really . . . no . . . but several times there are quite good . . . good cases that are kinda presented in a . . . nice way,

16 that I have for instance told my daughters that there you are, did you notice, there's a good example how you can say and handle an issue . . . it has sort of . . . I . . . of course,

17 Of course you cannot take it as advice as such but I mean . . . there are

18   there are things can come up in ordinary life quite as well, quite the same way.

One way of utilizing this type of text as research material is to analyze it expressly as a story with a certain plot. Any text or part thereof can in principle be studied as a whole story with its own 'structure'.

What is a Story?

Texts may include many different kinds of structures, but the specific focus here is on how, or to what extent, a text as a whole has a chronological plot. Not all texts have this feature. According to Prince (1973) the simplest possible story contains three interrelated events, of which the first and third state a certain situation, while the second is active. The third event depicts a change in the state of affairs as compared to the first event. An example of this type of story is typically: John was happy until he met Mary and then he became unhappy.

A story, as a specific form of discourse, is a unique example of the variety of ways in which the parts of a text link up to form a whole. A poem or an instruction manual, for instance, will no doubt exhibit its own distinctive structure. Of all the different types of discourse, stories have probably received most research attention because they are so easy to study. Perhaps, though, a story is also a type of discourse with considerable cultural significance. Mass communication, for example, largely consists of stories with plots. Typical examples would be entertainment stories, films and series; news broadcasts and current affairs programmes also include stories about logical and chronological chains of events. Stories transmit, among other things, temporal change, a characteristically modern experience of history. An essential part of modern people's world of experience is the idea of change and individual development with time. We can also talk about a specific biographical consciousness and a way of experiencing which is reflected in many ways, especially in the fact that the telling and writing of life-stories are essentially phenomena of modern times and modernization.

The element of narrativity in the research material can be taken into consideration in many ways and for many reasons. It may be assumed that the researcher is only interested in a specific topic or theme which the text deals with in certain places. For example, Falk and Sulkunen (1983) have studied drinking habits and the conceptual world related to drinking in Finnish films. They limited their analysis to only the scenes where drinking took place. Even by this they found out quite a lot about the meanings and the changes of meanings related to drinking, but the analysis might have reached entirely new dimensions if the role of the total narrative structure had been considered as well. From the perspective of its function, an individual scene has meaning beyond what is stated in that particular place. The meanings of drinking are present not only in the drinking scenes themselves; they have a function in terms of the structure, plot and chronology of the story as a whole. The entire thematic of the story may be expressed in these 'drunken' episodes. For example, according to the research of Falk and Sulkunen (1983), the objective of men in drinking situations is to have fun, and even though they also appear to be talking about life seriously, their personal open-heartedness remains superficial. Nevertheless it may be assumed that the actual situation is preceded by many private and everyday problems. Thus it could be suggested that the elements which are not present, those not spoken about in drinking situations, are also meaningful. The fact that personal problems are not discussed (at least directly) in a drinking situation can be seen as significant silence about these problems, which opens up one perspective on the meaning of the 'babbling' of intoxicated men. Through this babbling the drinker stresses the difference between drunkenness and everyday life, the fact that drinking is a matter of relaxation, freedom from everyday worries and obligations.

Technically speaking, the analysis of narrativity is not at all difficult. Teun A. van Dijk (1980) has provided a set of rules which are quite precise and which are applied in the work he calls discourse analysis. To get at the 'macrostructure' of a discourse he suggests that one should proceed by applying certain reductive *macrorules*.

The first rule, named *deletion/selection*, 'deletes all those propositions of the text which are not relevant for the interpretation of other propositions of the discourse and which do not denote facts which may be subsumed as normal properties of a more global fact which is denoted a macro-proposition of the discourse' (1980, 46–47). The second macrorule, called *strong deletion*, is merely a stronger variant of the first one. It means that one deletes detail that is locally relevant, but irrelevant from the point of view of a more 'global level'. The third rule, *generalization*, means that 'we do not simply leave out globally irrelevant propositions but abstract from semantic detail in the respective sentences by constructing a proposition that is conceptually more general' (1980, 47). When applying the fourth rule, that of *construction*, we 'take together' propositions by substituting them, as a joint sequence, by a proposition that denotes a global fact of which the micropropositions denote certain components. Finally, the *zero* rule leaves propositions 'intact' by admitting them directly at the macro-level. Especially in short discourses it is often the case that 'microstructure' and 'macrostructure' coincide. Everything said in that case is equally relevant or important, as in simple orders like 'Come home!' (1980, 49).

Actually the rules van Dijk lists are just a formalized description of the familiar procedure known as *summarizing* a story. To apply those rules may be useful for two related reasons. First, by following them we can make sure that we do not disregard or forget about some aspects of the texts we are studying, or that we are at least aware of the level of abstraction on which we move. Secondly, by presenting the analysis stepwise, following van Dijk's macrorules, we can better convince the reader that the results are not based just upon an impressionistic reading of the material. However, one must beware of not being totally immersed with a close and time-consuming reading of the material and, as a result, forgetting about the larger picture.

Let us take another look at the story above. The actual plot begins from statement 3 and ends in statement 9. By assigning a descriptive name to each turn of the plot, which I have separated numerically into discrete statements, we can present the following plot summary:

3   Mother gets sick.
4   Father gets sick.
(5   Statement with no relevance in terms of plot.)
6   Son is given authority within family.
7   Son orders the girls around.
8   Girls complain to parents.
9   Mother has to get well and assume family authority.

Narrative Analysis within Social Research

What is the point of making such plot summaries? The pioneer of narratology, Vladimir Propp (1975 [1928]), created his 'morphological' method first and foremost to improve the classification criteria for stories. He was not satisfied with the external classification criteria applied in the study of folk tales where the most common division was into tales with fantastic content, tales of everyday life, and animal tales. The problem was that an individual tale could contain features of several different types. Propp maintained that the accuracy of all further study depends upon the accuracy of classification, and that is why a classification must be the result of certain preliminary study.

> What we see, however, is precisely the reverse: the majority of researchers *begin* with classification, imposing it upon the material from without and not extracting it from the material itself. (Propp, 1975, italics in original)

According to Propp, a firmer basis could be created by classifying the tales according to their narrative structure. If two fairy tales are made up of similar constituent parts (which Propp calls functions), it can be said that they belong to the same tale type. As a result of the analysis of the material Propp studied, 100 Russian fairy tales, he showed that they represented the same type. This tale type consisted of 31 consecutive turns of plot or 'functions', which Propp named according to their content. In other words, the individual tales studied could be seen as variants of a single 'macrotale'. These tales start out with one of the family members leaving home, so that the villain harms either those who remained in the home or the one who left. After many complications in the plot, all of which do not necessarily happen in an individual tale, the tale ends in a wedding.

Propp's pioneer work has, among other Russian formalists, had an influence both on Lévi-Straussian structuralism and on other trends of narrative and discourse analysis. More recently, the 'Proppian' narrative analysis has been used for classifying stories by, among others, Will Wright (1975), who used the method to categorize Westerns. I myself (Alasuutari 1992a, chapter 4) have applied it in research to classify life-stories – where it turned out that the life-stories, with just one exception, all followed the same plot type. In another study (Alasuutari and Kytömäki 1986) we applied the method to categorize episodes of the TV series *Der Alte*.

However, the use of narrative analysis as a method of classification is by no means a simple and straightforward mechanical procedure. Say that we set out to explore people's plot summaries of sitcoms or episodes of the *Bill Cosby Show*. We cannot assume that the same twist (such as both parents falling ill at the same time) will recur in several different episodes. And if it did, its relevance to the development of the whole narrative might be entirely different. The idea of Propp's method is to compare different stories and their plot summaries with each other at a somewhat more abstract level than their apparent contents. According to Propp, the constituent unit of a story (or its 'function') must be defined and named from the point of view of its relevance to the plot. For example, in the previous story the relevance of the parents falling ill lies in the effect that they are out of the picture, which then results in a change in the family's power structure. At this level it would no doubt be much easier to find common features between this episode and several other episodes of the *Bill Cosby Show*; we might even find a large number of episodes where, for one reason or another, the family's power structure is upset. This results in all sorts of frictions and problems which are resolved at the end of the episode as the family's power structure returns to normal.

In the search for such common structural features we are nevertheless forced to interpret and decide on which level of abstraction the similarities between the events in different stories are studied or in which direction the visible content will be abstracted. The stories may also involve several different levels. For instance, our analysis of the detective series *Der Alte* revealed a kind of dual structure. On the one hand, at the level of presentation, the narration of each episode proceeds so that the chain of events related to the crime is gradually revealed to the main character and to the viewer by dropping clues here and there. On the other hand, the final solution is a story in its own right, namely a reconstruction of who committed the crime and how it took place. A typology of different episodes devised on the presentational level may differ greatly from a typology devised according to 'the plot of the crime'.

It cannot be argued, then, that the decisions made in the classification of stories are the only possible ones. Classification is not the main issue at all; it is a tool that often comes in handy during research. To study the structural features of stories by creating plot summaries and by summarizing those summaries is helpful in the comparison of texts which may often be of extensive length. It is a means to discover both uniting and separating features. It is, after all, a prerequisite of qualitative analysis that the researcher is able to say something absolute, something that holds throughout the text corpus under scrutiny. From this follows the demand that even in the cases where representatives of different plot types are found in the material, the various types have to be defined in relation to each other. When Will Wright found four different plot types in his study of Westerns, he described them in relation to each other by stating that they depict different ways of resolving the tension between the individual and society. On the other hand, the research design may demand that even the most delicate nuances are brought under scrutiny. For instance in her study *Reading the Romance*, which deals with the Harlequin romance series and its readership, Janice Radway (1984) asked her informants to list examples of both ideal and failed romances published in the series. Thus it became Radway's objective to discover the differences between good and bad stories, quite regardless of whether they, in terms of Propp's definition, represented the same narrative structure type or not.

In this way narrative analysis is helpful in locating the differences and similarities between different stories. In addition it is also a key to studying the meaning structure of stories.

For example, Will Wright's idea in studying the narrative structures of Western films was to see how the changes in the world-views they portray reflect changes in American society. First he does a narrative analysis of the films in the sample, and then he interprets the results as reflections of world-views.

Wright found that there were four story types in the Westerns he studied: the classical plot, the vengeance variation, the transition theme and the professional plot. Wright names the functions of the classical plot thus:

1 The hero enters a social group.
2 The hero is unknown to the society.
3 The hero is revealed to have an exceptional ability.
4 The society recognizes a difference between themselves and the hero; the hero is given a special status.
5 The society does not completely accept the hero.
6 There is a conflict of interests between the villains and the society.
7 The villains are stronger than the society; the society is weak.
8 There is a strong friendship or respect between the hero and a villain.
9 The villains threaten the society.
10 The hero avoids involvement in the conflict.
11 The villains endanger a friend of the hero.
12 The hero fights the villains.
13 The hero defeats the villains.
14 The society is safe.
15 The society accepts the hero.
16 The hero loses or gives up his special status.
(Wright 1975, 48–49)

Wright describes in a corresponding way the three other plot variants, and analyzes the world-views that they represent by applying Lévi-Strauss's ideas. As a conclusion, it is shown that these historically consecutive plot variants represent different ways of dealing with the tension between individual and society. While, for instance, in the classical plot the hero helps the society, because society is weak, in the vengeance variation and in the transition theme the hero steps outside of society for the same reason: the weak society cannot punish the villains, and therefore the hero himself revenges the injustices he has suffered. In the professional plot the hero is permanently outside of society, and the question of good and bad, right and wrong, has lost its meaning. Gunfighting is the hero's profession and a source of excitement.

Even though the Westerns representing different plot variants have been produced contemporaneously to some extent, they generally follow each other historically. The classical plot Westerns were produced in 1930–55, the vengeance variations in 1948–61, the transition themes in 1950–54 and the professional plot from 1959 onwards. According to Wright, this corresponds to the shift in American society from market capitalism to corporate capitalism.

Wright's study is a good example of how, in order to get at sociologically relevant results, one must not be content with mere observations. Narrative (or 'syntagmatic') analysis led him to an analysis of the ('paradigmatic') structures of meaning embedded in the plot structure, and thus to questions discussed in the previous chapter.[1] But he did not even stop there. At the end of the study he shifts our focus from Western movies to changes in American society. According to Wright, the emergence of especially the radically different professional plot reflects changes in the social institutions which shape attitudes and actions. The professional plot offers a new structuring of the relationship between individuals and society; a solution that corresponds to the actions and attitudes necessitated by the transition from a market to a managed economy. The managed economy then leads to the birth of a technical élite, and thus to the attitude reflected in the professional plot:

> Let us look briefly at some aspects of the human relationships that industrial technology creates and its ideology legitimates. First, technology requires group decision-making. The individualistic, self-reliant entrepreneur is gone. Now the requirements of specialized knowledge and skills, together with the need for detailed planning and complex organization, necessitate reliance upon a group of men each of whom contributes information needed to make decisions. This is the group Galbraith calls the technostructure. It consists of specialized men, professionals, who work together for a common goal. (Wright 1975, 178)

Although Wright's effort to link the plot variation to the structural changes in American society may be loose and sketchy, it is still a challenging and suggestive work. The result of the structural analysis of the

---

[1] In fact, these two aspects of discourse can be separated only for analytic purposes; in actual practice they intertwine. Both of these perspectives to texts – cultural distinctions and narrativity – also represent the *emic* approach: the aim is to uncover structural features from the texts themselves rather than to impose a grid or model upon the material from without.

plots – the finding that the genre of the Western is divided into historically consecutive plot variants – is not left without any reflection. Interpretations can always be challenged, but without them there isn't much point in cultural studies.

It is easier to search for structures within the texts when the number of texts under scrutiny is relatively large. Instead of attempting to study the innumerable details of the story, the focus can be shifted to the features that unite and separate different texts at the level of their narrative structures. Of course, a narrative typology is not a research result in itself. It merely improves our ability to perceive the stories under scrutiny in such a way that we can draw conclusions about reality other than that of the texts themselves.

Consider the narrative analysis of life-stories, which has recently gained much popularity.[2] As such, it is a very simple research programme. The method of narrative analysis is applied to life-stories, texts which are usually, within the 'natural attitude', considered as more or less accurate or reliable documents giving us information about a life-course or life-history. Yet this simple idea opens up whole new perspectives.

First, by underscoring that life-stories are necessarily retrospective accounts of a personal past, it casts doubt upon their status as histories. Instead, they are seen as documents reflecting the story-tellers' current, situation-bound theories and constructions of selves. For instance Kevin Murray (1989) considers the telling of stories of a personal past as a means of identity construction. He distinguishes two sides to identity. 'One must find a *social identity* – an honoured place in the social order – yet also attempt to maintain a *personal identity*, in the sense of a biographical uniqueness' (1989, 180). On the other hand, he classifies different types of narratives, of which two types are of particular interest here. *Comedy* involves the victory of youth and desire over age and death, whereas *romance* 'concerns the restoration of the honoured past through a series of events that involve a struggle – typically including a crucial test – between a hero and forces of evil' (1989, 181–182). In his study dealing with the accounts of people who had decided to run a marathon for the first time, he shows that those concerned with the *social* identity 'project' employed a *romantic* narrative structure of tests, whereas those keen on the *personal* identity project gave their account by means of the idiosyncrasies allowed in a *comic* narrative structure.

Secondly, to follow the line of thought shown by narrative analysis of life-stories, the 'self' as the hero of the story can be seen as a product of a narrative, as something made by the life-story and continuously remade by biographical narrating. For instance, from this viewpoint Freud's theory of personality can be seen as a particular construction, compiled from his patients' narratives. The lines of action, in concert with things usually

[2] For instance Gergen and Gergen (1984); Gubrium (1993); Gubrium et al. (1994); Hankiss (1981); Labov and Waletzky (1973).

considered pleasures, sins or socially unacceptable behaviour, are – as options for future action or as views of past action – named 'libido' or 'desire'. The views of action usually thought to be in accordance with socially esteemed values, moral codes or with an individual's long-term interests are named 'super-ego' or 'self-control'. After constructing this typology of separate lines of action into two classes, the next step is to conceive of them as object-like elements in an object-like structure called personality.

As has become clear, narrative analysis often opens up an avenue to interpretations about the meaning structures of the stories. A classic example of this is found in the work of Claude Lévi-Strauss, who has studied the structure of myths. He does not have a group of stories, but a single story suffices as an object of analysis. According to Lévi-Strauss, its substance lies in 'the *story* which it tells' (1963, 210), in the structure of the myth, not at the level of its individual terms or concrete events, even if he does not always follow his own sometimes obscure methodological rules. In any event it can be said that once narrative analysis has helped to establish that the stories concerned are variants of a limited number of narrative structure types, the study can proceed by suggesting conclusions as to why the narrative structures are what they are, and what they reveal about other reality.

The Use of Narratology in Analyzing Other Types of Text

It is useful to look for chronological structures also when studying types of texts other than narratives. Suppose we are studying the reports of state committees, published during a certain time-span, to analyze the ideological currents underlying changes in policy and legislation. First, by identifying the typical structure of reports we could restrict our analysis to certain sections of the reports rather than cover the full texts. In this case it would make sense to focus our attention on the parts where the problems in the present state of affairs are described and where the measures to be taken are stated and justified. To manage the mass of material, the parts of the reports with more detailed technical descriptions of the problem and the suggestions for further action could be skipped. Next, we could proceed to analyze the narrative logic of the justifications: how they perhaps begin by defining the present situation, go on to describe the inherent problems, then present possible solutions, and eventually justify the rationale of the solutions.

In an ongoing project of mine the task I have set for myself is to look at the ways in which the Finnish welfare state, a society based upon central planning, has been developed since the Second World War in certain fields of policy. My intention is to focus on the structures of argumentation and on the discursive structures that can be identified through the different stages of development in different social spheres. I want to see how legislative changes and reforms have been explained and motivated, what kinds of notions of good society underlie those reforms, and what kinds of justifications politicians and interest groups have had in their recent criticisms of the legislative system and contracts that have grown up over the decades. One of my main sources consists of a corpus of editorials in *Helsingin Sanomat* (*HS*), Finland's biggest newspaper. The idea in studying the editorials published between 1946 and 1994 is to analyze the changes in the public discourse.

Again it is useful to begin with an analysis of the structure of presentation. A preliminary examination of editorials seems to point at the following type of structure: initial motivation of the issue discussed by reference to a recent news event; presentation of the problems involved; the treatment of solutions suggested by different instances involved; possibly the author's own suggestions for action; and often, in conclusion, an attempt to link the problem to a broader political context.

The overall structure of an editorial seems to apply to any editorials, not only those of *HS*. As an example, consider the following editorial published in the *New York Times* on 22 November, 1994:

New York City's Budget Cuts

The New York City budget for the current year is at least $1 billion out of balance. Mayor Rudolph Giuliani has proposed cuts to balance it, and City Council members seem ready to accept his overall estimate. But they do not accept each and every cut he would make to reach that total, especially cuts in social service programs. Negotiations to resolve their differences are under way – in secret.

Past practice indicates that a settlement will be reached and immediately approved with no more than a momentary public glimpse of what was agreed. Given the huge impact of cutting so much from programs that have already been cut once this year, the public deserves thorough hearings on the agreement and the rationale behind its cuts.

The budget adopted by the Council in June provided $31.6 billion for the 12 months beginning July 1, including virtually all the $1 billion in cuts the Mayor proposed in May. Despite official word that the budget was balanced, principal players knew it was not; they were agreed, however, that bigger cuts would have been politically unacceptable at the time. Now they must catch up.

The state requires the Mayor to update the budget outlook during the year, and to propose changes to close any new gap, as Mr. Giuliani has now done. As a general rule, the Council cannot vote on separate items but must accept or reject his revisions in toto. It can, however, offer counterproposals and negotiate with him to change the plan before the vote is cast.

This is what is happening now. Tomorrow is the target date for an agreement and a Council vote. While the yes-or-no procedure is generally thought to be required under the city charter and other fiscal statutes, it is possible that the Council might test a legal loophole to vote on separate items. That would surely provoke a confrontation with the Mayor, and would be surprising from a Council that has been relatively docile so far.

The Council's concerns are valid, however. Members are particularly unhappy with proposed cuts in day care and other youth services, mental health care and aid for food distribution programs. Their counterproposals include a tougher crackdown on billowing outlays for overtime work, most notably in the uniformed forces; consolidation for some city agencies, and generally squeezing small agencies to trim staffing more than Mr. Giuliani already seeks.

The Council's alternatives make sense because they appear to save money in ways that will not hurt the services the city provides, and these savings could then be used to soften the blow to programs for the city's poor. Mr. Giuliani insists the savings he proposes will not hurt services, because he aims to improve the productivity of city offices. That is all to the good, but he should also be open to Council proposals to save more.

With negotiations incomplete, and still secret, it is not possible for outsiders to assess what is going on. But the Council is on the right track in accepting the Mayor's target figure, while at the same time pushing alternatives to cuts to a social services system that is already lean.

This editorial is more or less set out in accordance with the basic structure of presentation outlined above. The first thing it does is to present a problem: that the budget is out of balance. It then moves on to express the writer's view that the public deserves thorough hearings on the rationale behind the cuts proposed. After presenting some background information concerning the reasons for the unbalanced budget, it describes the situation and the two parties', the Mayor's and the Council's proposals concerning the best ways of balancing the budget. The writer concludes by emphasizing that the blow to programmes for the city's poor should be softened by alternative cuts. Yet it is obvious that the editorial is not a narrative; there is no plot structure in it. How can this type of writing be summarized to facilitate further analysis?

Even though there is no plot in the leader, it does nevertheless have an intentional structure of argumentation. The author presents a certain set of premises, the objectives aimed at, and discusses the factors that stand in the way of the attainment of those objectives as well as the factors that promote its attainment. One possibility is to apply A.J. Greimas's (1987) actant model, which he has reduced from the structure of a number of folk tales. In the folk tale you will have the villain taking the King's daughter; then the hero appears on the scene, wins back the daughter and returns her to the King. According to Greimas, all texts follow this same structure in which it is possible to identify a sender (some morally important and acceptable principle), an actant object (such as the King's daughter or the social issue at hand) and a receiver, who should receive the object, pure and intact. In addition (and this is important), the story involves an actant subject and a countersubject with helpers.

In Finland, Greimas's actant model has been applied for research purposes among others by Ismo Silvo (1988), who analyzed Finnish television politics as a discourse. It seems that not only folk tales but other types of discourse do indeed follow this structure. The model is really quite exciting in its innovativeness, but browsing through the studies that have applied the model it is hard to avoid the impression that Greimas's actant model has served as a frame upon which the structural characteristics of the texts are imposed. What is more, the actant model would not allow us to take into account the presence in editorials of two simultaneous levels: the

Table 7.1 *The coding frame for editorials*

The goals of activity	Means of activity
Balance the NYC budget Preserve services for the poor Achieve an agreement between the Mayor and City Council	Cuts to the budget Alternatives to cuts to social services Vote on separate items
Obstacles or opposition	**Reasons for obstacles**

Budget out of balance
Mayor argues that the cuts do not affect
  social services
Yes-or-no proceure
	In May bigger cuts were politically
	  unacceptable
	Mayor aims to improve productivity

author, on the one hand, is presenting an interpretation of a certain situation, and, on the other hand, is putting forward his or her suggestions about other possible solutions to the problem.

Instead of just adopting Greimas's actant model as a coding device, it is sensible to approach the structural analysis of the editorials more inductively, although it is true that, to manage a large corpus, at some point one just has to come up with a model or models for summarizing and coding the texts. After experimenting with different models, it turned out that a more useful model for the analysis of the editorials is provided by one which identifies the *goals* of the actors involved in the situation, the *means* applied to attain those goals, the *obstacles* and *opposition* faced, and the *reasons* for obstacles or opposition or the ways in which the factors concerned prevent the attainment of the goals. The same items can also be examined in relation to the author's own proposals, in which case the elements may change places: opponents are presented as proponents etc. In the example above this is not necessary, however, as the author does not present his or her own proposal of how to resolve the problem. Instead, the writer just sides with the Council's proposals. On this basis the editorial can be analyzed according to the model illustrated in table 7.1.

The example already reveals how complex and many-sided editorials are. The four-field 'coding frame' only partially captures the way in which the parties of, for instance, a political dispute often honour or at least refrain from disagreeing on a principle valued by the other party; they just present an alternative solution. In the sample editorial, the Mayor is not said to oppose the aim of preserving the social services system; he just insists the 'savings he proposes will not hurt services, because he aims to improve the productivity of city offices'. Furthermore, the four-field frame fails to capture some sideline remarks by the writer, for instance that '[p]ast practice indicates that a settlement will be reached and immediately approved with no more than a momentary public glimpse of what was agreed'.

These weaknesses of the presented coding frame show that formal models can never replace inductively advancing textual analysis and interpretation of the data. However, although such models or coding frames are always more or less approximations, and as such insensitive to particular features of texts, they are useful in helping one in better managing a big text corpus. In my study under way I have used the coding frame just for that purpose: it has helped me in handling the data consisting of several hundred editorials.

Greimas's actant model as well as the above model of means–end rational activity both show that narrative analysis and similar methods can also be applied to stories that do not necessarily have a plot. This is explained by the fact that goals, means and obstacles can always, in principle, be presented in the form of some sort of story, even though the original account is in a different format. Consider the above structural analysis of the *NYT* editorial. It can easily be rewritten in the form of the following story:

> The New York City Mayor and Council realized that the city budget was out of balance, and that further cuts were thus needed. The Mayor's proposal would have hurt the social services programmes targeted to the city's poor, although he insisted that the cuts would be balanced out by improvements in the productivity of city offices. Although the yes-or-no procedure was thought to be required, the Council decided to test a legal loophole to vote on separate items. That provoked a confrontation with the Mayor, but the changes made to Mayor's proposal saved more money in ways that do not hurt the services the city provides. These savings could then be used to soften the blow to programmes for the city's poor.

Plot Structure and the Story as a Whole

So many texts have characteristics of a narrative. However, not even stories proper – that is, the ones that have a plot – can be reduced to the narrative structure. The story is always a whole, a complete presentation in which the narrator in one way or another justifies why he or she is telling the story. Take someone who is telling a joke: he or she will never (unless this is a joke-telling contest or a book of jokes) set out to tell the story without some introduction or warning as to what is coming up, such as 'have you heard the story about the . . .', or 'that reminds me of the story where the . . .'. It is also common for the story- teller to insert comments of his or her own, such as 'I'm not really very good at telling jokes, but this is quite funny . . .', or, after telling the joke, 'the poor guy must have been quite surprised'.

The example reminds us that there is more to a narrative than just the plot. The plot is told in the section which Labov and Waletzky (1973) call *complication* by using what they call *narrative clauses*, but in addition to them there are *free* and *restricted clauses*. They are distinguished from narrative clauses by the fact that the place of free clauses can be freely changed without this affecting the plot, while the place of restricted clauses can be changed within certain limits (Labov 1972; Labov and Waletzky

1973). These clauses constitute four additional sections in the 'overall structure of narratives'. In addition to *complication*, Labov and Waletzky distinguish *orientation*, *evaluation*, *resolution* and *coda*. The *orientation* serves to orient the listener to the story, told in the *complication* section. The *evaluation* establishes the point the story-teller makes by the story; it is 'that part of the narrative which reveals the attitude of the narrator towards the narrative by emphasizing the relative importance of some narrative units as compared to others' (Labov and Waletzky 1973, 37). *Resolution* 'is that portion of the narrative sequence which follows the evaluation', whereas *coda* 'is a functional device for returning the verbal perspective to the present moment' (1973, 39). Coda is often expressed by *deixis* – by using the words 'that', 'there', or 'those' as opposed to 'this', 'here', or 'these' – and in that way pointing to the end of the narrative, identifying it as a remote point in the past: 'And that was that.' Not all narratives may necessarily include all these sections. For instance, the resolution section may coincide with the evaluation, and not all narratives end with a coda.

Even if one is primarily interested in the plot of the stories, it is often useful to analyze sections other than just the narrative clauses: the points where the narrator comments on the story or speaks directly to the listener or reader. These different parts of narrating have different functions. For instance, in a life-story the plot is a (retrospective) presentation of the logic of action that took place in the past, whereas in the evaluative, *free* or *restricted* clauses the story-teller expresses his or her relation to the events told about. What does the person think about a past event or his or her past action now? What was the point in telling an incident? I suggest that the overall narrative organization recurring in many life-stories reflects the cultural conceptions of reality and of persons, with their typical motives for action. Instead, the evaluative clauses reflect the ways in which individuals make sense of that reality; how they relate to the perceived conditions of action.

Stories can also be approached from the point of view of the relationship between the story-teller and the implied or real listener or reader. Recorded interactive story-telling situations can be analyzed, for instance, with the help of the methods of discourse analysis or conversation analysis, discussed in the next chapter. In the study of written texts, such as biographies, one can look at the different ways in which the writer addresses his or her reader. Vilkko (1988) uses the concept of *writing subject*, by which she refers to the character who has been created by the writer and who is encountered by the reader – and who enters into an interactive relationship with the implied reader. Vilkko refers in this context to the concept originally coined by Philippe Lejeune (1989), that is, that of the *autobiographical pact*, but broadens its scope: 'The interpretation I have is that the writer proposes to the reader, so to speak, an autobiographical pact in which she hopes the reader can recognize and accept a set of codes according to which the life-story has been put down on paper' (Vilkko 1988, 84).

In the main body of this chapter we have discussed approaches which concentrate on the narrative clauses which establish the plot of a narrative. In that way we have neglected many other perspectives to narratives. Many interesting findings in the study of narratives and narrating have undoubtedly been left undiscussed, but that is partly because some of them have already come up or will be discussed elsewhere in this book. For instance, if one focuses attention on story-telling situations, on the way in which the situation and the story are interactively constructed by following certain rules of conversation, one is led to the areas of discourse analysis and conversation analysis, to be discussed in chapter 9. On the other hand, if one concentrates on the ways in which the narrators present themselves and address their recipients, a theme already touched upon in this section, one begins to approach the domain of rhetorical analysis, which is discussed in the next chapter. Stories are an inseparable part of language and interaction.

8

The Interaction Perspective

Some years ago when I was doing a case-study on a tavern and its clientele (see Sulkunen et al. 1985) I took the opportunity to interview a couple of waitresses at the same time. I had my research assistant transcribe the tape-recorded interviews. With one interview completed, she came back and said there was one place where she definitely thought I should have pressed on with a follow-up question. She was referring to a situation where I had asked whether the waitress's job was a hard one. The waitress had said that in physical terms it wasn't, but the mental stress was frequently a problem. I recorded the response and left it at that, moving on to the next subject. My assistant emphasized that if I had followed up the lead that was clearly there I might have been able to uncover some useful information that as it was now remained hidden. I could have asked in what way the waitress regarded her job as mentally strenuous, what kinds of situations she considered particularly difficult, and what sorts of strategies she used in trying to cope with those difficulties.

From the factist perspective, the qualitative interview and other methods of data collection are regarded as ways of generating information about the object of study. The interview situation, specifically, is normally considered in terms of the reliability of the information it yields. What we will usually see is some sort of evaluation as to how the situation and the interviewer have influenced the interviewee and by the same token the nature and reliability of the data. For instance, the inference might be made that on more delicate issues (such as drinking habits) people will not always be quite honest but try to portray themselves in as positive a light as possible. In other words, from the factist perspective the interaction situation is defined as a potential source of error. As was noted in chapter 5, one of the ways in which researchers have tried to overcome this problem has been to interview the same people on several occasions in order to gain their confidence. In the interview situation where I was talking with the waitress, I was probably just about to get beyond the surface level and witness some of the conflicts that a waitress experiences on the job – but I moved on and failed to take advantage of the opportunity.

However, this chapter approaches the interaction situation from another perspective. Instead of concentrating on the respondent's speech as the source of information, as the 'data', let us take the entire interaction situation as the object of analysis. Where this approach is adopted we will be asking slightly different questions of our data. We will want to know what the interviewee's reactions to the question, or my reactions as an interviewer to the interviewee's reply, tell us about the phenomenon being studied. For example, when people are asked 'How are you?' and they say 'Fine thanks', that provides important information about the rules of interaction that apply in the encounter between two people. One thing we can infer is that the question is automatically interpreted as a 'rhetorical' one; in most situations it would be quite an embarrassing violation of the rules of interaction immediately to set out on a detailed account of all our troubles and problems.

The gist of what I call the interaction perspective is simply to study the recorded interaction situations in their entirety. Instead of rushing in to draw conclusions from this or that statement in the data, one studies the cases as specimens of interaction. From this perspective, for instance, an in-depth interview is not a more or less successfully handled tool used for getting confidential information from an individual. In the study as a whole it may be all of that as well, but the interaction perspective goes one or two steps farther by asking how the interviewer and interviewee co-produce the 'in-depth interview': how their interpretation of, and adaptation to, the particular context is visible in the structures of interaction or in concepts they use. The same applies to any interaction situation analyzed as data. For instance, one does not consider the statements of a specialist interviewed on television as more or less 'biased' information. Instead, the interview is regarded as data open to a whole range of analyses: how the interaction is orchestrated, how different speaker positions are constructed or challenged, etc. From the interaction perspective, one does not think that there are 'unbiased' statements or speaker positions. There is only situated speech that one can use as data when trying to make sense of social and cultural phenomena.

Moreover, texts and speech are more than just a means of communication or data which reflect cultural models and world-views. As speech act theorists (Austin 1962; Searle 1976) have pointed out, speech (and text) amounts to action; it produces states of affairs. Every expression can be examined from the point of view not only of its meaning but also of its effects. For example, when a priest at a wedding ceremony declares the couple husband and wife, he will be producing a new state of affairs. It is important to note, however, that the effects of speech as 'acts' can only be distinguished from their meanings in analytical terms: a promise is a promise and a directive is a directive only insofar as they are interpreted as such.

The Research Relationship and Interaction Perspective

Feminist research has devoted much attention to interviews and other forms of data collection from the viewpoint of the research relationship.

For instance, gender differences as evident in the forms of interaction have been discussed. The ethical aspects of different types of interview situations and of research relationships more generally have also been a particular concern (Smith 1974, 1977; Stanley and Wise 1983).

The example of my interview with the waitress could also be approached from the viewpoint of gender differences. How did my reactions as an interviewer possibly reflect my role as a man?

An unstructured interview comes quite close to a normal conversation situation, and the interviewer, especially if he has practically no training for the interview job or for therapy, will behave in much the same way as he would when talking with a friend. The interviewer will follow the pattern of behaviour that he has learned more or less instinctively to follow as a representative of his gender and cultural group. In this sense the interviewer's reactions do indeed constitute part of the research data; they are documents of this type of gut-instinct knowledge possessed by the interviewer.

In the interview situation concerned, my behaviour was probably representative of the male gender in Finland, known for its reluctance to talk about anything too serious or intimate. To talk with another man about your personal, psychological problems is to risk embarrassment; the most probable response will be an immediate diversion into a less grave and serious topic. Any support you get will be in the form of non-committal comments, such as 'Don't worry, things will turn out alright'. This might be something of a caricature of the male attitude and the (non-existent) confessional conversation among two men, but the fact still remains that the men we studied in local taverns (Alasuutari 1992a, 22–37; Alasuutari and Siltari 1983) very rarely talked about their problems with any openness. And the more delicate the problem, the more certain it was that any discussion that did go on would be shrouded in a veil of humour. Similarly, Falk and Sulkunen (1983) observed in their study of drinking episodes in Finnish films that men do not exactly pour out their feelings and emotions; in fact they say very little, and the person they are talking to will not pay very much attention. So one inference we may suggest here is that it is consistent with the male pattern of behaviour not to follow up on delicate issues because that would be regarded as an unwanted intrusion. A man will talk to another man about his private matters only if he wants to and only to the extent that he himself regards it appropriate.

In order to pursue this clue further, we would need to first of all do a systematic analysis of the data from this particular perspective. We might also want to collect material giving more prominence to the rules that govern conversations between men. For purposes of comparison it might be interesting to collect examples of interaction between women.

Gender differences are clearly highlighted in a study by Margareta Willner-Rönnholm (1990). In her interviews with men and women who had studied at the Turku Drawing School in 1950–1, the interview situations and the atmosphere in those situations was very different.

Talking with women, Willner-Rönnholm found that the conversations were friendlier and more informal, as if she were talking with a friend. As for her male interviewees, many did not even ask whether she wanted a cup of coffee, and the orientation on both sides was much more formal (which was evident, for example, in the way that the participants dressed for the interview). Some of the men were very brief and even blunt, and there was very little of any kind of informal chatting. When the interviewer switched off the tape-recorder, so too did the male interviewee switch off; it was almost as if he had been talking straight to the tape-recorder rather than to the interviewer.

When stressing the ethical aspects of the research relationship, feminist researchers have stressed that the methods of gaining knowledge that contributes to women's liberation should not be oppressive (Acker et al. 1991). The ideal is to have a situation where the two parties involved face each other on a par, as two equal subjects, instead of an objectifying power relationship. It seems that it is easier to achieve a more equal relationship when women are studying women, or at least such a situation reveals the complex relationship between the knower and the object of study (Westkott 1979).

On the other hand, examined as a relationship between two human individuals, the interview situation always and necessarily involves an aspect of power. Ronkainen (1989, 70–71), for instance, has pointed out that during one interview the frame of the situation may change and that it may do so more than once. In a home environment, an encounter between two women is often modelled, initially, on a normal visit among friends: 'two women meeting over a cup of coffee'. On the other hand, since the interviewer in this particular case was considerably younger than the people she was interviewing, she became the young girl next door who could be given advice; the interviewee was the more dominant party in this interaction context. Occasionally, however, Ronkainen deliberately over-turned the natural order of things:

> I reminded the respondent of who I was, what I had come here to do, I called upon the university to back me up. I was a researcher or a researcher trainee once again; I came from the University of Helsinki. I was in a position to ask questions that the girl next door couldn't, I could present possible explanations and analyses that were taken seriously. (1989, 71, my translation)

Still another frame of interaction that Ronkainen identifies in the dynamics of the interview situation is that of confiding: two women are disclosing their intimate matters or innermost thoughts to each other. This frame of conversation requires a degree of reciprocity.[1]

---

[1] Ronkainen (1989, 74) assumes that the exchange of experiences and disclosure is – at least among relatively distant women – a 'deeply feminine feature'. In the light of my own research experience I would say that such reciprocity is a universally human, not just a feminine, trait. To overstep a certain line of privacy and intimacy requires a measure of reciprocity also in interaction between men, although it is evident that the limits of the degrees of intimacy vary between individuals, genders and cultures.

An encounter between two people who are beyond and outside all hierarchies and all power relations is unthinkable; it is quite simply not a possibility. It is also important to recognize that the interview situation and the research process are two completely different things. An objectifying method of data collection (such as a questionnaire) may quite well be used in a study where the aim is to uncover the power relations prevailing in society. On the other hand, data collected in confidential in-depth interviews can be used unethically, against the interviewee's wishes.[2]

It is true of course that the qualitative interview must first of all be regarded as a situation in which all the parties to the conversation use their 'sociological imagination'. They are active producers of the research material. Through their speech acts and through the roles and attitudes they adopt, they produce concrete examples of how people act and behave or can act and behave in different cultural situations. In this sense the in-depth interview can be compared to many other forms of data collection, such as the role-playing method (Eskola 1988; Ginsburg 1978) or memory work (F. Haug 1987, 1992). However, with the possible exception of memory work carried out among a group of researchers, the actual analysis of the material will normally remain the job of the researcher – even though it is often a good idea to ask the interviewees for comments on the manuscript. At this stage the researcher is no longer just one party in the conversation.

The research relationship is of great interest from the interaction perspective, but not from the viewpoint of research ethics. Nor does one make the automatic assumption that a certain type of research relationship (for instance, one based on close mutual confidence) necessarily produces a better quality of research material than a formal relationship or a superficial discussion. The value of the data depends ultimately on the questions asked of that material. Willner-Rönnholm (1990, 47), for example, notes that even though her interviews with men were more formal and in a sense less pleasant situations, the quality of the data she obtained was in fact better (for her purposes) than in her conversations with women. She had perhaps understood her female interviewees 'too well'; and since she thought she knew the answers anyway, she had not gone to the trouble of asking any follow-up questions.

---

[2] Research ethics is a multi-faceted problematic. On the one hand, there are ethical problems related to the research relation and situation. On the other hand, they have to do with the research report. Consider, for instance, the identification of the individuals interviewed and observed in a study. In the study *Miehisen vapauden valtakunta* (The Realm of Male Freedom) (Alasuutari and Siltari 1983) we gave pseudonyms to the neighbourhood, the tavern and the study subjects, although they said that they could be referred to by their real names. However, we thought that the subjects had no way of knowing what the publicity caused by the research would be like and how wide it would be. Instead, there was nothing we could do when the darts players whom we had studied took a newspaper clipping containing a cartoon about the study, published in *Helsingin Sanomat*, and put it on the bulletin board of the tavern.

From the interaction viewpoint all aspects of a documented conversation have important use value in that they serve as clues for the analysis. The way in which power relations are reflected in the research relationship, for instance, will not be seen as an ethical problem but on the contrary as a factor that makes possible the analysis of those power relations in the first place. The interaction situation is not examined as a factor with this or that 'influence' on what the respondent says, instead the purpose is to draw inferences from what the interviewee says in a certain situation; the concern is with the whole constellation of questions and answers, comments, reactions and counter-reactions. Within the interaction perspective the aim is to interpret the rules that govern interaction, and the frames of interpretation applied by the participants. One studies the participants' definitions of the situation which help to make sense of the whole conversation and its various details.

The Frames of Interviews

In order that aspects of interaction can be studied as sources of information rather than merely as potential sources of error, we will often need to have hypotheses or explanations as to how the parties to the interaction situation have interpreted the situation, or how these frames of interpretation evolve as the situation itself unfolds. Whatever the situation, people always have some idea of 'what is going on'.

In studies based on qualitative interviews, for instance, it can be safely argued that no interviewee will answer any of the questions presented without giving at least some thought to the purpose of those questions; people will want to know what the research is really about and by the same token which questions are 'relevant' to the underlying research interest. These definitions of the situation help to orientate the interviewee. This is most clearly seen in unstructured interviews where the respondents always have to make the choice between what they want to tell and leave untold. When the interviewer asks something surprising, the respondent will have to reconsider the interviewer's intentions; and his or her response will be directed by the interpretation of those intentions. Indeed, the interviewee might even ask the interviewer what he 'means' by this or that question.

The same applies of course to social surveys as well: before answering the question the respondent will try to form some idea of the meaning of the questions presented. The very decision to take the trouble to answer or fill in a questionnaire implies that the person has in fact formed some opinion. In many cases the researcher will try to help out the respondent here by presenting a more or less detailed and truthful account of the purpose of the study.

The frames of interpretation and orientation applied by the interviewees are not situational throughout. Instead, initially people will orientate themselves by applying the frame of a familiar situation that best applies to the situation they are looking at. In modern society every adult has at some point filled in some kind of form and answered some kind of inquiry, so on this basis the 'questionnaire' may be regarded as a standard situation of everyday life; but the interviewee's orientation may also be based on some other situation that is familiar to him or her. For instance, a 'visit' is itself a frame or 'schema' which may be invoked in interpreting and organizing a situation (Chafe 1977, 222–224).

It would be overly simplistic to suggest that people only use one stereotypical frame of interpretation within which they define a situation. On the contrary they always employ a multitude of frames which overlap and flow into one another. When confronted with questions concerning morally sensitive issues (such as drinking habits), people probably try to portray themselves in as positive a light as possible regardless of who the stranger is who is asking those questions and regardless of how they have interpreted the particular situation. Amongst male cronies, heavy drinking and the ability to tolerate drink may sometimes be a matter of bragging, whereas experienced therapists say it often takes a lot of time before patients at therapy sessions will give an honest account of how much they have been drinking and of the problems that their drinking has caused. This may even be the case where the patient has decided he will go to therapy with an open and sincere mind, convinced that the best way to help himself is to come out and talk about his problems.

Personal Interviews and Group Discussions as Data

Because people always try to form some idea of what is happening in the situation as it unfolds even before they answer the questions and during the interview itself, different types of interaction situations also yield different types of research material. For example, in unstructured personal interviews many interviewees seem to apply some sort of modified 'therapy frame'. There are not very many people who have actually been to therapy sessions in which the client is expected to describe how he or she as an individual feels about different things, but as a frame the situation has become familiar to large numbers through television serials, films and other mass media. Or perhaps the model of 'individual therapy' is simply an adapted version of a 'confidential conversation' among friends. On the other hand, since the 'social scientist' or 'sociologist' is not a very familiar profession to the general public, he or she will easily be associated with the more familiar professions of 'psychologist' or 'social worker' (Peräkylä 1989). This might be so especially if the sociologist does not use the survey method but instead conducts unstructured interviews. When people are asked about their private life, they will tend to concentrate on what they think about things and how they perhaps differ from other group or family members.

In this regard the group discussion produces a very different type of research material. Particularly in the case of natural groups the participants will usually apply an everyday interaction frame. In this kind of situation the discussion will turn on what is common to the individuals concerned as group members, whereas individual differences and subjective, personal feelings will often be filtered out. The conversation will not remain a game of questions and answers between the interviewer and interviewee, but (as Willis [1978] observes) every now and then the researcher will recede into the background as the group members start asking questions of each other, discussing typical attitudes within the group and possibly beginning to argue over their interpretations. The researcher will now be in a position to see, hear and analyze aspects that do not surface in individual interviews: the terms, concepts, perceptions and structures of argumentation within which the group operates and thinks as a cultural group.

Group members can of course be asked about these things in personal interviews as well, but there is a very clear difference between the two situations. In a personal, face-to-face interview the respondent can describe his or her group and its culture, but in a group situation that culture is actually present in the sense that when they speak to one another, members of a cultural group can use 'insider' terms and concepts.

Given this special nature of the group discussion, the researcher may occasionally find that he or she does not fully understand what the group members are saying to each other or what they are arguing about. However, it is these situations that are particularly valuable as sources of information. The researcher can intervene and ask the participants to explain what they are talking about. This can be done either during the conversation or afterwards in a later discussion, after listening to the conversation on tape. The researcher can also submit to the group his or her preliminary interpretations formed on the basis of observations and the material collected.

However, the group should not be regarded as a tribune that has the authority to accept or reject the researcher's interpretations (cf. Marsh et al. 1978). Basically, a group acceptance neither strengthens nor weakens the validity of the researcher's interpretations. The group's judgement may be based more on how flattering than on how accurate the interpretation is. The researcher's interpretation is valid when and only when it makes understandable the observations made, when within the frame of that interpretation a logical explanation can be given as to why the people concerned act and talk in the way they do. Nonetheless it is important to test one's preliminary interpretations with the group, who may come back with counter-arguments that were not known to the researcher or that either corroborate or run counter to the interpretation. The feedback may suggest new important questions or interpretations to the researcher, or push him or her towards collecting new material that will facilitate the testing of the interpretation or the analysis of the meaning of the new discoveries.

In general, then, it may be said that individual interviews and group discussions produce material of a different type and quality; and that this difference must be borne in mind in interpreting the material. This is not to say that one or the other method of data collection is 'better' than the other, or that one produces more interesting or in-depth data than the other. Whether the material is good or not depends on its relevance to the questions addressed.

One reason why some researchers are reluctant to use group discussions or 'group interviews' is that they suspect people will not want to talk about their private lives in front of others; and that instead of seriously addressing the group's internal conflicts people will want to represent themselves in terms of yes-we-agree-on-everything. They want to convey the picture that theirs is a harmonious group, but that may be nothing more than a façade dictated by the group's leading authority.

Behind this line of critique against the 'group interview' there lie two different misconceptions about the analysis of qualitative research material. First of all, there is the assumption that the researcher always has to accept the statements made by the group as statements of fact. This is not so. In the analysis of the group situation it is important also to look at the hierarchy and at the interaction structure that prevails within the group: who answers the questions first, who is or who are in a position to interrupt when someone else is talking, to what extent are interpretations debated. The conversation situation can also be compared with the rest of the research material collected and the picture given by this material of the organization concerned. In that way one may be able to construct an explanatory model which, for instance, explains the contradictions between different sources of information. Consequently the analysis of interaction within the group situation provides one further piece of evidence that the organization is a hierarchical one, supporting the evidence from other components of the study.

Secondly, this critique against the group interview is grounded in the assumption that any personal and private account is a particularly valuable type of material. Indeed in some studies this may well be the case; but it will have to be a study where this information is of direct use, where conclusions can be drawn from the information that are relevant to the problem of the study. From the factist perspective detailed and intimate accounts appear as a particularly valuable source of information because it is assumed that this is the only way we can get down to the 'truth' and get to know what people 'really' think, whereas from the interaction perspective confessions and critical self-assessments are regarded simply as one form of discourse among others. There is no assumption that there exists one ultimate truth, that it is even possible to say what people 'really' think. 'Honest talk' and 'confiding' are approached as activities and forms of interaction that in themselves require explanation and interpretation. What do people say when they 'open up'? How do people know when someone is 'confiding' in them? How do they tell it apart from other forms of talk? Or conversely: How do people communicate that they are making personal confessions?

It is also against the idea of the interaction perspective to assume that group discussions are better than individual interviews because the situation is more 'natural', that the group 'culture' is authentically present in the situation. We have to remember that a tape-recorded group discussion in which the researcher asks the group various questions and submits different interpretations would not take place at all if it were not for the research. The reason why group discussions provide valuable information is that the situation encourages the people involved to talk about things that would otherwise remain outside the conversation because they are so self-evident. Where people talk about things that they normally do not talk about, we are bound to obtain interesting material. As Rabinow (1977, 119) observes, the researcher's job is to help people objectify their life-world. The group discussion is in this regard a useful method of data collection in that the subject at hand will be covered from different angles; group discussions can produce different types of discourses within which people talk about the subject at hand.

Organized Situations and Naturally Occurring Data

It is in the very nature of all scientific inquiry that the core question addressed in a study is never directly observable. No matter how honestly individuals tell about their innermost thoughts, their disclosures do not equal research results. Regardless of how freely and naturally group members engage in a discussion with each other, their 'culture' is not directly observable. The data are never the same as the object of research, because they are always framed in a particular way to shed light on the question addressed in the investigation. What can be seen or heard are just observations to be used as clues and evidence in presenting the results.

Consider a video tape-recorded by a hidden camera of people walking in a shopping mall. It is authentic material in the sense that it is not affected by the actual research process. However, even here the validity of the conclusions based on the tape will depend on the research design: the questions asked and the way they are framed. In the natural sciences, the most interesting discoveries of natural phenomena are often made in 'unnatural' circumstances. The same applies in large part to the human sciences, where most observation, conversation and interview situations are in themselves 'unnatural' settings. This, however, has nothing to do with the quality of the material or with its 'objectivity'. From the interaction perspective it makes little sense to look at the method of data collection as a more or less distorting lens that could be adjusted according to how 'natural' the setting is, and then take a picture of 'reality as such'. The material should always be examined as activity occurring in a certain situation.

It is nevertheless useful to make a distinction between data acquired by bothering people in some way as opposed to the type of data which exists or which can be collected without having to trouble anyone. Textbooks refer to *unobtrusive measures* (see Webb et al. 1966) or *naturally occurring data*; and examples are provided by films, books and magazines. Passive observation (such as recording interaction situations on tape or video) may be slotted into the same category of data collection methods. However, the latter are not wholly unproblematic as far as research ethics is concerned. On the other hand, one should not exaggerate the 'effects' of recording upon an interaction situation that is specially arranged for research purposes, even where we have the participants' consent to go ahead with the recording. For example, discourse and conversation analysis have typically looked at tape-recorded interaction situations (such as telephone conversations or therapy sessions) and sought to draw conclusions about the type of rules that the participants in the conversation usually apply in these situations. The intention is not to examine these situations as situations recorded specifically for research purposes.

In designing a study, a researcher has basically two options as to how to collect the data. In addition to using already available data one may use unobtrusive measures by, for instance, recording everyday interaction. One can also make different kinds of interventions in people's lives by, for example, sending questionnaires, doing participant observation, interviewing or arranging discussions. In both options, one is actually gathering specimens of discourses in different contexts; it is only that in the latter case one is not restricted to naturally occurring contexts. The interaction perspective simply means that when drawing conclusions from any type of data one always considers it as a totality; as a particular kind of interaction situation, not as statements extracted from their context.

Rhetoric

The study of rhetoric is a method of reconstructing or laying bare the interaction context that the speaker or writer has constructed in the text. How the speaker presents him- or herself, and from what position; who the text is addressed to; what the argument is and how it is justified. The analysis of rhetoric starts from the idea that text and speech is always created in a social context in which it is possible in one way or another to identify the roles of *speaker* and *audience*. The new rhetoric, a line of inquiry influenced most particularly by the studies of Chaim Perelman and Lucie Olbrechts-Tyteca (Perelman 1982; Perelman and Olbrechts-Tyteca 1971), is concerned with the means applied in the attempt to influence the audience, for instance to convince them that what has been said is true and honest. The relationship between speaker and audience is reflected in how the argumentation proceeds.

A distinction is routinely made between two sides in rhetoric, that is, argumentation and poetics. In the domain of poetics the concern is with concepts, distinctions and underlying metaphors; while in the case of argumentation the focus of attention is on the strategies employed to persuade the listener or reader.

A key concern in the analysis of argumentation has been with the audience construct that can be distinguished within the text or speech. If a speaker addresses his or her words to a particular audience, he or she can appeal to the private interests of that audience, but in scientific argumentation (and with certain reservations in political persuasion) the target must be a universal audience.[3] The attempt to persuade and convince a universal audience implies that the arguments must appeal to reasons and grounds that are widely accepted and regarded as true within the culture concerned. For instance, the chain of scientific argumentation is expected to proceed in such a way that, given the same premises, any adult of judgement would arrive at the same conclusions.

The 'rhetoric of inquiry', concentrating on scientific argumentation and writing has indeed been a vivid area of rhetorical analysis.[4] To take an early example, consider Gusfield's (1976) analysis of how the issue of drinking and driving is discussed in research papers. To pass as science, the articles he analyzes follow a particular 'literary style of Science', a form of presentation that is supposed to convince the audience. In this instance Gusfield speaks about the 'windowpane' theory: the style of the scientist 'insists on the intrinsic irrelevance of language to the enterprise of Science' (1976, 16–17). This means, among other things, that the active voice is rarely heard; it is as if the reality itself or pure reason alone dictated the operations and revealed the results. Gusfield treats one of the articles as a paradigmatic case:

> In the lead sentence the author (by inference) writes: 'It is increasingly becoming apparent . . . .' But to whom? Throughout the paper the conclusion or result is portrayed as emerging from an external world of data or tables. 'Differences were found . . . .'; 'This finding necessitates the reevaluation.' (1976, 20)

However, the drinking driver research – or other fields of research, for that matter – does not persuade the audience just by adhering to the rules of science. Many choices of forms and words result from and reveal implicit choices of perspective guided by common sense. For instance, the exemplary article writer's choice to speak about the 'drinking driver' instead of 'drinking driving' reflects the perspectives of psychology and sociology, the difference between a drama of agent and a drama of scene (1976, 24). With this move, the writer pulls the audience into the perspective of psychology and into a search for abiding characteristics of the personalities of persons. From this perspective, it is then a short step to suggest a common-sense distinction between the *social drinker* and the *problem drinker*, between 'normal' and 'abnormal' drunken drivers. Then,

---

[3] In public political debate it is necessary for the speakers, when expressing their views, at least to pretend to appeal to the general good (Elster 1986, 103–132).

[4] See, for instance, Atkinson (1990); Brown (1977, 1987, 1989, 1992); Edmondson (1984); Hunter (1990); Nelson et al. (1987); Simons (1990).

after the writer has reconceptualized the drinking driver from a delinquent to a patient, an alcoholic, he can express understanding and compassion. 'The courts have moved off center and to the side. In their place the medical and paramedical practitioners of alcoholism have taken the starring roles' (1976, 27).

The implicit premises on which the argumentation is based can be studied as clues about the audience to which the text is addressed, and to whom the voice of the speaker belongs. Consider the Finnish government's 1987–91 plan for the development of housing conditions in Finland:

> During the period under review no substantial increase in government subsidies to the housing sector will be possible. Since the majority of the population already enjoy at least satisfactory housing conditions, special attention shall now be devoted to better targeting of housing subsidies. The housing conditions of the underprivileged can be improved without any dramatic increase in direct expenses. By contrast we do not see sufficient grounds to continue a policy of supporting the demand for housing across the entire population, because that will effectively undermine efforts at striking a balance on the housing markets and at the same time keep prices at a high level. . . . In accordance with the above principles . . . decisions with regard to the deductibility of interest on housing loans will increasingly be based on means-tested considerations. (quoted in Summa 1989, 163)

The main purpose of this argumentation is to convince the reader that changes are needed in the current system of tax deductions granted for interest on housing loans. The starting point for the argumentation, that is, the 'truth' with regard to the government's budget restrictions, reflects the views of the party presenting the argumentation as to what the audience considers a significant shared domain. At the same time it is clear from the argumentation whose voice is speaking – the people who are in charge of the state budget.

Another focal concern in research has been with the precontracts made between the speaker and the audience, or with such domains of unanimity that are utilized in the process of argumentation. The speaker adapts to an audience by choosing theses the audience already holds as premises of argumentation.

Among the points of agreement from which the speaker draws the starting point for his or her discourse, one can distinguish those which bear upon *reality* from those which bear upon the *preferable*. The points of agreement that bear upon reality include facts, truths and presumptions, whereas those concerning the preferable have to do with values, with the principles of rank-ordering different values, hierarchies, and the loci of the preferable (Perelman 1982, 23). Two main loci of the preferable can be distinguished: the locus of quantity and the locus of quality.

> We state the general *loci* of quantity when we assert that what is good for the greatest number is preferable to what profits only a few; that the durable is preferable to the fragile; or that something useful in varied situations is preferable to something that is of use in highly specific ones. If we give as our reason for preferring something that it is unique, rare, irreplaceable, or that it

can never happen again (*carpe diem*), we are stating the general *locus* of quality. It is a locus that favors the elite over the mass, the exceptional over the normal; that values what is difficult, what must be done at the very moment, what is immediate. (Perelman 1982, 30)

An example of the locus of quantity is provided by democracy: here reference is made to what the majority of the people think and believe. The locus of quality, on the other hand, is typically adopted by the speaker who is in the attacking position because the justification of change usually requires calling into question the value of 'normal'. In this case the very foundation of the locus of quantity appealing to commonality will collapse.

In the analysis of the poetic elements of rhetoric, the basic idea is to identify in a speech or text sequence any tropes or metaphors and, particularly, to uncover 'dead' or 'dormant' metaphors that are not visible to the 'naked eye' but that often add extra suggestive force to the argument. For instance, in the policy-planning rhetoric, as evidenced by the documents preparing policy and budgetary decisions on housing policy, one often encounters such dormant metaphors as 'efficiency' and 'flexibility' (Summa 1992). When the metaphorical expression is the sole way to designate an object in a language, it is called a *catachresis*. We may, for instance, speak about the *legs* of a table or the *arm* of a chair (Perelman 1982, 122).

However, the study of rhetoric does not need to look at a text whose specific aim is at scientific or political argumentation. For instance Matti Hyvärinen (1994, forthcoming) has applied rhetorical analysis in his study of life-stories. Although Hyvärinen is concerned in his analyses to study the biographies of left-wing student activists of the 1970s, the gist of rhetorical analysis is not to try to find out how interviewees defend their position or a certain interpretation in relation to the interviewer or some wider audience. Rather, the choice of method highlights the point that the biographies produced in the interview are records of a certain interaction situation and that the material on the whole is above everything else a linguistic construct. A text is always a representation within which the speaker arrives at the conclusions he or she does on the strength of the rhetorical means and metaphors he or she has used, no matter how conscious or unconscious the choice of the logic of representation.

Consider one of Hyvärinen's case-analyses, where he looks at the rhetoric of conversion and continuity in the story told by a former student activist (Hyvärinen, forthcoming). He starts out with the observation that the interview with the woman, Anu Rantanen, is somewhat contradictory; at least it does not flow very well, in fact it is almost chaotic. The interviewee has no single interpretation that she wants to advocate, instead she is weighing the pros and cons of different interpretations. For instance, at one point where Anu is asked why she decided to join a radical left-wing student organization, she raises several possible factors and says 'perhaps one should discuss in a different way why one went . . . along'. 'Might' and 'perhaps' is the rhetoric that prevails.

In discussing the nature of the life-story, Hyvärinen refers to Norman Denzin (1989), who has suggested that the factor which makes life-stories such valuable material is their 'thick description':[5] 'Biographical, situational thick descriptions re-create the sights, sounds, and feelings of persons and places' (Denzin 1989, 93–94). From this point of view the interview with Anu Rantanen could have been regarded as a failure. In terms of a description it is rather thin, abstract, it makes sweeping generalizations – and there is no logical or chronological structure to it.

However, if we look at its 'root metaphors' (Perelman 1982, 124), it does in fact appear to exhibit a more or less coherent structure. The pre-dominant aspect in the narrative is its rhetoric of the self. Rhetorically, she makes in her account a radical distinction between the concepts of 'self' and 'true self' (cf. Perelman and Olbrechts-Tyteca 1971, 415–457). The story by Anu Rantanen of joining the radical student movement and about her membership in the movement amounts to an interpretation of what kind of human being she is and what was expected of her. The ideal member, as far as the organization was concerned, was a 'militant youth', a 'committed agitator and propagandist'; Anu herself says she was and is more inclined to withdraw and be on her own. The organization's ideals clashed with her self-image. Anu's account, closely bound up to years and dates and concrete events but hopelessly disorganized, is a story of how she gradually began to accept the kind of person she really is.

The rhetoric of self is of course in itself a linguistic and interpretative construction, even though it may consist in implied speech, in a construc-tion of one's self-image and in convincing oneself that this construct is true and honest. The ultimate 'true self' who is independent of the construct generated does not even exist because the self-construct is at once the manuscript for the activity to come. It is for this reason that it is so common for people to write their autobiographies at major turning points in their lives, in situations where they have to start thinking about things differ-ently or at least stop and think about their lives more seriously.

So truthfulness is not really a good concept for assessing self-constructs; instead, they have to be believable and persuasive. The utility of the self-construct that leans on past events for evidence as a manuscript for future activity correlates directly with its correspondence to one's own experi-ences and memories. In order that one can live one's life in accordance with this manuscript, one has to believe that the self-image is true and accurate. On the other hand, the person one is is not the only one that matters: one also has to be able to tell a believable and convincing story about one's conversion to others. This at once shows how profoundly social the self is and that rhetorical analysis is useful in studying life-stories. As

[5] The concept 'thick description', with 'thin description' as its opposite, was originally borrowed from Gilbert Ryle and introduced by Clifford Geertz (1973). By it, Geertz refers to the descriptions anthropologists doing fieldwork write about their objects of research.

Griffin (1990) has emphasized, the role of rhetoric in the conversion process is more powerful than has been realized.

When seen from the general interaction perspective on qualitative materials, the study of rhetoric is an interesting and very promising research programme in that (unlike conversation analysis, for instance) it can incorporate in its analysis the interaction context even where the material does not consist of an actual conversation situation. This means we can explore, say, administrative documents or newspaper articles.

New rhetoric critically distances itself from the old concept of rhetoric which is based on common sense: from the view that it is possible to identify in everything that is said something that is 'only rhetoric' and something that is more, something that is true and genuine. The premise of new rhetoric is that linguistic constructs are always rhetorical. The purpose of rhetorical analysis is to find out how linguistic choices and practices construct reality, how they bracket off alternative solutions and create commitment to certain thought patterns.

Rhetorical analysis is one of the means by which one can approach qualitative data as glimpses of interaction situations. It emphasizes the situational nature of meaning and, by the same token, the meaning of situations and interaction. In addition to it, and the remarks made in this chapter about different types of qualitative data as seen from the interaction perspective, there are, however, many other methods of getting a grasp of speech and conversation as interaction. Let us continue this discussion in the next chapter.

9

The Structures of Interaction

In this chapter I am going to discuss approaches and methods which particularly address the ways in which speech amounts to reality. They show how situations and realities are co-produced in face-to-face interaction or in other speech contexts. Following the pattern in this book, I will discuss how they can be applied in actively producing observations to be used in addressing social and cultural phenomena.

Conversation Analysis

Conversation analysis (CA) is an inductively advancing research programme which has been developed over the past few decades on the basis of Harvey Sacks's lectures and writings. Its objective is to study one of the bedrocks of all social life, conversations, as they occur in their natural contexts.[1]

In conversation analysis, speech situations and the rules people follow in those situations are not explored in order to make inferences, indirectly, about the reality outside the conversation; rather, the conversation is itself the prime object of study. As Schegloff puts it, Sacks started examining talk 'as an object in its own right, and not merely as a screen on which are projected other processes, whether Balesian system problems or Schutzian interpretive strategies, or Garfinkelian commonsense methods' (1992, xviii). What kinds of activities does conversation include? What kinds of structures do 'speech acts' exhibit? How do the people involved in the conversation produce an intersubjective conception of what they are doing? These are some of the more general questions that are addressed in conversation analysis. In a crude description one might say that this line of inquiry is interested in how the conversation moves from one turn to the next. So whereas narratology is interested in the logical and chronological structure of the narrative, the focal concern in conversation analysis is with the logical and chronological structures of the interaction between the individuals involved. Compared with the plot of the narrative, the only difference is that the structures of the conversation are constituted through the interaction of several individuals.

[1] For an introduction to conversation analysis, see Heritage (1984, 233–292); Nofsinger (1991); Peräkylä (forthcoming); Silverman (1985, 118–137; 1993, 125–143).

In any conversation, the type of given expression (that is, the actions contained within the expression) is largely dependent on the turn that has gone before; and that expression will for its part largely determine the conditions for the next turn of speech. For the parties involved in the conversation these structures are normative standards in the sense that they will orient themselves to interaction situations according to those rules and standards (Heritage 1984, 247–248; Nofsinger 1991, 53–54). If someone deviates from the rules, he or she will be expected to provide some sort of account of the reasons why. An example is provided by the common question–answer sequence of conversations. If you fail to answer a question within a reasonable space of time, the question will be repeated or you will be expected to give an account for not answering. The same applies to an invitation: whoever presented the invitation will assume that in reply you will either accept it or turn it down.

So, when analyzing a conversation, should the researcher try to interpret whether an utterance is or isn't really meant as an invitation? This is not needed nor even acceptable because a fundamental principle in conversation analysis is that the focus of analysis is restricted to those observations that are available to all participants in the conversation: to the information that is contained within the conversation itself. For instance, neither the analysis nor the interpretations suggested on the basis of the analysis should resort to background information such as where the conversation is taking place or what kind of institutional positions are held by the participants in the conversation. If, for example, the gender or rank of the people is not in any way visible in a conversation or in any of its episodes, then it may be inferred that such factors are not relevant to that particular situation. Accordingly, the researcher should not, and need not, try to figure out whether this or that turn of speech was intended as an invitation. Consider the following brief excerpt from a conversation:

B: Why don't you come up and <u>see</u> me some[times
A: [I would like to
(Atkinson and Drew 1979, 58)

In expressing her consent, A is indicating that she has regarded what B said as an invitation. In other words we have here an *adjacency pair*: an invitation and its acceptance (unless A continues her turn of speech by 'but', which then leads to a polite refusal). If, on the other hand, A had taken B's turn of speech as a question and answered it, we would have had another adjacency pair: a question–answer pair. If in the latter alternative B had in fact intended her statement as an invitation and therefore not immediately received an appropriate answer, then she might perhaps have rephrased her turn of speech as an invitation. If, on the other hand, no invitation were to follow later on in the conversation, then the rules of conversation analysis say that the researcher should make no attempt to infer what B 'really' wanted to say in her turn of speech. In CA one does not speculate on the 'true' meaning of an utterance, but instead studies the means and rules by which the participants make their intentions clear and work out a common understanding. As Heritage puts it: 'To summarize, conversational interaction is structured by an organization of action which is implemented on a turn-by-turn basis. By means of this organization, *a context of publicly displayed and continuously updated intersubjective understandings is systematically sustained*' (1984, 259, italics in original).

The example above also serves as a good illustration of the transcription technique that is employed not only in conversation analysis but also in certain types of discourse analysis. The purpose is to transcribe what is said in the conversation verbatim and as meticulously as possible. For this purpose there are various special symbols that are used. For example, pauses are indicated in brackets down to one tenth of a second. Similarly, emphases are underlined (or italicized), and overlapping speech is indicated by using square brackets as in the example above. The reason why this is done is that these aspects of the conversation carry information that is relevant and important to the conversationalists. And by the same token they are relevant to the analysis of the conversation.

Recently CA researchers have become increasingly interested in what is called 'institutional talk', such as press conferences, cross-examinations and interaction situations between experts and clients. Many of these topics and observations were initially pointed out by Harvey Sacks in his now published lectures (Sacks 1992a, 1992b), to be later studied more thoroughly and meticulously by his disciples and followers. The idea has been to study how the parties to interaction produce their roles as 'expert', 'interviewer' or 'witness' and how this differs from the process in ordinary everyday conversations (for an overview, see Drew and Heritage 1992).

The CA programme, with its roots in ethnomethodology, has a love–hate relationship to phenomenology, the 'forefather' of ethnomethodology. Following the founder of ethnomethodology, Harold Garfinkel, it denounces phenomenological attempts to interpret meanings. According to the CA perspective, the study of meanings amounts to an effort to look inside the heads of human beings. In that respect it has the same tendency as behaviourism to bracket off the *geisteswissenschaftlichen* assumption of the soul or of thinking. Yet the objective of CA is to study how people in an interaction situation produce an intersubjective understanding of what is going on, and in that sense it carries on the phenomenological tradition. The solution is to make only second-order inferences: to refrain from interpreting what people mean, and instead only study the ways in which individuals interpret each other's utterances and behaviour. In CA, one is not allowed to use common-sense thinking as a 'resource' in the analysis of speech.

But is this really true; is it possible that conversation analysis does not use lay understanding as a resource? Strictly speaking, it would be more to the point to say that one attempts to minimize it. CA intends to be an empirical, scientific research programme concentrating on naturally occurring interaction, and that is why one wants to base all inferences on visible or audible details in the data. However, such a programme can only be based on a basic level common-sense understanding. Consider a conversation analysis of a 'trial'. When in these cases we say that we are studying 'interaction in institutional settings' (Drew and Heritage 1992) and comparing that with 'ordinary conversation', we have to assume that there is really a difference. Besides, we have to presume or suspect that there are more or less permanent institutions or (to avoid such a big premise) 'institutional settings' where 'trials' regularly take place.

In fact, the gist of CA often is to point out a distinction between the 'literal' and the 'common-sense' meaning of an utterance. Consider the following conversation:

```
11   S:   G'n aftuhnoon sir, W'dju be innerested in subsribing
12        to the the Progress Bulletin t'help m'win a trip tuh
13        Cape Kennedy to see the astronauts on the moon shot
          . . .
17   R:   Well I live in Los Angeles. I don't live around here
18        but these fellas live here, you might- ask the:m, I don't
19        know
```
(Jefferson and Schenkein 1978, 156)

In the excerpt, S's utterance in lines 11–13 is understood as a polite request to buy a newspaper subscription, although literally it is phrased as a question of whether the man would be *interested* in buying one. Similarly, the man's response in lines 17–19 is understood as a 'no' answer, although he did not actually say no. Conversation analysis studies and pinpoints such details of everyday conversation. As the late Harvey Sacks put it: 'What we want then to find out is, can we first of all construct the objects that get used to make up ranges of activities, and then see how it is those objects do get used' (1992a, 11). The fact that in CA we are able to point out the actual, exact ways 'that persons go about producing what they do produce' (Sacks 1992a, 11) is premised on our ability to immediately understand the 'common-sensical' meaning of an utterance.

One could say that one of the functions of CA as an empirical research programme is to start off from common-sense concepts and differences and to show how they relate to the details of naturally occurring interaction. The idea is not to argue with lay conceptions, but the CA programme nevertheless builds up knowledge that provides us with a new way of looking at social and cultural phenomena. The empirical research, for instance, provides a list of the features which distinguish 'institutional talk' from 'ordinary conversation' (Drew and Heritage 1992, 22) and what exactly is a 'press conference' or a 'trial' from the CA perspective.

Contextualizing the CA Perspective

Conversation analysis is an interesting research tool with a lot of untapped potential. It shows how human interaction is socially organized also at the microlevel. Yet the research has shown that the social patterns of interaction are by no means deterministic. The participants in the interaction may at any point intervene and push the conversation in the direction they want.

Another important advantage of CA is that its rules are very clear and that the method advances in a genuinely inductive fashion. It produces reliable, positive information about conversation and its structures. When one applies CA in studying social and cultural phenomena, it is, however, important to place conversations in a broader context.

First, it is important to notice that in CA we are dealing with conversations, not with interaction generally, although this distinction sometimes becomes blurred when someone in CA talks about 'structures of interaction'. As Moerman puts it: 'Conversation analysis focuses on talk. But talk, and other human sound, is only one component of interaction. Like all components, it is neither impermeable nor functionally specific' (1988, 2). Conversations are only one type of social interaction and relations. There are other sites and ways of constructing realities and establishing relations between groups of people, and these types also have a bearing on the sites of conversation. As a particular form of social interaction, conversation is premised on certain assumptions shared by the parties and, consequently, the possibility of CA is premised on the same assumptions. That is why we must be aware of these social premises.

Consider the regulative rule of conversation where you are supposed to respond to a question posed to you or you are held accountable for not doing so. It implies a certain kind of obligation to the person who asks something, and in that sense it implies a degree of alignment. The same goes for all structures of conversation.

Now, there are sites or episodes where not even such minimal 'politeness' is honoured. Yet they are also part of human interaction or social life generally. Consider a drunkard or an otherwise annoying person talking to strangers on a bus or in a public place. Most people respond in no way at all; even 'addressed recipients' (Goffman 1979) may fail even to excuse themselves for not responding.

As trivial as the example above may seem, it points to a more general feature of society's institutional structure and power relations within it. Social institutions are designed (although not necessarily consciously and deliberately) to control and regulate the amount and forms of face-to-face interaction between such groups of people as are able to impose conditions and constraints on each others' lives. This applies to social institutions from traffic lights all the way to written language, money and mass communication. In other words, 'ordinary conversation' is a special case which occurs between equals (in that situation). And the greater the difference in rank or power position, the more 'institutional' the conversation is.

To take an example, have you tried to talk to an important, hierarchically superior person? Recently I called the president of our university. His secretary did not put me through, but instead she asked what my business was. I told her, and she passed it along to him in the next office. To answer a question I asked, she put me on hold and talked to him, and then she answered. At one point during the conversation the president yelled a response from his room, so that I could hear him down the line, but I never talked directly to him.

Conversation analysis has in fact paid attention to the phenomenon. In his 1964–65 lectures, Harvey Sacks (1992a, 51–52) discussed the problems faced by journalists because they are not allowed to pose a follow-up question in a press conference. As a consequence, journalists may try to put long, involved questions: 'Would you do so-and-so or not, and if not, then . . .?' Nevertheless, by not being able to ask follow-up questions they have limited control of the situation.

Given the far-reaching implications of that phenomenon, one would assume that the research on 'institutional talk' is just the right direction for CA to take in future: in that way it seems to tackle an important issue. That is certainly true, but to move ahead requires that one takes distance from the strictly inductive CA research programme. For instance, although the hypothesis presented above, according to which institutions can be understood as ways of controlling and regulating the amount and forms of face-to-face interaction, is perfectly in concert with the findings of the CA research on institutional talk, we could never come to that conclusion inductively.

If one wants to study institutions or social interaction in a broader sense, as outlined above, CA may help in producing hints about the phenomena, but some of its specific features impose restrictions on its applicability. For instance, there is the problem that the special rules of talk in an institutional setting are hardly ever decided in that very setting. Institutional settings of talk are like games with special rules. Of course, the rules are never detailed enough to determine each move in a game. If they were, we would be talking about not a game but a clockwork process. The idea is to define the general rules within which the parties can try to pursue their own ends. Actual game situations consist of different parties trying to achieve their goals within the given rules, and of negotiating or even bending them. Yet, it would be silly to say that there are no preset rules, or that the whole concerted action is locally produced.

The decisions about the general rules of institutional games are not necessarily made in particular accessible sites of interaction, such as meetings. By weighing the pros and cons as they are framed and presented in, for instance, the memos for a meeting or discussions in the mass media, people may make up their minds in the lonely hours of the night.

However, even if we were to get access to conversations where institutional arrangements were made, CA would not be the right method for that purpose. The undoubtedly great invention of CA is to restrict itself to those details of a conversation which the participants themselves take up when responding to the others' turn of speech. By letting the conversationalists confirm the meaning of an utterance or a word used the researcher can, in a way, hide behind the 'members'' backs, which makes an interpretation (of an interpretation) rhetorically convincing. However, this restriction also means that the researcher is at the mercy of the conversationalists. For instance, the members' shared understandings or an individual speaker's insinuations, which are evident in particular choices of words or framings of a topic but are not taken up by others, are beyond the scope of CA, no matter how systematically a cultural distinction or frame appears in the material. Besides, even the 'confirmed' meanings of utterances are only approached from the point of view of their function for the course of the conversation. Because of this kind of formalism in the CA perspective, it does not address the cultural contents of conversation but only the structures of interaction evident in that particular setting. If we are interested in studying the reasons and rationales for following or challenging institutional rules, the structures of meaning inherent in the speech are a more promising aspect of the data. As has been discussed in the previous chapters, there are many other things going on in interaction besides the structures of conversation. People share a world-view or a view of life; they may try to appeal to principles or frames; play rhetorical tricks on each other; or they may threaten each other with force.

Imagine a trial where the judge says to the witness: 'The next time you do that I will hold you in contempt.' From the CA perspective the transcript of the trial would show how the interactants co-produce on the spot the 'testimony' as an example of 'institutional interaction', with certain constraints on what the witness says or does in the stand. If the breach of the rules of proper conduct on the part of the witness were something else (for instance, 'improper' language) than, say, the constraints on turn-taking, the whole conflict would not even emerge as a topic. Yet the normative rules of proper conduct, stated and sanctioned in the law and applied and negotiated by the participants, are obviously vital in making sense of courtroom behaviour.

Like any methodological perspective on qualitative data, CA abstracts away from some aspects of the material in order to shed light on other aspects. But we can, of course, make use of the tools CA provides in addressing some of the questions that fall outside the scope of the CA framework, by combining them with other approaches or methods. *Pure* CA deliberately abstracts away from the contents and material conditions of talk to a more formal level, at which one only studies the rules followed in a conversation. One does not allow the use of background information or common knowledge as a resource in interpreting and making sense of a conversation. Everything has to be based on the material made available to the participants during the conversation and explicitly referred to by the conversationalists. If, say, the gender of the participants is not explicitly evoked in a speech situation, it does not exist as a relevant category for the CA researcher. Therefore, more macrosociological questions cannot be addressed by assuming and making inferences from discourses which guide and organize human thought as well as the workings of organizations. On the other hand, we can talk about *applied* conversation analysis, where the method is used to make further observations from qualitative data, to be then used as clues in addressing social and cultural phenomena.

Both branches of CA have their function. Pure conversation analysis provides basic knowledge about the rules and structures of conversations and institutional talk. Applied CA can, for instance, help make visible distinctions based on cultural understandings and explain how those notions are put to use in real situations.

Let us consider here the article by Silverman and Peräkylä (1990) which discusses the treatment of 'sensitive' issues. According to their analysis, reference to a sensitive topic, for instance sex, will be marked in the conversation by hesitation or pauses between words. This provides a better means than intuition to locate 'sensitive' topics of conversation.[2] The next question could then be: why are these particular topics so 'sensitive'; what do 'sensitive subjects' really mean? Accordingly, conversation analysis can produce observations (such as lists of 'sensitive topics') and make a distinction between those situations in which the participants 'mark' a certain topic (such as 'sex') as sensitive and those in which they do not.

The methods of CA can also be applied in identifying more subtle reflections of discriminating or underprivileged social categories, such as gender. Although the same basic rules might be applied to all participants, and although the category that makes a difference is not invoked, it may be that the participants have a tendency to treat those falling into that category in a particular way more often than others. For instance, Victoria Leto DeFrancisco (1991) shows that in ongoing interactions between heterosexual married couples, the women were more likely to be silenced by men than the other way around. As complex and interpretative as the work of identifying conversational components is, counting such cases can sometimes be useful, at least as a means of coming to grips with interesting further questions. The same goes for CA in general: it is one useful way of generating more observations of qualitative material than are visible to the naked eye. The potential uses are virtually endless.

The Concept of Face

In terms of its theoretical and methodological approach, conversation analysis comes quite close to Michel Foucault's theory of discursive practices and also many research ideas inspired by Erving Goffman. These

[2] Silverman and Peräkylä (1990, 294) state that, increasingly, ethnographers are resisting the naïve assumption that phenomena like 'the family' or 'science' are only (or most 'authentically') constituted in single sites, such as households or laboratories. They suggest that the same be true about 'sexuality' or 'death'. This suggestion refers to the discourse-theoretical viewpoint, represented particularly by Michel Foucault (1980), where for instance both 'sex in itself' and 'sexuality' are considered in a nominalist fashion as phenomena that exist in the form of various speech- and other practices – that is, discourses.

(not to mention many other) lines of inquiry share with CA the premise that language is not just a way of conveying ideas and information about reality or of expressing cultural views and distinctions about the world that surrounds us. It is also and importantly a way of producing and constructing states of affairs. This aspect of human interaction is always linked with questions of morality.

A shared understanding among the parties to interaction as to 'what is going on' is always tightly intertwined with notions as to what kinds of things people should respect as moral values. Erving Goffman has looked at the rules followed in social interaction from this particular point of view. According to Randall Collins (1988), Goffman is here, in his analyses of how social and symbolic order is maintained by means of rituals, following the tradition that was started by Émile Durkheim in *The Elementary Forms of the Religious Life* (1965).[3] In the modern world, however, rituals are not impressive religious ceremonies but often small little things that are part of ordinary social etiquette. 'In situations where we feel momentarily embarrassed and annoyed as people do not give way in the street, as someone in the lift comes too close or as someone wholly impolite interrupts a joke, we are dealing with the sacred that is ingrained in the etiquette prevailing in modern society' (Heiskala 1991, 97–98). In everyday interaction the role of the sacred, comparable to divinity, is reserved for the individual person. Goffman (1967, 73) quotes Durkheim, who indeed deals with the same question: 'The human personality is a sacred thing; one dare not violate it nor infringe its bounds, while at the same time the greatest good is in communion with others' (Durkheim, 1974, 37).

In what way is the person sanctified in everyday rituals? One interesting perspective on this question is opened up by the concept of *face*, discussed by Erving Goffman. According to Goffman, 'face may be defined as the positive social value a person effectively claims for himself by the line others assume he has taken during a particular contact' (1967, 5). Goffman argues that a sacred principle prevails in conversation situations whereby the parties to the conversation reciprocally maintain and defend each other's face. This means, among other things, that the people involved in the conversation are considerate towards each other and try to sustain each other's self-image.

Let us briefly go back to the excerpt given earlier where the first speaker presented an invitation (Why don't you come up and see me sometimes?) and the second answered in the affirmative. First of all, the fact that a reply is given to the invitation may be seen as an example of a considerate act, the aim of which is to keep intact the face of the person who asked the question. Secondly, the invitation may be seen as an example of an act

---

[3] According to Randall Collins (1988), one can identify a Durkheimian ingredient in Goffman's theoretical orientation throughout his production. That is partly because as a student several of his teachers were followers of Durkheim.

Table 9.1   *Types of face-threatening acts*

Act threatens	Speaker's face	Addressee's face
Positive face	Apologies, confessions	Criticism, ridicule, challenges, irreverence
Negative face	Expressing thanks, excuses, acceptance of offers	Orders, requests, advice, offers, promises

which jeopardizes the listener's face because it pressures her into acting in a certain way.

Brown and Levinson (1987) propose a detailed classification of different types of face-threatening acts. It is based on a distinction between acts threatening positive vs negative faces; and on a distinction between whether the act primarily threatens the face of the speaker or of the listener. Table 9.1 illustrates the classification and examples of it.

In everyday situations it is impossible to avoid face-threatening acts, but we do have various strategies for making them less threatening. For example, we can make an indirect apology, as in the previous example. The invitation was presented in the form of a question, so that the listener could easily have turned it down without causing any offence, preserving the speaker's face by interpreting the invitation as a question and saying: 'I'm sorry but I've been so busy recently.' There are also many ways in which a person may refuse an invitation and still preserve the invitor's face. Heritage (1984, 273) uses the same extract of a conversation as an example of the 'preferred action format' *acceptance*, in which case the replies commonly occur 'early'. Instead, the dispreferred *refusals* often occur 'late', thus also allowing for the first speaker to reformulate the invitation. And of course the preferred, 'affiliative' action format can be used as a 'polite' way of refusing an invitation: 'I would like to but . . .'

Analyses of face-protection in rituals of everyday life touch upon the very core issues of sociology in the sense that, ultimately, they have to do with how society is possible in the first place. From a Goffmanian point of view – as Heiskala puts it – 'even in modern society social order is founded upon this sacredness that is ingrained in micro-situations' (1991, 98). The status of sacred is afforded specifically to the individual person. On the other hand, it is clear that a secularized everyday religion which sanctifies the individual as god cannot be the only glue that holds together modern society. In his discussion of this same theme, Mäkelä (1991) stresses that the assumption of human individuals as rational, goal-oriented actors is one of the main preconditions for fluent interaction and at the same time a mainstay of social order. Microsociological analyses have disproved the common assumption of the sociological tradition and shown that moral and means–end rational activity (or *homo sociologicus* and *homo economicus*) are closely intertwined and stand as prerequisites for one another.

Frames and Discourses

Erving Goffman's contribution to the analysis of interaction is not confined to the concept of face. Another important aspect of his writings has to do with the way in which he looks at the self as a social construct flowing from the structure of interaction. This line of analysis highlights the fact that identities vary across different situations. Individuals are always constituted in different situations as different kinds of identities, and even in the same situation the determinants of self may rapidly change. This line of argumentation critically distances itself from the view that the individual's personality is a quality or characteristic which changes very slowly, if at all.

This approach is most clearly seen in Goffman's (1974) concept of frame. By frame, Goffman refers to sets of rules that constitute activities so that they are defined as activities of a certain type. When in everyday life we form some picture of 'what is going on', we have located a frame that makes the situation (at least partially) understandable.

The concept of frame lies somewhere in the middle ground between interactionism, structuralism and discourse analysis. On the one hand, the concept can be approached from a cognitive point of view, looking at it as a framework for interpretation, in the spirit of symbolic interactionism. Different frames can be applied to a certain situation or a certain phenomenon to make them appear in a different light, or to throw light on different aspects of them. The structuralist undertones in the concept of frame are highlighted in the absence of any assumption that actors are free to produce their own interpretations; the interpretation of meanings is regulated by the frames existing within the cultural context and within which expressions take on a meaning (and the interpretation of meaning takes place by combining those frames). The discourse-analytical and ethnomethodological approach, on the other hand, is seen in the argument that in situations which are always 'framed' in one way or another, it is not so much that the situation is interpreted within this or that framework; rather the point is that the framework constitutes the situation. When, for instance, one of the participants in a situation is engaged in a long extended monologue at the front of the room while the others are listening, we have a situation which is described as a 'lecture'; but when the audience begins to comment on the lecture or pose any questions, to fill in the spaces occurring in the monologue and make use of turn-exchange mechanisms, the situation turns into a 'conversation'.

What does all this have to do with the production of identities? When a frame changes from one into another, so too do the situational identities of the participants change. For example, when a 'lecture' changes into a 'conversation', the 'lecturer' or 'teacher' changes into a 'participant in the conversation'.

In a study on the hospital treatment of terminal patients, Anssi Peräkylä (1989, 1991) applies the method of frame analysis to explore the material he collected by way of participant observation. He found that all activities that had to do with his patients in hospital could be slotted into one of four frames: Activities within the *practical frame* have to do with everyday routines such as making up the beds, washing the patients, getting the meals done. Activities within the *medical frame* are concerned with examining the patient, monitoring and controlling processes occurring within the patient's body, running different tests on the patient. Within the *lay frame* emotions are expressed that are called forth by illness and death: crying and embracing relatives are typical activities that are found in this category. Finally, the *psychological frame* is where these same emotions are analyzed and where one attempts to control those emotions; for instance, nursing staff will keep records of the patient's reactions and present their interpretations of those reactions.

There are fixed assumptions linked to these frames about the individuals, with certain identities involved in the interaction. For example, within the medical frame the patient is regarded simply as a physical body, whereas in the psychological frame the patient is thematized as a set of emotional and cognitive processes.

In everyday practices and in everyday speech, frames often flow into one another and change very quickly. Let us look here at one excerpt from Peräkylä's fieldnotes:

> The neurologist enters the room with a medical student. They go over to see Mr K. The neurologist asks the patient something. There is no reply. He then turns to the wife and repeats the question: are we doing any better? He is very brisk and cheerful. The wife says, slowly and dryly, no, we're not doing any better. The doctor then proceeds to carry out some neurological tests (moves the patient's hands, examines the back of the eye) and at the same time talks to the medical student. After the examinations the neurologist says (speaking separately to the man and his wife) that he'll now be transferred to ward 101; hopefully the situation will improve up there. The wife asks the doctor what is causing the trouble. The neurologist says it is impossible to say for sure; perhaps it is the illness itself, or then the recent discontinuation of cortisone treatment. This will now be resumed. – Observation: the patient's wife is very matter-of-fact as she discusses her husband's situation with the doctor, very careful in what she says. (1990, 20)

Most of what is happening here is taking place within the medical frame; but there are also two other, parallel frames. Early on in the excerpt there is a reference to the doctor asking, in a cheerful sort of way, how the patient is feeling; this points to the lay frame, to the patient's and his wife's experiences. Towards the end of the excerpt the psychological frame emerges as the researcher draws his inferences about what is going on from the behaviour of the patient's wife.

A focal concern in Goffman's frame analysis is with the relationship between different frames, and this is clearly seen in the above study by Peräkylä. He draws our attention to the fact that the psychological frame was used for purposes of problem-solving in conflict situations: serious analysis of the patient's emotions started most particularly in those situations where something had gone wrong in activities belonging to other frames. This kind of situation will emerge, for instance, when a dying patient refuses to have treatment that artificially maintains his or her life-functions. Since the continuation of life is a more or less self-evident objective as far as medicine is concerned, refusal to receive treatment will be handled as an abnormal reaction that will be interpreted and taken under critical scrutiny within the psychological frame.

A strictly formalistic frame analysis, which focuses on practices as constituted by particular frames, is elegant in its clarity, but on the other hand it abstracts away from the contents of speech taking place within such frames. Sue Fisher's (1991) analysis of medical consultations shows that a look at the contents of discourse or the more cognitive side of frames reveals how complexly intertwined different frames, discourses and practices are. For instance, medical encounters can be sites for discussing or struggling over the meaning of marriage, women, work and nuclear family.

In her article she compares the ways a nurse practitioner and doctor communicate with women patients during medical encounters. In a doctor–patient encounter she analyzes, in the 'medical discourse', within which the doctor prefers to discuss the patient's problem, he uses the 'discourse of the social' as a resource to draw practical conclusions from his diagnosis. He has diagnosed the patient's problem as hyperventilation and tension. When it turns out that the woman, who has a small baby, goes to work, and that her husband has been frequently out of town because of his work, the doctor says:

> Well, you know, if this continues to be a problem, you know, if you have any more episodes then you know you might need to look into ways that you could limit the amounts of any work that you have to do, uh and I think that that would be a good place to start. (Fisher 1991, 164)

In the other example, where a nurse practitioner deals with a woman patient's problem, the discussion is consciously focused on the social context of the patient's life. In the course of the consultation, the reason for her fatigue is traced back to her being overburdened by work and household chores, and the husband being too 'suffocating'. As a conclusion, the nurse practitioner advises that she continue to try to change her job so that she is no longer working next to her husband. She also urges her to take up running again, because these changes would reduce her stress.

Fisher's case examples show that frames or discourses, whatever one calls them, are embedded in each other in many ways. For instance, medical diagnoses are informed by and premised on larger cultural notions, and vice versa.

It is of course natural that professional frames, such as the 'medical' frame or discourse, are influenced by or embedded in other frames, because they are an integral part of culture. The gist in frame or discourse analysis is not to first separate a professional discourse from its social contexts and then to reveal that it is 'biased' by them. Rather, frame analysis attempts to distinguish and point out the linguistic and non-verbal practices by which phenomena and subjects, commonly known to belong to particular classes, are constructed.

Consider my own analysis of alcoholism as a cultural phenomenon (Alasuutari 1992a). In this study I did not undertake a detailed frame analysis of speech or activity, but, rather, used the notion of frame as a sort of umbrella concept to conceptualize the way in which 'alcoholism' is produced in everyday practices. The notion of drinking as an activity that may lead to an addiction is reproduced in everyday life in such a way that people deal with drinking in the context of two different frames – that is, the *everyday-life frame* and the *alcoholism frame*.

The everyday-life frame here has a very broad meaning. It refers to all those specific frames that organize everyday life both conceptually and practically and which guide the meaning of drinking in those situations. Everyday life is organized by, and around, different frames such as 'party' or 'going to work'. Within the everyday-life frame, drinking is understood in the context in question as an ingredient in an everyday-life situation. In social interaction, drinking may have different functions. First of all, a drink may be used as a signal which carries a special meaning; for instance, people may drink a glass of champagne in celebration of an important day. On the other hand, the everyday drinking situation may in its entirety define or constitute 'what is going on'. This will be the case in the situation where colleagues go out together for a drink after a hard day at the office.

In the alcoholism frame, drinking is the object of reflexive attention, and as such it is isolated or seen apart from its particular social contexts. Instead, attention is focused on the individual and on his or her habits or style, on the specific way in which the individual plays his or her role in the situation that involves alcoholic beverages. In any situation any individual can of course shift his or her attention from the communicative meaning of activities to the style of behaviour, and vice versa. The alcoholism frame is a special case amongst those frames which construe the modern person as an individual distinct from others with distinctive characteristics. The identity of the 'alcoholic' is produced from this perspective in such a way that the individual and the people around that individual repeatedly apply the alcoholism frame to his or her drinking (or abstinence) so that it structures different situations of everyday life. However, the role of the alcoholism frame in the structuring of social reality is not confined to the production of 'alcoholics'. It is applied not only to extreme situations or to deviant drinking habits; people use it commonly in interpreting and evaluating their own and other's drinking habits. That is why it structures, to a certain degree, all drinking situations. This also means that theories of problems related to alcohol use must be seen as an integral part of these problems and not only as observations or theories of some illness.

The way I used the concept of frame in analyzing alcoholism is actually closer to Michel Foucault's concept of discourse than Goffman's concept of frame. Both concepts are keen to stress that linguistic interaction consists not only in the exchange of information but also in the production of different states of affairs, positions and identities. Goffmanian frame analysis particularly emphasizes the situational nature of speech acts. A frame analysis à la Goffman would probably show that even in therapy situations alcohol problems are not dealt with in a single alcoholism frame, but that several frames are employed and therefore several identities are produced for the client. Instead, the Foucauldian concept of discourse stresses the institutional and organizational side of discursive formations. Discourses, such as the alcoholism frame, may often be challenged in speech situations, but some of them have materialized in institutions built in accordance with them. The 'true nature' of alcoholism can be challenged and speculated upon, but the alcoholism treatment institutions and other existing societal and legal arrangements set up to handle identified patients impose their very concrete and practical limits and conditions for the formation of subjects and identities.

Power and Knowledge in Discourse

Discourse analysis is sometimes associated with a voluntaristic and idealistic notion of social life. According to this notion, reality only consists of constructs and subjective perceptions, which can thus be freely changed by just starting to think differently. Although there might be some truth in that image of discourse analysis, it is also ironic as far as the Foucauldian concept of discourse is concerned. For Foucault, 'it is in discourse that power and knowledge are joined together' (1980, 100). Admittedly, also for Foucault discourses allow for re-readings or reconceptualizations of dominant power/knowledge couplets. However, he not only refers to speech or discussions; institutions organized according to certain forms of power/knowledge are part of the discourses. In this sense, the Foucauldian notion of discourse is an enlargement of the meaning of the interaction perspective. Our interaction with institutions and built environments can be seen as part of it. Within the Foucauldian concept of discourse, interactants are not separated out from their social and material conditions, or treated as free-floating bodyless minds that are engaged in a conversation joyfully playing with words and ideas. The concept of discourse refers to the ever-renewing unity of words and realities: speech and language convey meaning, produce states of affairs, and construct subjects and identities all at once, and a change in any of these aspects has a bearing on the other ones.

10

Cross-Tabulation and Quantitative Analysis

The basic principle of qualitative analysis is the unconditional nature of observations: on the basis of individual observations, we must be able to formulate rules which are valid throughout the material. We cannot base our argumentation on statistical relations between the variables describing the observation units.

This methodological requirement often leads to presentational problems, when a rule which holds true throughout the material is based on combining raw observations. In such a case the meta-observation is formulated on the basis of several variants which can be seen on the level of raw observations. If there are a sufficient number of cases, it becomes impossible to present them all as direct quotations from the material – at least if we do not wish to stultify the reader and swell the research report to mammoth proportions. If, on the other hand, there are only a limited amount of case examples, the reader may doubt whether the observation clause is really valid for all cases.

I have dealt with this problem by giving some examples of all the different ways a meta-observation manifests itself in the material. This technique was used in my research *Blue-Collar Men's Life-Stories and Alcoholism* (Alasuutari 1986; for a shorter English version see Alasuutari 1992a) in which I dealt with the narrative structure of men's life-stories on the basis of narrative interviews. The narrative turns, or phases as I called them, within the discovered structure of the life-stories assume different forms in different stories. When I selected examples of the ways the phases appear in the stories, I grouped the variants into different categories and chose dissimilar examples from the representatives of these categories.

For instance, while studying the appearance of the phase called 'man decides to become independent' (Alasuutari 1986, 42–45), two examples describing the dramatic breaking away from home are chosen. Here is one of them:

> When I was fourteen, it was Christmas eve or something like that. . . . My younger brother had some mishap and Pop, who was drunk, started to administer some discipline. I got up and said you'd better quit beating him right now. So I hit Pop, the rocking chair and Christmas tree came down with a crash, and so did Pop. . . . First he went and got out an axe, I was fourteen and felt fourteen feet tall, he didn't scare me none. I took the axe from him – then he went for a knife. During the fight I hurt myself enough to draw some blood from my nose, and that was the end of it. . . . I finished school, alright – but having

finished it I left home straight away and didn't go back for years. . . . Mom used to visit me. (Alasuutari 1986, 43)

In a similar way I selected two examples of stories in which becoming independent relates to school. School becomes repulsive as the protagonist of the story wants to become independent by earning money for himself. I also quote a story in which independence leads to estrangement from former friends. Furthermore, I present a quote from a story in which becoming independent entails an experience of insecurity: 'It was hard to get a job. And it ain't easy to get used to working and bear responsibility for one's own doings' (1986, 45).

Arranging the Observations in Tabular Form

In examples like these it is also possible to present all of the cases, divided into different types, in a tabular form. This was done in another section of the same study (Alasuutari 1986, 86). In the table I classify the life-stories into three types according to the main organizing principle of the narrative – namely economic career, human relations and changes of mood – and calculate the proportions in which the life-stories of the two groups, the customers of the A-Clinic, a treatment centre for alcoholics, and the metal workers who acted as a comparison group, are divided into these three types.

In such classification and counting of the cases we are not yet really dealing with quantitative analysis – that is, presenting conclusions based on statistical relations. Tabulation is only a handy way of presenting the material on which qualitative analysis is based. It shows that the material is being used systematically; not merely as a search for text passages to support our intuitive interpretation.[1]

However, even this type of presentation in tabular form is proving things with quantitative relationships in the sense that by arranging the cases in a tabular form we can prove the existence of a rule which is true for all the cases. For example, in his paper analyzing the alcohol quotes from general magazines and women's magazines in 1955 and 1985, Heiskala (1988) presents a table in which he classifies the cases according to consumer groups and sample years, as well as whether the quotes deal with intoxication use or instrumental use (table 10.1).

As his conclusion, based on the table, Heiskala states that in 1955 'a sign of woman cannot be associated with the sign of alcohol without the mediation of a sign of man'. There was one superficial exception to the rule, which Heiskala had to analyze in order to prove that the observation clause is unconditionally true for all the material:

[1] It is of course possible, at least in principle, that a scholar applying both qualitative and quantitative methods of analysis is simply cheating: presenting claims about his or her tables or other material which are not true. However, when the arguments are presented in tabular form or otherwise explicitly, it is easier for a doubtful reader to check the results by asking to see the original data.

Table 10.1   *Mentions of alcohol in general magazines and women's magazines in 1955 and 1985 according to types of use and the construction of the user groups*

	Type of use			
User group	For purposes of getting drunk	Instrumental use	Not classified	Total
1955				
Male or group of males	6	4	2	12
Female or group of females	1	–	2	3
Male and female	–	2	–	2
Mixed group	–	5	–	5
Not classified	1	–	3	4
Total	8	11	7	26
1985				
Male or group of males	11	6	1	18
Females or group of females	2	6	–	8
Male and female	–	6	1	7
Mixed group	–	1	1	2
Not classified	4	2	5	11
Total	17	21	8	46

'Male and female' user group refers to a couple; 'Mixed group' includes more than two people and both sexes.

Source: Heiskala 1988, 5

As a matter of fact, this single reference also confirms the masculinity of drinking alcohol with the purpose of getting drunk. It is namely a joke, where a man returns home late after a night out. Instead of the nagging wife he fears to encounter, what he sees is his wife leaning against a floor lamp in an advanced state of intoxication. She manages to sputter between hiccups, 'Too bad, too bad, honey, that you didn't come home earlier! Now I've lapped up all your best whisky!' (1988, 5)

In a similar way Heiskala sums up his observations about magazine quotes of alcohol usage according to who is the controlling agent. There are six cases including a control perspective in 1955; in four of them the controller is the wife, in two the police. When it is further noted that both of the latter cases take place abroad, Heiskala can state that the structure of meanings built around alcohol use in the 1955 material is organized almost exclusively according to the model 'man drinks – wife controls'. On the contrary, in 1985 the picture of male intoxication use has become more complicated. First, it does not always build up into a problem calling for control. Secondly, other controllers, like the state, have entered the picture along with the wives.

Boolean Algebra and Qualitative Comparison

This type of analysis based upon qualitative argumentation can be developed further under certain conditions. In his book *The Comparative*

Method Charles Ragin (1989) presents a method based upon Boolean algebra where the idea is to investigate under what conditions a state of affairs is realized. The precondition of this method is that the possible factors influencing an object are simplified into a binary form: either some factor is influential or it is not influential. After this the cases are presented in a truth table where different types of cases are represented by variables in their own rows, the last variable being presented as the conclusion or answer to the problem. To illustrate this method Ragin (1989, 90) takes a hypothetical example from research that investigates what conditions cause the collapse of military regimes. The three research conditions are: a sharp conflict between older and younger military officers (A); the death of a powerful dictator (B); or CIA dissatisfaction with the regime (C). In the truth table, 1 indicates realization of conditions and 0 that it is not realized.

The examined results can be presented by listing all the combinations of conditions whose final outcome (F) results in the collapse of the regime. In this form of presentation upper case letters (ABC) indicate the condition realized and lower case letters that the condition is not realized. In this way the above truth table can be presented in the following form:

$$F = Abc + aBc + abC + ABc + AbC + aBC + ABC$$

The familiar multiplication and addition signs in Boolean algebra have their own significance: the plus sign indicates a logical OR operation and multiplication (like Abc) indicates the logical operation AND. Boolean algebra also has its own rules for simplification, of which the most important is that if two terms differ from each other by only one state, but still produce the same final result, the state can in this instance be ignored. So that in the above expression, since the fourth term is ABc and the last is ABC, these two terms can be simplified to the form AB. When all possible simplifications are carried out in this expression the end result is as follows:

$$F = A + B + C$$

This means that the military regime will fall if even one of these conditions is realized.

Ragin's research examples represent an approach that is quite quantitative, variable-oriented and aimed at explaining causal factors. How well does Boolean algebra apply to cultural studies' characteristic problem settings, like qualitative analysis of unstructured interviews? Is there anything about this model that is fundamentally incompatible with cultural studies?

Let us do a small analysis exercise. As research material let us take eight personal interviews that deal with listening to the radio.[2] These are taken from the material consisting of 48 interviews, where the idea was to obtain

[2] The collection of the data in question was funded by the Finnish broadcasting company YLE. The first publication based on it is *Radio suomalaisten arkielämässä* [Radio in the Everyday Life of the Finns] (Alasuutari 1993).

an overall picture of the role of radio in everyday life. Therefore one part of these interviews was to get as much detailed description as possible about the situations in which people listened to the radio. As well as other questions, the interviewees were asked: at what time and where did they listen; what else were they doing; was anyone with them; was there any group discussion about what was heard on the radio; did other tasks prevent concentrating on listening; do they remember what the programme was, what was discussed, what records were played; and which station did they listen to?

From these eight interviews I found a total of 42 listening situation descriptions which were so detailed that each situation could be coded with variables describing listening location (A), character of listening (B), social situation (C) and programme type (X).

The first problem with applying Ragin's method is that the variables have to be simplified into binary form, thus excluding typologies containing considerably more alternatives, describing, for example, the programme type. It is quite difficult and arbitrary to decide how this simplification is to be accomplished. Furthermore, in spite of this simplification, the alternatives do not correspond to what Ragin means by his conditions affecting a state of affairs: the method includes the precondition that in each investigated case certain conditions are either realized (code alternative 1) or not realized (alternative 0).

Another problem is that, when we try to explain the role of radio in everyday life in terms of interpretative sociology, it does not make sense to think that the explanation is causalistic: it is by no means self-evident that there are some independent variables and one dependent variable. Any situation describing property can be the variable that needs to be explained. In any event let us construct a coding model that describes the characteristics of a listening situation:

Variable A: Place
1 = at home or during the weekend
0 = at work, in the car or in a public place

Variable B: The nature of the listening
1 = listening is the main mental activity
0 = the radio (or cassette or record player) is for background music

Variable C: Social situation
1 = a person is alone or a passive member of a group
0 = a person is in an active interaction situation

Variable X: Type of programme
1 = news or other speech programme
0 = music, record or cassette player

In the research example discussed, the problem associated with the analysis is that, as certain conditions are realized, the dependent variable is

Table 10.2 *Truth table showing three conditions for listening to music*

| Conditions | | | Music | | |
A	B	C	Number of cases	Listening cases	Outcome
1	1	1	14	4	1
1	1	0	8	1	1
1	0	0	4	2	?
1	0	1	0	0	?
0	1	1	10	7	0
0	1	0	2	0	1
0	0	0	0	0	?
0	0	1	4	4	0

given the value 1 in some situations and in others the value 0. This indicates that the conditions are not sufficient; that many additional situation variables would be required. It is unclear whether one could even theoretically find so many explicit and unambiguous conditions that the final result, in every instance, would be one or the other of the given alternatives. One would think that in extreme cases each listening situation described would represent its own type. In this case it would be back to square one: with this approach nothing generally useful could be said about listening to the radio.

To this, however, Ragin has a solution which can be appropriated. At the same time it approaches an analysis in quantitative research. The idea of this solution is to count how many cases the variable to be explained realizes the alternative 1 and in how many 0. If either alternative forms a definite majority then it is assigned as the value of the final result. Again if the events are evenly divided then the final result is assigned a question mark. In this way we arrive at the table depicting the researched cases (see table 10.2).

According to the Boolean algebra and the simplification rules applied to it, the examined results can be presented in the following form:

News or other speech programme = ABC + ABc + aBc = AB + Bc

This means that in all probability people listen to the news or to other speech programmes when, for example, at home they listen attentively to the radio, or wherever they, as a group, are concentrated on listening to the radio.

The analysis appears to produce results that seem logical. Its usefulness lies most of all in the fact that making truth tables forces one into disciplined thinking. Additionally it helps one in noticing how different factors are linked together in the data. Ragin stresses many times that the idea of his suggested theory of qualitative comparison is to produce a method that can be used in the typical situation in social scientific research where naturally occurring social phenomena display such limited diversity that traditional statistical hypothesis-testing is not possible. A solution is offered to this by the method of qualitative comparison. First, different causal factors are not isolated from one another. Instead, the method preserves the systematic nature of the causal relations involved: a factor affects a state of affairs in combination with a certain other factor, but not individually. Secondly, the method allows one to take into account missing cases: these can be examined symptomatically, as if adjuncts alongside the real events. The fact that all US presidents have been white males, for example, is an obviously meaningful instance of limited diversity (Ragin 1989, 104). In this sense the method comes close to the characteristic qualitative research design with its small number of observation units. The case-study is an extreme form of it.

Yet the research example shows that the application of Ragin's method to cultural studies has its problems. The type of research described above does not aim to present generally applicable rules which describe only one type of listening set apart from all others. The idea is rather to make sense of *different* listening situations, radio relations, or forms of discourse dealing with radio listening. From this basis, the research tries to be able to say something of general interest about the role of radio in everyday life. When applied in the way described above, the Boolean method side-stepped those interesting 'exceptions' where an individual mentions listening to music attentively at home. Yet these cases tell us about a different function of using radio or some other media.

These problems could be solved by incorporating more distinguishing factors. For instance, in the exceptional cases mentioned it was often the case that recordings, not radios, were being listened to. The problem could also be solved by analyzing different listening situations, one at a time, and searching for their causal conditions.

The problems are partly related to my research example. First, the analysis of this kind of material should preferably be more text-oriented. If the interviews are examined from the factist perspective as pictures of behaviour, the spectrum of factors related to these pictured situations is endless. Instead, at the level of discourse and the forms of orientation it reflects, one could quite well find a structure that could be qualitatively analyzed. Ragin's method could well be used to highlight this.

Secondly, in the data in question there was no problem with a limited number of comparable cases. In these eight interviews 42 listening situations were described; in the entire material there were 489 instances! Thus, in those parts of the final research report where I used descriptions of the listening situations as observation units, I decided to use conventional statistical analysis to cross-tabulate variables and to interpret the results alongside qualitative analysis. In that case I was not committed to the fact that the variables would have to have been assigned binary values. Boolean analysis is most appropriate when there are so few examplary cases reflecting the phenomenon to be explained that traditional statistical hypothesis-testing is not possible, but numerous enough that one does not necessarily come to think of all logical possibilities. In other words, one has to proceed as far as possible by other means, especially by further raising the level of abstraction, before there is a sufficiently small number of cases so that the above mentioned method of qualitive comparison becomes sensible. It may help (or become useless) in the final stage of analysis as support for logical conclusions, but it is not a substitute for sociological imagination.

However, the method has a premise that is foreign to cultural studies. The method of qualitive comparison is based on the supposition that there are causal factors which can be found by comparing cases to each other. In this method the different elements or dimensions of the phenomenon being studied are thought of as causal 'factors' – that is, independent variables, linked to each other by (possibly complex) mutual causal relations. This underlying model presumes that, in a case, each independent variable either affects or does not affect. This method does not favour the typologies so characteristic of the social sciences where a variable divides the observation units into a number of types. We may try to get around the problem by making a sufficient number of truth tables. However, processing the variables mentioned in the research example in such a way that the code alternatives would not be simplified to two types (style: 1 = listening to the radio in the car, 0 = listening elsewhere) would produce 126 truth tables instead of the one presented. Additional work would not eliminate the basic problem. The method's in-built premises about the characteristics of the total phenomenon being studied implies the presupposition that the phenomenon can be described as some kind of systematic causal model. The case-study design typical of qualitative analysis is instead based upon the idea of finding the teleological logic of an activity.

Let us imagine that the Boolean method is used to present an explanation about why the Finns are so interested in sauna bathing. Culture could be described by different variables, and the variable to be explained could be phrased as: does the said culture use a sauna? This would not lead very far since cultural phenomena are often arbitrary or contingent, so that to build an explanatory model looking for causal factors would not be successful. This does not, however, mean that it would be impossible to study the meaning of sauna bathing in a culture, nor that Boolean algebra could not be used in testing the interpretations. The more general lesson to be learned from the comparative method introduced by Ragin is that it is instructive to cross-tabulate typologies and to present the examined cases in tabular form. From this, we can locate the missing cases and ponder why they are absent.

Quantitative Analysis

It is also possible to build an argument on quantitative relations, such as percentages and statistical relations between different factors, while analyzing qualitative material. The only prerequisite is to have a sufficient number of cases.

If the amount of the qualitative material is measured by the number of interviewees or collected text samples, for instance, the common finding is that quantitative analysis is impossible because of the modest amount of data. However, in that case it is taken for granted that the observation unit is an individual or a text sample.

This is a presupposition adopted from survey research. In it the standard approach is to treat the individual as the observation unit, and to analyze statistical relationships between the variables characterizing individuals. The reasons for this are tied in with the theoretical framework of 'behavioural science'.

First, it reflects the underlying tendency to look for causal factors explaining individual behaviour. The individual's permanent properties are usually chosen as the independent variables, and the variables describing the individual's behaviour are typically chosen as the dependent variables. Therefore it is practical to consider the individual as the observation unit. For example, from a causal perspective it is logical to explain the prevalence of smoking by gender, as smoking cannot change a person's sex. However, gender is a social and cultural construction. From the viewpoint of the social construction of gender identity, the link between gender and a given behavioural pattern is not a causal relation. Rather, it is a relation of meanings; smoking is one of the symbols and expressions of gender. This link only manifests itself as a formal causal relation in statistical analysis.

Another reason is that in survey research the problem of generalization is solved by studying the data as a sample of a particular *population*, to which the results can be generalized. In this context, we are talking about a population as the concept is used in statistics: it refers to any larger group of observation units out of which the sample is randomly selected and to which the results of statistical analysis are supposed to be generalized. It is only that in survey research the population is a human population, usually the people inhabiting a defined geographical and municipal area. In survey research these concepts are defined by using the individual as the observation unit mainly because it is so easy and practical. This means that social phenomena are reduced to the level of individuals. Institutions, social and class structure, and social groups exist in this research approach only as typical combinations of an individual's background variables characteristic of the members of the institutions, classes or groups. These 'secondary groups' are, for their part, defined by using various individual-level variables as criteria, so that, for instance, 'class-position' can be used as a variable explaining the individual's action or consciousness. Structural, situational rather than individual, features of the actors' mutual interaction are left out of the analysis due to methodological limitations.

The use of the individual as the observation unit leads to a situation in which easily measurable and assessable generalizations of the population are achieved at the expense of representative variation in the individuals' actions. For example, the informants have to estimate how they 'typically' act. It of course depends on the truthfulness of the generalizations individuals make about their behaviour, but generalizations made at the population level on the basis of such individual generalizations do not necessarily reach the core of the matter. Let us imagine a linguist who studies the usage of 'but' by asking respondents how they typically use the word. Even on the basis of carefully planned question and answer alternatives, the core of the matter would not be reached because a sentence containing the word 'but' is in this case a much more fitting observation unit than the individual. The answers would not even validly measure a given individual's personal way of applying the grammatical rules guiding the use of 'but'. It would be more sensible to obtain a text sample from all the people being studied.

Even when the material consists of personal interviews, it is useful to study qualitative materials from exactly this perspective: as samples of speech, action or text, whose structures we can study in the search for answers to the questions posed in the research design. If a part of the analysis is to operationalize the problem setting by defining a certain observation unit, it will most often be something other than an individual. If the data contain numerous observation units, then statistical methods may also be applied in making the observations we are using to solve the riddle.

If we use something other than the individual respondent as the observation unit, we cannot actually define the 'population', or universe from which cases are picked as a sample. Therefore, one cannot assess whether the sample is big enough to be representative of the (hypothetical) universe. Apart from being foolish, it would also be just about impossible to define the universe for the usage of 'but', and to pick a statistically representative sample of it. However, many statisticians agree that this does not prevent us from applying statistics. In such a case we generalize to a *hypothetical universe*. 'It is the universe of all possible samples (which may be limited universes) which could have been produced under similar conditions of time, place, culture, and other relevant factors' (Hagood 1970, 66). To generalize to a hypothetical universe means that one simply assesses whether the number of cases is big enough to allow the inferences drawn from the breakdown of cases in terms of different variables used in classifying them. The validity of the results – the explanatory model to be presented – does not depend on the representativeness of the sample, although tests of significance can be consulted in assessing the clues. Instead, the judgement of reliability and validity will be made by the present and future scientific community. The explanatory model has to be valid not only in regard to the sentences within the material, but also in regard to sentences that are yet to be uttered.

I have applied statistical analysis in the way described above in a study which dealt with television viewing habits and programme preferences of families living in Tampere, Finland (Alasuutari 1992b). The idea of the analysis was to study television viewing as a moral issue. By this I mean that, in discussing their viewing habits, people make implicit or explicit references to ideal or preferable programme choices, which are separated from actual behaviour. People imply that they ought to behave differently from how they actually do. The moral nature of the interviewees' television discourse can be discerned in how they speak about different programmes. So I chose as the observation unit the particular way in which the people talked about watching different programme types when a certain programme type was mentioned for the first time in an informal interview. In 99 interviews there were as many as 79 such observation units, so that I could consider the relationships between the various types of discourse and the other variables (like the programme type in question) statistically significant. In this context statistical significance means that the results may be assumed to be generalizable in relation to an imaginary population; if another, comparable data set could be gathered, the results would be similar.

I distinguished five different types of discourse. First of all there is the plain statement that one watches a certain programme or likes a certain programme. The second, opposite type is represented by the equally straightforward statement that one does not like a certain programme or never watches it. The third type of discourse may be described as reflective. Here the speaker comments in one way or another on the fact that he or she watches a certain programme. For instance, the interviewee may explain why or in what frame of mind he or she watches a certain programme, or analyze the programme itself and its attractions. The fourth type is analogically the reverse case, where the individual explains his or her reasons for not watching a certain programme; this type of discourse occurred only in the category of documentaries. In the fifth type, I have distinguished as a separate discourse the statement that one used to watch a certain programme but that one has 'given it up' or lost interest in it. Additionally these informal interviews included the sixth possibility that the person does not mention a single programme belonging to the programme type in question, and the interviewer does not bring it up by asking about it.

In table 10.3 it may be seen how often the various types of discourse have been used in connection with various programmes. As mentioned, the analysis is based on the categorization of the discourses of 99 individuals.

I made use of this table in several different ways. First of all it can be used in suggesting many quantitative interpretations. The larger the proportion of the references to different programme types that consist of either 'watches' or 'explains-why-does-not-watch' statements, the higher is the programme type in a general moral or value hierarchy. At the top of that hierarchy we find documentaries and nature programmes, whereas at the bottom we see detective serials, action serials and family serials, in that order. In other words, factual programmes are the most prestigious, and fictional serials are least esteemed.

Table 10.3   *Discourses by programme types*

Discourse type		Programme type						
		A	B	C	D	E	F	G
Watches	(N)	45	32	29	13	6	6	10
	(%)	85	86	58	72	33	9	29
Explains why does not watch	(N)	2	0	0	0	0	0	0
	(%)	4	0	0	0	0	0	0
Does not like the programme	(N)	1	1	10	0	2	24	6
	(%)	2	3	20	0	11	35	18
Given up or lost interest	(N)	0	0	0	0	1	8	0
	(%)	0	0	0	0	6	12	0
Reflective	(N)	5	4	11	5	9	31	18
	(%)	9	11	22	28	50	45	53
Total of references	(N)	53	37	50	18	18	69	34
	(%)	100	100	100	100	100	100	100
No mention	(N)	46	62	49	81	81	30	65

Programme types:

A   Current affairs and documentaries
B   Nature programmes
C   Sports programmes
D   Situation comedies (*Golden Girls, Kate and Allie, Bill Cosby Show*)
E   Detective serials (e.g. *Murder She Wrote*, Agatha Christie serials, *Bergerac, Hill Street Blues*)
F   Soap operas (*Schwarzwald Clinic, Dallas, Dynasty, Colbys, Öman's Varuhus* or *St Elsewhere*)
G   Action serials (e.g. *Spencer for Hire, A-Team, V, Miami Vice, Hammer, Magnum, McGyver*)

Source: Alasuutari 1992b, 565

It must be noted that this hierarchy reflects a collectively adopted moral code in the sense that it is independent of the programmes the individual watches. The moral 'judgement' of a certain programme type is passed not only by those who say they do not like the programme. The way in which the general moral hierarchy was detected means that those who reported watching a serial type could also contribute to lowering its ranking by excusing themselves for doing so or by otherwise spontaneously commenting on it.

The table in question was a starting point for other observations leaning on both qualitative and quantitative analysis, so that the conclusion to the article reflects on the culturally subconscious presuppositions of western culture. Underlying the moral discourse surrounding television viewing the article detects a view of fictional programmes which is permeated by the idea of the Enlightenment, that is, that programmes should provide ethically sound models of life.

In his article 'Appealing to the "Experience" of the Patient in the Care of the Dying' (1989) Anssi Peräkylä uses quantitative analysis in a similar

Table 10.4   *Frequency with which staff members, or the researcher himself, introduced the identities of the researcher in different frames*

Frame of the identity	Staff member	Researcher	Total
Medical	24	51	75
Practical	52	32	84
Lay	43	3	46
Psychological	145	30	175
Research			
as work	28	5	33
as ethical thinking	17	6	23
Others	15	3	18
Total	324	130	454

Source: Peräkylä 1989, 129

way. He pays particular attention to the identity he is offered as a researcher in his encounters with the staff members of a terminal care department of a hospital. To test the impression that as the sociological field researcher he was often assumed to be particularly interested in psychological issues, Peräkylä studies his fieldnotes quantitatively regarding his discussions with the staff members. He counts the frequencies with which four frames of identity – practical, medical, lay and psychological – exist in the encounters, and whether a frame is introduced either by a staff member or by the researcher (table 10.4).

With the help of the table Peräkylä shows how his role *qua* researcher was not restricted to the identity of the researcher. He was offered an identity of 'counsellor' for the patients, and as a 'therapist' or 'a supportive person' in relation to the staff members. The figures show that staff members offered identities located in the psychological frame to the researcher much more often than he did himself. The same goes for the lay frame: he was offered the identity of a feeling and experiencing subject in the face of a fellow man's death. The opposite is true when it comes to the medical identity, a subject who knows the medical situation of the patient and deals with medical interventions. He had to show an active concern with medical questions; the staff members did not spontaneously regard him as interested in them. As a sociological fieldworker Peräkylä was incorporated into the psychological frame in several ways. He was an incarnation of the new socially and psychologically conscious medical discourse. 'The knowledge and the criticism, however, were in the field before me: I could only adopt the identities waiting for me, the social researcher' (Peräkylä 1989, 130).

If there are a sufficient number of observation units when we are analyzing qualitative material from a certain perspective, there is really nothing that prevents us from analyzing them even by using three- or four-dimensional tables and multivariate analysis. For example in my research on the use of the radio in Finnish everyday life (Alasuutari 1993), mentioned above, multivariate analysis could have been used. In the

Table 10.5 *Listening place by sex and residential area (per cent)*

	Female		Male	
Listening place	City dweller	Country dweller	City dweller	Country dweller
Morning at home	10.1	14.7	10.6	9.9
Car	8.4	16.2	17.4	21.0
Evening at home	16.2	16.2	17.4	16.0
Public space	10.6	7.4	8.7	3.7
Daytime at home	9.5	11.8	8.1	7.4
Work	11.7	10.3	11.2	11.1
Leisure	33.5	23.5	26.7	30.9
Total	100	100	100	100

interviews a total of 48 individuals were asked about different situations in which they listen to the radio. If a particular use of the radio did not automatically come up, the interviewer posed follow-up questions about an individual's radio listening, say, in the morning, in the car, at work, in the evening, during weekends, or at the summer cottage. The interviewees were asked to recall the latest radio listening occasions, and to describe what the programme was and how attentively they had been listening to it.

Since each interviewee described roughly a dozen listening occasions, I ended up with a data set of 489 observation units. Therefore, I was able to form observation matrices, in which the observation units were all of the various listening occasions the interviewees had recalled and described. The 'situational variables' included the listening time and place, whether the individuals were alone or in company, how attentively they had listened to the radio, and whether they themselves had chosen the programme listened to. On the other hand, each observation unit could also be given the 'background variables' of the person who had produced the description of the listening situation: age, sex, occupation and residential area.

Such statistical analysis, applying the factist perspective to the data, operated in this study mainly as an incentive for qualitative analysis, an aid in the search for new questions. The results show how many useful clues can be found by applying statistical analysis. Let us take an example (table 10.5).

The table indicates that, compared to men, a smaller share of women's radio listening takes place in a car, because generally speaking women drive cars less than men. Correspondingly, it seems that in the countryside radio is listened to more in the car, because the distances are greater and the car is used more. There is also an interesting difference in morning listening between rural men and women, namely that it is more usual among women. This could be due to the fact that in farm families – represented by all the adult rural interviewees in the data – a woman is usually indoors, near to a radio in the mornings, while the man is out in the fields, where it is difficult to listen to the radio.

However, when statistical relationships are produced in this way one should not think of them as representative of the total population. It is simply that within the data certain variables describing the observation units are on the average associated with other variables in a certain way. When we are looking for a sensible interpretation for the relationships, we have to go back to the same data and find out which concrete descriptions and statements have produced the statistical relationships. It does not matter if the distribution of the data into different groups of people has nothing to do with the normal distribution of the population. Nor does it matter if the interviewees are far from being typical representatives of their gender, age group or occupation. At the unriddling phase, interesting statistical relationships are explained *locally*. This means that the explanatory model must be as valid as possible as regards the empirical data it is based on. It is only on the basis of local interpretations that we may make inferences about the explanatory model that can be generalized to the level of culture or society.

Qualitative and Quantitative Analysis as a Continuum

Qualitative and quantitative analysis provide two different means of actively producing observations and of combining raw observations based on qualitative data. The theoretical and methodological framework may thematize the data in such a way that we can identify several parallel and comparable observation units. In such a case we may, within particular limits, proceed by employing either qualitative or quantitative analysis.

On the one hand, we may proceed qualitatively. This means that we have to be able to say something that is unconditionally true of all data, of all the raw observations thematized from the particular perspective in question. Thus we are searching for one or more common denominators for the raw observations. In this way the result may be a rule without exceptions, formulated as an observation clause, or a typology containing relatively few categories. In this case typology means that one is able to formulate an unconditional rule which holds for a certain group of raw observations. There are as many of these rules as there are types in the developed typology.

To proceed in terms of qualitative analysis from this point onwards means that we should also be able to unequivocally define the relations between the various types of the typology. We should be able to formulate rules which describe the typology as an internally logical whole. Let us consider the typology of the types of social action by Max Weber (1978a, 4–6), which makes a distinction between instrumentally rational, value-rational, effectual and traditional action. According to Weber, these ideal types of social action are not mutually exclusive: it would be unusual to find concrete cases of social action which were oriented only in one or another of these ways. Even though Weber says that his classification is not meant to exhaust the possibilities of the field, in an important sense it is assumed to be comprehensive. It is meant to formulate 'sociologically important' aspects of social action, which are, furthermore, assumed to 'constitute its elements'. To prove useful, and thus worth presenting, the typology is supposed to make sense of all 'essential' or 'relevant' societal phenomena. That is precisely what Weber thought he was able to do in his investigation. A valid typology does not need a 'garbage category', into which all the cases that do not fit in any of the types can be thrown.[3]

The comprehensive nature of a typology does not mean that all the types should be found also in the material being analyzed. A typology may be constructed by deducing it logically on the basis of the cases actually identified in the material. Missing cases often give us a clue about the cultural structure being studied: how it sets the limits for internal variation.

On the other hand, quantitative analysis may prove to be a better direction to take. There may be such a vast number of observation units that a sensible typology cannot be constructed. It may also be that the relations between the defined types are difficult to determine qualitatively, by the means of unconditional rules. In such cases it is possible to describe the observation units through different variables and to analyze the statistical relations between them.

The 'values' of the variables can be defined either with qualitative criteria as mutually exclusive types of observation units in regard to the variable in question (in this case we speak of a nominal variable) or by cutting up a quantitatively defined continuum into parts. In the radio listening study mentioned above I used the number of listening occasions an individual described in the interview as a 'background' variable. The number varied from one to twenty. Here we are dealing with a variable presenting a quantitatively defined continuum, which in this case was simplified into four classes. On the other hand, the variables classifying the described listening occasions, for example the place where the radio was listened to, are nominal variables. No matter how the variables are formed, the percentages or the average relationships between the variables may be used as clues while solving the riddle.

The fewer observation units there are, the stronger must be the statistical relationships between the variables if they are to be considered as worthwhile clues in unriddling. In that sense qualitative and quantitative analyses may be regarded as a continuum. If there are only a few

---

[3] It may, however, be commented that Weber's typology of social action limits itself only to such action which is social. By this he means action which has a meaningful relation to the action of other people (Weber 1978b, 1375). This division into social and other action does not completely stand up to criticism, or at least it does not correspond to modern views. When, for example, pedestrians react to a shower by opening their umbrellas, Weber claims that it is not social action, but 'homogenic mass behaviour' instead. Weber's concept of meaning and social action is limited in the sense that it does not take into account the culturally conditioned meaning structures, within the framework of which people react to things and events, whether they be caused by other people or by natural phenomena.

observation units, we should stick to qualitative analysis. When analyzing a slightly larger number of units, obvious quantitative relationships will suffice as weak clues, even if we cannot build the whole solution on them. If there are hundreds of observation units, we can even attempt to make observations by applying multivariate analysis. However, in the last instance the validity and reliability of the research results depend on the coherence of the *local explanation*, the number of clues in the material supporting it, and how relevant the explanation appears to be when applied outside the material in question. There is nothing mystical about numbers and figures; they offer clues like any other observations.

PART III

UNRIDDLING

11

Asking Why

In the chapters above we have been looking at some of the methods for generating observations from qualitative research material, or for extracting more from the material than is visible to the 'naked eye'. These methods provide important tools for evaluating the material as more or less reliable descriptions of people's behaviour or of what has happened; for highlighting the different structural features of texts; and for exploring the research material as documentation of interaction situations. However, although the rigorous application of a certain approach or method can produce absolutely fascinating discoveries even of the most mundane situations, it is important to realize that these are, as yet, nothing more than that: discoveries or observations, clues produced by means of conceptual tools and research craftsmanship. This provides the foundation for resolving the puzzle, for answering the question of why. Observations are merely answers to the question of what.

A common (but rather sloppy) argument that one often hears repeated in this context is that the phenomenon which is at the centre of attention in the study is in fact 'inherently' what it looks like from the vantage point of the method adopted: that, say, a life-story (from a factist point of view) is a description of a life lived, or (from a narratological point of view) first and foremost a story and a linguistic construct, or that an interview or conversation (from an interaction point of view) is above all an activity consisting of speech acts in which the participants produce a certain institution 'on the spot'. It is pointless to try to rank-order different approaches or perspectives on qualitative materials. The purpose of these approaches is not to present totalizing interpretations of the 'distinctive characteristics' of the material, but rather to gain a clearer view of something that might prove useful in resolving the mystery. It should also be stressed that the different perspectives are not mutually exclusive. In many cases it will be necessary to apply several different perspectives even with the same material. On the other hand, where just the single perspective is employed it is useful for reasons of testing validity, for instance, to look at the material from other points of view as well.

Sociological inquiry does not consist only in making observations and in reporting findings; they do not yet count as results proper. As well as addressing the question of what, sociological research is always concerned, in one or more ways, with the question of why. The purpose is to use the material to unravel a given 'mystery'. In this chapter my intention is to look at how one extracts and generates these why-questions so that one can proceed to address them.

In light of what we have traditionally learned from textbooks on statistical social research, the search for why-questions may seem like a rather curious exercise. Most textbooks will say that the first step in the research process consists of formulating the research problem and generating hypotheses. The research problem, in effect, refers to what we have been calling the why-question; while the hypothesis is the same thing as the answer provided, the validity of which is tested against the empirical material.

Reality often differs from the textbook description of the research process. The research plan generally outlines a crude and general statement of the problem addressed; the more detailed why-questions (and the answers to those questions) unfold only with the analysis of the material. In many cases you will also find that when you read the material the preliminary why-questions turn out to be trivial or impossible to answer. Particularly in the case of qualitative research it is in fact very rare that one addresses the hypotheses formulated in the original research plan. A thorough reading of the material will often provide new insights and suggest completely new questions that one could never even have thought of before getting to know the phenomenon more closely. Research consists of more than just corroborating what is expected or known.

The impression one tends to get from detective stories or research reports is that resolving the mystery is no big deal. Many research studies will set out the problem right at the start and then unravel that problem by analyzing the material. In detective stories you will have a murder occurring at the early stages of the story and then the reader, working closely with the story-teller and the leading character, will have to try to find out who did it. However, the why-questions do not come as a free gift; the investigator (and the writer) will have to work them out and extract them from the material.

In the process of data collection, in reading the material one has collected and in analyzing the data, it is important to try to find as many good why-questions as possible so that there are plenty to choose from by the time one gets to the final analysis and the writing stage. The most trivial mysteries as well as those that have been resolved earlier can now be eliminated, as can those questions that cannot be fruitfully addressed with the material at hand.

The objective is always to detect paradoxes within the material or the phenomenon studied, but the problem is that these will not always become evident all by themselves. Especially in situations where you are looking at something that is closely related to your own culture, most things will often appear more or less self-evident and trivial. However, there are various methods that can help to generate the why-questions.

Cross-Cultural Comparison

In an ethnographic study of a foreign culture the why-questions will often stem from the researcher's failure to understand why the people concerned are living the way they do, or why they think the way they do. The researcher's own way of life differs to such an extent from the culture he or she is exploring that it is simply impossible to understand or accept what is going on. The researcher may feel threatened; or that his or her role is inadequate or dishonest. In this sort of situation, where two different cultures clash, one way for the researcher to extract useful why-questions is to take a hard look at the underlying foundations of his or her own patterns of thinking. From this vantage point it should be possible to generate hypotheses as to how the presumptions in the culture concerned differ from those that prevail in one's own culture; and whether in spite of the differences appearing at the superficial level there are in fact certain aspects that both cultures share in common. The research process thus moves in at least two directions at the same time: it lays bare the latent presumptions of the culture represented by the researcher, on the one hand, and the subjects, on the other (Alasuutari 1989; Rabinow 1977, 119; Willis 1978, 197–198).

The case is very different in studies of one's own culture. Everything seems so clear and so self-evident that it all verges on the banal. In order to generate those all-important why-questions, the researcher must be able to see beyond the horizon of the self-evident. How, then, does one problematize the self-evident? How do we study phenomena which we master in practice but are not reflexively conscious of?

One way is to try to find a point of comparison in a different culture that you do not know so well. For instance, you could look up research that has been done on the same or similar problems in different cultures. By looking more closely at a world where things are different from home, you can try to make the familiar look strange and alien. This, of course, is the whole idea of anthropology: to compare different cultures in an attempt to make visible and understandable the unique way in which any given culture perceives the world and to detect and conceptualize the limits to intra-cultural variation.

Cross-cultural comparison can also be done in the imagination, as we are instructed by C. Wright Mills in his magnificent introduction to the sociological imagination and the craftsmanship of research. For instance, you can play games with the relative sizes of different phenomena; imagine how small things would appear if they were big or vice versa. What would be different? 'What would pre-literate villages look like with populations of thirty millions?' (Mills 1973, 236).

Contradictions with Other Research

Another useful way of generating why-questions is to compare the picture you have from the study at hand with the picture that emerges from a reading of other studies. If there are any discrepancies between these two pictures, you will be more than half-way to some good whys. First of all it is possible that you yourself have gone wrong somewhere, that the picture drawn by other studies is more reliable and more accurate. However, even in this case there remains the interesting question of why one was misled. What caused that?

Not uncommonly, however, it will turn out that earlier research has missed something important, that it has asked the wrong questions, failed to ask more than one type of question, or that the interpretations are wrong. This is the area in which qualitative research can really show off its greatest strengths: that is, while surveys do provide all sorts of interesting information on statistical associations between different variables, the interpretations as to what lies behind these correlations will often be more or less perfunctory. It is useful, therefore, to read the results of surveys for their statistical findings since the qualitative material you have could offer a meaningful or better interpretation. Indeed the entire research project can be geared at disproving earlier results and possibly at offering an explanation as to what has been feeding those false notions.

For example, in his study of how parents talk about their children's television viewing habits, Juha Kytömäki (1991) found that parents are not usually very concerned about their children's behaviour; on the contrary, they say they rarely have to impose any restrictions on their children's viewing because there simply is no need. Their children never watch violence, for instance – although when specifically asked they might mention that their children sometimes watch action serials.

All of this seemed very contradictory when Kytömäki compared his findings with earlier reports on parental control in family television viewing. On the one hand, the picture that he formed on the basis of interviews with 90 families was quite consistent with earlier studies. Only 32 per cent of the families said they actually controlled their children's television viewing. Earlier research had considered this a rather disturbing indication of parental indifference with regard to children's viewing habits. However, none of these earlier studies had given any thought to the question of what control or the absence of control really means; that question quite simply was beyond their scope as they addressed it on a dichotomous yes/no basis. Kytömäki decided to reconstruct the earlier findings, and by reducing the responses he had obtained to the same yes/no format he arrived at roughly the same figures as those given in earlier reports. However, the responses of all the parents he spoke to were in the form 'no, but . . .'. Looking more closely at what came after these buts turned the results completely upside down. The parents said they did not control the contents of what their children watched because they were not allowed to watch the late-night shows that were for adults only, or because they agreed on what is suitable viewing for children and what is not. Therefore, active control had become unnecessary. On the other hand, in those families where the parents said they did control their children's television viewing, that control did not seem very effective, or parents and children did not have a very clear agreement on the rules of television viewing. In contrast to what earlier studies had led us to understand, the problems were worse in those families where the parents said they did control their children's viewing.

Relationship to Public Images

Useful whys can be extracted also from a comparison of the picture emerging from the research material with the picture prevailing in the public sphere, with what is thought about the matter by the public at large. For example, public images can be studied separately by looking at newspaper articles on the subject, or sometimes the popular notion will be revealed in an interview study where people compare their own views with what 'other people' think or do. This was what we saw in our previous example of controlling children's television viewing habits; to a certain extent the parents were unconcerned about their children's viewing because they had read or heard about studies which portrayed scenes of totally indifferent parents and children spending hours on end watching violence on television. There was no way that these people were going to recognize themselves in these studies.

This leads us to the intriguing question of how public images or prevailing notions and the behaviour of individual people are interwoven and how they interact with each other. The publicity that surrounds a certain subject or phenomenon thematizes it in a particular way into a social issue or individualized problem. The way in which individual people talk about a subject can always be approached in terms of how their notions are related to the ongoing public debate. A why-question can also be formulated if something that is close to the hearts of the interviewees is not discussed in public at all. In this context we refer to discourse in the sense that Michel Foucault uses the term, which now has become so very popular. By discourse, Foucault refers to the way in which a certain phenomenon thematizes knowledge, deliberation, action and institutionalized practices as an object of discussion. It includes what is taken for granted in that discussion and how disagreements on the issue occur. In this definition discourse also includes silences. The question as to who is expected to remain silent or which topics are not to be spoken about forms an integral part of the discourse, just as does the question of how it is appropriate to address the topic (Foucault 1980, 17–18).

Even in a situation where public discourse on a certain issue appears very strange and biased from the point of view of individual people, they have no option in explaining and describing their attitudes but to do so within the dimensions and argumentation structures offered by the discourse itself. Reverting again to the television viewing study quoted above, it seemed that, paradoxically, parents were not really alerted and concerned by the descriptions in the public debate of widespread indifference with regard to children's viewing habits (which was the intention), but on the contrary they felt reassured that the situation in their own family was much better than in these problem cases. The important thing about this discovery is not that the campaign to alert parents didn't work or was counterproductive but the why-question that is raised by the contradiction between the everyday reality of families and the public discourse: why does it appear that children's television viewing is thematized by necessity as a problem and more specifically as a concern that parents are not up to their job and let their children watch the most atrocious horror and violence films? From the point of view of the families concerned the problems related to children's television viewing were of a very different kind; they were much more practical. For instance, violent scenes were a problem to parents if and when their child had bad dreams the next night. The public image of overly lenient parents and of kids sitting in front of the television for hours on end definitely has a role to play: it serves to give parents some peace of mind.

The Search for Incomplete Typologies

In many cases it will be very difficult to identify 'silences' within a given discourse; at least for the researcher who comes from the same culture one of the first questions asked is not usually why this or that subject is discussed while some other subject is not. A useful method here might be to produce different kinds of typologies and to cross-tabulate those typologies; in other words, to generate as comprehensive a typology as possible of different ways of talking about a given subject and to tabulate instances of using those ways of talking by creating another typology of different kinds of speakers, speech situations or various cases related to the subject. If in this sort of table one is left with blank columns, it may prove a useful exercise to try to explain and interpret them. This is what David Silverman (1985, 10–11) refers to as the search for incomplete typologies.

Internal Contradictions within the Research Material

The discovery of inconsistencies within the data will also point the way to some useful why-questions. Kytömäki, in his viewing habits study, also detected one such inconsistency: why did the parents say their children never watched violence on television but in the next sentence mentioned several action serials which frequently contain scenes of fighting and shooting? The answer, according to Kytömäki, was that, by 'violence', parents understood programmes that caused nightmares. From this point of view, realistic scenes of violence often have deeper effects than the violence of television serials.

I myself have seen this sort of logical contradiction in a participant observation study of a self-help group for people with alcohol problems (Alasuutari 1992a, 107–148). At their meetings members of the A-Guild, a self-help group for former alcoholics, would often more or less boast about how much they used to drink; at the same time they tended to understate the amount of drink that other people could handle. Bearing in mind that this is a group whose purpose is to encourage members to stay off the bottle, it is of course somewhat contradictory that they boast of their earlier drinking. The explanation eventually offered was that, being manual labourers, these men had a higher regard for practical experience than for theoretical knowledge. A long and heavy drinking career was therefore an indication of extensive 'field experience', that the man concerned really knew what he was talking about and was therefore in a position to pass on advice to others.

The Search for Norms

One rather effective way of generating why-questions is to look for normative statements within the corpus of texts that serve as the data. By this I do not simply mean cases where someone expresses an opinion as to how one should go about doing something. A norm may find expression in the research material in someone denying, preventing or reprimanding someone else; on the other hand it may also be seen in someone urging someone else to do something. Further, normative conceptions are reflected in people's accounts of their own behaviour, as in someone describing how he or she follows a certain moral principle. You might also see people who are ashamed of their actions defending what they are doing, saying that they really 'should' be doing this or that, or that they 'shouldn't' really be doing what they are. For instance, someone who is lighting up a cigarette might briefly pause and say, in more or less apologetic terms, that they should really give up the habit. Or conversely, you might have someone bragging and boasting about what they are doing. For instance, someone might comment when another person lights up that they managed to kick the habit years ago with no difficulty at all.

Whenever you find a clue in the material suggesting that a norm might exist, you have in effect encountered a contradiction. Adherence to a certain normative principle means that people know there are other options as well; they are very much aware of the temptation to act differently, or they may want to upgrade the status of their preferred behaviour by representing that behaviour as consistent with their moral principles (Alasuutari 1992a, 9–20, 169–180). In each case the researcher may try to find out what in fact lies behind the statements. Another useful question is: why and how does the normative principle acquire its high moral status? Being ashamed of one's behaviour, covering up and defending one's actions, also raises many why-questions. For instance: Why the reference to the norm if the individual concerned acts against it anyway? Why do people repeatedly point at a normative principle if they go against it? Whenever a norm crops up in the research material you can always ask why people take a normative position on this particular subject, why they regard it as a moral issue.

In a recent study where I was concerned with the different ways in which interviewees talked about their television viewing habits (Alasuutari 1992b), my attention was frequently drawn to the ways in which they spoke about what they 'should' and 'shouldn't' do. The analysis was grounded in an observation I had made while reading the material: television viewing seemed to be a profoundly moral issue for these people. There are very few programmes that people regard as legitimate viewing which requires no explanations or excuses. Many of the interviewees who said they watched serials would have some sort of qualifier attached, for instance:

Q: What sort of programmes do you like yourself?
A: I watch all the sloppy stuff. I don't know, like *Dallas*, I always watch it, even though it's stupid really, but every time it's on I watch it.
     (Alasuutari 1992b, 569)

From this vantage point I worked out the basic notion that the more often people said they watched a certain type of programme without attaching any qualifying statements or excuses, the more 'respectable' that programme type must be. On the basis of this idea, I went on to create a value hierarchy of different types of television programming. This, in turn, provided a useful basis for an interpretation of the moral nature of television viewing: what are the implicit principles that make certain programmes more acceptable or less problematic than others?

So the search for clues which point to the existence of norms is just the starting point for research. This is not adopted from norm theory, that is, that a given cultural phenomenon or mode of behaviour can be explained simply by the fact that an applicable norm prevails in the community. References to norms may have many different functions. In each case the researcher can ask: why does the norm exist and appear, and what is its meaning?

The Search for Analogies and Umbrella Concepts

Another way in which you can turn a phenomenon that is deceptively familiar into a foreign one, and in this way generate why-questions, is to think about what you can compare it with. For instance, compare the way in which Finnish people talk about television viewing with the way in which they talk about their sauna habits. In the case of sauna it is totally inconceivable that the majority of the interviewees would be ashamed of admitting that they go so often. However, people would probably talk about their drinking and smoking habits in a similar vein as they talk about television viewing; some of the interviewees in my study, for instance, said they used to watch a certain series but then decided to drop it, much the same way as you might hear someone describing how he has given up smoking. In this way a given phenomenon (in this case television viewing) can be slotted into a broader category which could be labelled 'moral issues'. Therefore, it may be asked how well or how poorly it fits in with discussions of addiction or illness. And further, we may ask what television, alcohol and tobacco have in common as addictions.

In practice you can go about the search for differences and similarities with other phenomena by replacing focal terms within texts with other terms. For instance, consider personal interview stories of (usually famous) people in magazines: how they are characterized as individuals, how their everyday life is described, and how they themselves tell about their goals and views of life. Now, change the gender of the individuals. In which cases and to what extent do the stories appear as normal magazine stories, and in what ways do they strike you as odd or funny? The details that do not seem to fit in with the normal picture serve as clues about the culturally prevalent notions of gender; notions which may otherwise easily escape one's attention.

C. Wright Mills also draws attention to the benefits that can be gained from a study of antitheses: 'If you think about despair, then also think about elation; if you study the miser, then also the spendthrift' (1973, 235). It is very difficult to study a single isolated phenomenon; in order to fully grasp that phenomenon, in order to identify the dimensions on which the object can be compared and related to the reality outside it, you need to look at antithetical and parallel phenomena.

Comparison with closely related or more or less antithetical phenomena is not only a useful way of finding why-questions but also an important step towards the development of a theoretical frame of reference. The idea is to find a broader umbrella concept of which the phenomenon ·studied represents one example or special case. In this regard the researcher always has a choice. Television viewing can be examined equally as a leisure activity among many others, compared with other addictions and vices, or thematized as a moral problem in a broad sense like a religious issue. Discourses on what it means to be a man or a woman can be examined from the point of view of problems related to citizenship rights, identity construction or gender differences in health or average life expectancy.

The choice of research theme largely determines what kind of background reading you will have to do, even though it is always a wise policy to open the question in many different directions. It is not a good idea to look at research that has to do with only this particular empirical phenomenon. For instance, if you are undertaking sociological research that has to do in one way or another with drinking and alcohol, it is not advisable to concentrate only on reading alcohol studies or to keep in touch only with alcohol researchers – even though the field is so broad that the temptation must be there.

In the case of qualitative research, it is particularly important to set the phenomenon concerned in a broader context. That is because the answer to a certain concrete why-question often has more general interest-value only when it is examined in a broader framework as a model of explanation that, *mutatis mutandis*, is applicable to many other phenomena as well.

12

Generalization

The Standard View

The standard view of the strengths and weaknesses of different methods is that quantitative methods give you superficial but reliable facts, whereas qualitative methods provide more in-depth but poorly representative results. Therefore, as the standard view would have it, the logical thing to do is to use both methods, to combine them and make the best of their respective strengths. Qualitative methods are thought to be particularly well suited to pilot studies. Methods of fieldwork, for example, are applied where an in-depth understanding is required of a certain subject at the grassroots level. From this investigation hypotheses are then generated for testing and corroboration in subsequent analyses with statistical methods so that results can be presented with better generalizability.

Admittedly, the idea of using qualitative methods for this sort of groundwork is supported by the history of fieldwork methods. Qualitative methods have been developed in anthropology, which studies foreign cultures. They were a relevant way of responding to the need for information that grew up with colonial trade relations: in the project to 'appropriate' (in conceptual terms) a foreign society there existed no useful categories or classifications (such as 'class' or 'educational level') for identifying individuals and for explaining why some individuals behave differently from others. To move on to comprehensive surveys at the population level, one first needs to find the categories to be used in coding.

In studies of modern society it seems that sociology has needed qualitative methods in exactly the same sort of situation where social change has made old familiar categories and classifications useless. In the United States of the 1920s and 1930s, for instance, it was clear that the phenomena and problems linked with the massive influx of immigrants into large cities could not be properly explained in terms of the models and norms which applied to the rest of society. The Chicago School responded to this challenge by developing a toolbox of methods that were largely inspired by anthropology: instead of attempting to decode and interpret figures with an administrative intent, it advocated a research strategy of going out to the slums to see what sorts of lives people actually lived there.

The same thing happened in Finland in the 1970s as researchers set out to explore the problems that followed with the dramatic onset of urbanization. Outlining the objectives of way-of-life research in the late 1970s, J.P. Roos (1978) compared the goals and intentions of his own project to the interest that writers and researchers began to show during the nineteenth century in the 'way in which people really lived their lives'. One important difference, as Roos points out, is that while social researchers and novelists of the nineteenth century (such as Jack London) were explorers in a strange continent on which they had never set foot before, the objects of way-of-life researchers, suburbs and everyday life in suburbs, were much more familiar.

So why were qualitative methods needed in the study of suburbs? Because the old classifications and the old categories were unable to explain the problems and dilemmas related to a changing way of life. A qualitative research project was required to get an overview of those problems, and to gain a deeper understanding of the growth of suburbs and the process of rural depopulation. Once that qualitative overview was completed, the road was clear for social survey researchers to step in. There must be countless surveys where the population of Finland has been divided into four generations according to the classification suggested by Roos (1980; for an English language version, see Roos 1985), and based on his qualitative analysis of life-stories. In other words, the heuristic theory that Roos developed to describe the life-styles of different generations on the basis of a small sample has subsequently been proven correct at the level of the total population. Population surveys have shown that variables describing individuals are significantly associated with the generations they, according to Roos, belong to.

But surely this is the wrong way around? After all it is not the surveys which prove that Roos's theory is right; on the contrary it is the theory which provided the survey researchers with a tool for explaining the meaning and relevance of their statistical findings. So qualitative research does not fill the role of a pilot study; it is itself the result proper of the inquiry.[1] There prevails a curious division of labour between the use of qualitative and quantitative methods. Qualitative research produces classifications, conceptual tools and explanations for different kinds of phenomena. Empirical researchers who design and carry out surveys then import these classifications directly into their questionnaires as preset alternatives and use the explanations offered in interpreting the distributions and correlations in the data.

My intention in this chapter is not to argue that the standard view of qualitative research is all wrong and that the truth is the exact opposite. I merely want to point out that the recurring argument that qualitative research has a problem with generalizability is based on a number of latent presumptions about the very nature and purpose of social research. Many of these presumptions are such that when their foundation and justification is called into question, the whole problem of generalizability vanishes into

---

[1] It is equally misleading to refer to the testing of Roos's generation hypothesis. At the very best such a testing can help to demonstrate that this or that year of birth is associated with other individual variables; there is no way of proving that the dividing lines between different generations run exactly where they are supposed to according to the theory.

thin air. I will begin the discussion by looking at those cases where there is no such problem. Then, I will move on to look at how qualitative research – whenever this is necessary – seeks to produce results that go beyond the research material at hand.

Generalization is Not Always a Problem

The first thing that must be borne in mind is that the very requirement of generalizability to a certain population only applies with a certain ideal of scientific research. It can just as well be argued that the experimental testing of assumptions reduced to empirical statements is no longer a relevant task for a scholar. In cultural studies, for example, the idea is not so much to prove one's existing hypotheses as to try to reach beyond the old problematics. Instead of starting a study with a ready-made hypothesis 'Is it true that . . .?' one asks with an open mind 'How is it?' The researcher should always try to see beyond the horizon of the self-evident.

From this vantage point social scientific research is seen not as an institution which is concerned with producing practical information about society, but rather as a form of critical literature contributing to a more rational debate on society. The intention is to look at societal phenomena from fresh, unprejudiced, yet well-founded points of view. The basic idea is to call into question the self-evident. Michel Foucault formulates the idea as follows in the introduction to the second volume of *History of Sexuality*: 'The object was to learn to what extent the effort to think one's own history can free thought from what it silently thinks, and so enable it to think differently' (1986, 9).

From this point of view, it may be argued that if you do encounter the problem of generalizability and relevance, then you are already off-course. If you operate with means and averages and with statistically observable behavioural inclinations, then you are looking at the object of study from much too close a range. You will not see the forest for the trees. Cultural studies is concerned with the broader picture, with things that we master in practice but of which we are not consciously aware.

On the other hand, to say that one studies things that we know but haven't conceptualized does not mean that one is reluctant to demonstrate the generalizability of the results. If all readers of a study can recognize a phenomenon from the description presented, then generalizability is not a problem; the only issue of interest is the relevance of the explanation offered for that phenomenon.

The very notion of generalizability implies the assumption that, instead of trying to explain a unique event or phenomenon, the results of the study should apply to other cases as well. This does not necessarily have to be the case; historians, for instance, are usually concerned with explaining specific chains of events in history. This obviously renders irrelevant the issue of generalizability.

This is very much the same situation as we have in cultural studies, where the chief concern is with things that people know about but of which they are not very conscious. While the object of study is a phenomenon that recurs frequently in everyday situations, the descriptions and explanations are presented at such a level of abstraction that they are thought to apply to all individual cases.

A useful example is provided by the work of Fred Roberts (1982), an American anthropologist studying the way of life in a small village in southwestern Finland. Because of his outsider's point of view, Roberts was able to see and problematize interesting aspects of everyday life which are, because of their mundane character, largely left unnoticed by Finnish people. One of his observations concerned the central place of coffee-drinking in everyday life. Finns are very heavy coffee drinkers, and if you are visiting someone's home it is extremely hard to refuse a cup of coffee without offending your host. Yet there has been hardly any serious research into this phenomenon. For a Finnish researcher the subject is too close to be noticed.

For Roberts, coffee drinking represents an important ritual with a central place in Finnish culture. The scene of the ritual, as he describes it, is set by the coffee and foods, primarily baked sweet goods, which are placed on a table at one end of the room. The guests do not consume their coffee and food at the table but sit at benches or chairs around the periphery of the room. They must periodically fetch the various delicacies. Roberts pays particular attention to the reaction aroused by the hostess's invitation:

> After the hostess has already poured coffee into the cups on the table, she stands beside the coffee table, with her coffeepot in one hand, and usually announces to the group as a whole: 'The coffee is on the table. Please take some coffee!' This invitation inevitably produces tension; no one moves toward the coffee table, and the invitation must be repeated several times. Often guests pointedly glance away from the hostess, obviously ignoring her invitation. After several invitations have failed to elicit a response, a hostess (or her husband) may announce in an irritated tone of voice: 'The coffee is getting cold.' If all else fails, the hostess may turn directly to one person and choose some relatively insignificant reason to get her to go first (e.g., 'You come from the farthest away'). (1982, 251–252)

There are no doubt different versions of how the ceremony unfolds. The situation will be quite different, for instance, if the guests are seated at a table. In this case the ceremony will revolve around taking sugar and cream and having a biscuit. Among friends there will of course be much less ceremony; and at home there will be none at all. All of these different versions could be studied by means of statistical inquiries, but (even though they could produce quite interesting information) the important questions we need to ask are: What lies behind this phenomenon? What are the underlying reasons? Why won't the guests get up to fetch coffee as soon as they are asked to? Why are they so 'impolite'?

These are the questions that Roberts sets out to address. The behaviour is explained, he shows, by the strongly hierarchical emphasis in this ceremony historically. In the past the gentry (males and females) preceded the women of the farming and non-farming groups in the coffee ceremony. There had also been a hierarchical arrangement among the non-gentry guests, based primarily on landownership. In the 1970s, in the village Roberts studied, the gentry rule still applied as far as the parish's pastor was concerned; he could voluntarily exercise that privilege or be pressured into it. But in other respects the hierarchy has become more problematic. On the one hand, it has become much more diffuse than it used to be, and, on the other hand, many people in higher positions are, in the prevailing spirit of equality, particularly reluctant to go before others. To rush straight to the table at the first invitation might be interpreted as a sign that the person concerned believes he or she is higher in rank than anyone else among the guests. This explains the often apologetic, self-deprecating remark by the individual who goes first: 'Well, I am closest to the table' or 'Well, I'm so old, I guess I'll go.'

The case-analysis of the Finnish coffee ritual is a good example of a study where there seems to be no problem with generalizability. The aim in the analysis is to provide an explanation for a phenomenon whose existence does not need to be empirically proved, at least as far as Finnish readers are concerned. A detailed description of the ritual, livened up with a few direct quotations, will certainly suffice to bring to the Finnish reader's mind images and recollections of similar situations they have experienced themselves. The degree to which the explanation has general validity can then be compared with one's own experiences.

Indeed it is a distinctive feature of qualitative research that it intentionally concentrates on objects of study where generalization is not a problem. The focus of attention is on *explaining* the phenomenon, on making it intelligible. To *prove its existence* is not necessary.

Purification of Observations as a Generalizing Operation

There are also aspects of qualitative research which help to alleviate or even completely resolve the problem of generalizability. One of these aspects is the combining of raw observations into meta-observations. This process reflects the researcher's intention to explore the topic concerned not in terms of isolated cases but at a more general level. When several different versions are collected of the same theme and the object of study is defined at a metalevel so that it covers all the variation amongst the cases included in the material, then we are no longer operating with isolated, individual cases.

In the combining of raw observations into meta-observations you do not even need to be restricted to observations and cases found in the research material at hand. For instance, any typology compiled on the basis of the cases included in the material will be completed by way of logical inference to cover all imaginable versions and variations – including those that are not present in the material. The picture of the phenomenon that is being explained is formed on the basis of all the clues that are available which can help to resolve the mystery.

Alternatively these missing cases may in themselves be valuable clues in *local explanation*. A full typology in which the cases from the material are slotted as examples refers to the whole cultural structure to which the object of study is being related. While local explanation focuses on a particular phenomenon, the *relating* of that phenomenon to a broader entity is a generalizing operation in which the analysis of the specific phenomenon aims at conceptual appropriation of the broader phenomenon.

An example is provided by Kunelius (1994), who, as an outcome of his analysis of the news story, constructed a 'narrative force-field', where the initial object of study is located in a larger field and related to other forms of journalistic discourse. That field is structured around two axes, or narrative dimensions. The first dimension describes the *visibility* of the narrative voice. An extreme end is *transparent* narration, where the voice covers its own act of narration. The other end is *identifiable* narration, where the narrative voice gives definite hints about the time, place and context of the act of narration. The other dimension concerns the degree of *dependency* of the narrative voice. One extreme is exemplified by the narrator of a traditional realistic novel: a narrative voice that can be present anywhere, even when the characters are alone, and which can move freely in time and space. The other extreme is a totally dependent narrative voice, which merely repeats the utterances (and thus the discourse) of the sources. In terms of this force-field (figure 12.1), 'hard' news can be located in the 'southwestern' corner.

In some cases a typology or a table construed on the basis of certain variables may refer to a broader entity than the historically and locally specific cultural structure to which the cases in the material are *related* (and in this sense generalized). It may also refer to a logically possible domain. In this instance the cases that are possible but missing are interpreted as proof that they are not (for reasons put forward separately) possible in the culture concerned. In other words the missing cases provide some indica-tion of the cultural structure of the phenomenon concerned and of how that structure imposes its limits on internal variation.

Let us consider here a table I prepared for an article on the moral aspect of Finns' relation to television viewing. The table offers a detailed typology of the ways in which people explain, justify and defend their viewing of fiction programmes on television. Four different types were identified. The first was described as the *analysis of realism*: the speaker assesses the programme on the basic terms of whether its portrayal of the world is realistic or not. The second type of discourse, which also assesses programme contents, is called the *analysis of representation*: in it the

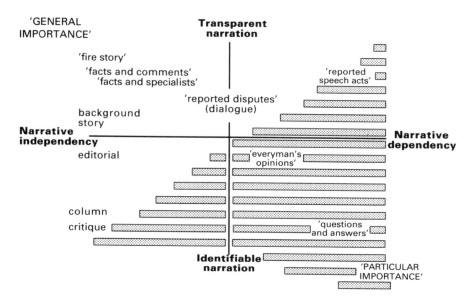

Figure 12.1   *The order of contemporary journalistic discourse in the narrative force field (Kunelius, 1994, 261)*

Table 12.1   *Forms of reflection on different types of TV serials*

	Realism	Representation	Psychological	Moral reference
Soap operas	5	13	14	31
Action serials	3	10	3	17
Situation comedies	0	2	1	8
Detective serials	0	6	3	8

Source: Alasuutari 1992b, 571

speaker evaluates what the film was like as a performance; how it was produced, directed, or how the actors performed in their roles. The third type of discourse was called *psychological interpretation*. In this discourse the speaker interprets or explains the reasons for his or her television viewing, or describes how he or she uses the programme, what sort of orientation he or she takes to viewing. The fourth and last of these types of reflexive discourse is *moral reference*. Here the interviewee somehow makes clear in one way or another that he or she is aware of the status of the programme concerned in the moral hierarchy of television programming. These discourses are not mutually exclusive; in one single account of a particular television programme people may resort to any number of them. Table 12.1 describes how many times the different discourses were used in the interviews when talking about different types of fictional programmes.

The missing cases in this table suggested one important conclusion: that is, references to (the lack of) realism were only made in the bottom two programme categories, i.e. soap operas and action serials. From this I could draw the inference that it is precisely a problematic relationship to reality that makes certain programme types less valued, so that people will then justify and explain their viewing of these programmes.

The operation of generalization is in a sense built into sociological explanations. To provide a sociological explanation of something means that one explicates the social and cultural conditions that guide people's activity in everyday situations and make those situations and models of action intelligible. Not only are the conditions identified; the specific logic of their formation and their impact are also explicated. Let us revert once again to our earlier example of the Finnish coffee ritual. The key to the explanation lies in explicating the *meaning* of fetching the coffee, the frame within which it is considered. When that is explained, the activities of the people concerned become intelligible.

By reading a good study based on qualitative research one often gets the impression that in this particular case generalization is no problem, that now we are dealing with a self-evident, common knowledge phenomenon. Such an impression, or a lack of concern for generalizability, is partly due to these generalizing operations. The common, simple, clearly distinguishable phenomenon which constitutes the research problem has been extracted from the endless complexity and monotony occurring in the research material (as well as in everyday life) by a method that abstracts the 'essential' from the 'non-essential', whether that method is narrative analysis, semiotics, rhetorical analysis or whatever. As the author submits to the readership a phenomenon for deliberation and explanation, the presentation is in itself an abstraction and a generalization at a certain level. One does not aim to provide an explanation for an empirical (non-representative) sample drawn from some hypothetical universe to which the results should be generalizable. The aim is to explain the *essence* of the phenomenon, although possibly captured with the help of very untypical and unrepresentative examples.

These types of generalization (or, more correctly, abstraction) form an integral part of all scientific research. Consider the well-known phenomenon that an apple falling from a tree will eventually hit the ground. The law of gravity that was deduced from this and other similar examples does not explain the falling of *apples*. Here, in the deduction of this kind of physical law, the notion that the observations must form a representative sample of the population, of all the 'corresponding' events, would hardly be very helpful. In the first place the number of possible 'cases' is endless. Secondly, someone who is not yet aware of the law of gravity would not necessarily realize that the sample should also include the behaviour of *rising objects*, that is, objects lighter than air; after all the concern was to explain *falling* objects.[2] The only benefit of the experiments would be in them providing a figure for the velocity of falling objects. Here, too, the explanation (that is, the law of gravity) takes into account the variation between different cases; higher up the velocity is lower than it is closer to sea level.

Even though people today like to cherish the idea of individualism, there are nevertheless various regularities in human behaviour, in social life and in products of culture that can be uncovered at a higher or lower level of abstraction by formulating a rule that applies to the whole. It might not be possible to have a rule that applies to all units of observation, but at least it will be possible to formulate other absolute rules that apply to different categories of 'deviant cases'. This does not imply the assumption that *individuals* in their behaviour follow certain laws, or even that they follow one particular rule or law without exception. It only means that *people orient to each others' behaviour as if it were guided by rules*, which constitute the meaning of verbal and non-verbal behaviour. This is the factor that makes it possible in the first place to combine raw observations into a limited number of observations.

Let us return to the question–answer pair that was discussed earlier in chapter 9 (which dealt with the structures of interaction). The discussants orientate themselves to interactive situations on the basis of the initial assumption that questions addressed to the individual will be answered. However, this assumption – a constitutive rule that the people involved take into account in their activity – does not restrict the individuals' freedom of action in any other way except that their behaviour will be interpreted on that basis in any case. If the individual fails to reply or interprets the statement as anything other than a question, then the other party may either repeat the question, ask why his or her counterpart is not answering, or draw his or her own conclusions from the information already received.

Conversation analysis that is concerned with the question–answer pair is obviously not based on a representative sample of conversation situations within a certain population; the requirement of a representative sample would simply be absurd. Besides, a random sample drawn from a random 'population' is hardly the best way to ensure that the evidence carries sufficient weight. Rather than trying to collect as large a number of cases as possible, it is more important to try to find examples of different types of question–answer pairs. The idea is to test whether a rule that people are supposed to take into account in their behaviour applies to all of these cases.

---

[2] Antti Eskola (1985, 110–132), quoting Kurt Lewin, refers to *Galilean* thinking in distinction to *Aristotelian* thinking. In Aristotelian physics it was an adequate explanation for falling to infer that heavy objects had a distinctive quality of falling downwards. The basic requirement for the breakthrough of modern natural science which grew up on Galilean foundations was *abstraction*; the distancing from the obviously self-evident in everyday practices and everyday thinking.

Unriddling as Generalization

Even at the stage of making the observations, in selecting the cases and in combining the raw observations into meta-observations, such principles are applied that the results of the analysis can be assumed to apply to other than certain individual cases. However, the problem of generalizability is largely dealt with at the stage of resolving the mystery. It is particularly important that the researcher personally clarifies in what way and in what respects he or she argues that the results have more general validity. There are innumerable directions of generalization and different ways of arguing for a broader relevance of the results.

In research based on sampling techniques, the solution to the problem of generalization lies in having a *representative sample* of the population. This means that, within certain limits, the researcher can be sure that the breakdown and the statistical associations between different responses obtained would have been the same if all the people included in the original population had been interviewed. The implication here is that generalization is always and inherently about generalizing the result to a certain *population*. This is not necessarily the case. In the results of any research there are different levels of generality.

In qualitative research the most important aspect of all is *local explanation*. The model of explanation must fit in as neatly as possible with the empirical material of the study. It must be coherent, logical, and it should be supported by as many observations about the material as possible. To demonstrate the broader meaning and relevance of the result is a separate task. The research result is examined in one way or another as an *example* of more than just the individual case concerned.

First of all there are probably not very many social scientists who seriously think it is even possible to find laws and regularities that can apply to all situations. On the contrary, the purpose is often to show that phenomena are historically and culturally conditioned. When one makes assumptions about the validity or generalizability of the explanation, it is normally wiser to adopt a strategy of caution than to claim universalism. As a general rule it should suffice to formulate a rule applicable to the whole research material.[3] If one makes the generalizing assumption that the phenomenon concerned applies, say, to Finnish culture in its entirety, it is important to stress (especially in the absence of evidence that clearly speaks for a different interpretation) that one does not automatically assume this to be specifically and only a Finnish phenomenon.

Matti Kortteinen puts the point succinctly by referring to the imaginary ornithologist who sees a raven and says, 'The raven is black'. 'This does not, by logical necessity, imply the conclusion that only the raven is black

---

[3] If in early attempts to formulate a rule one encounters 'exceptional cases', these can be used for checking the formulation of the rule or for suggesting an interpretation with regard to the limits within which it applies.

and therefore that every black bird is a raven. Even so the ornithologist may be quite right in saying that the raven is black' (1992, 78).

If the research is concerned with aspects of life that are central to the culture of the researcher and the readership, then it is not necessary to bother too much with the issue of generalizability. That will be more or less taken care of at the stage of purifying observations, where the researcher combines raw observations and explicates certain aspects of the 'cultural subconscious'; brings under reflective consideration something that any member can recognize and identify from the description. However, it is not always that easy to solve the problem of generalizability. For example, the reviewers of Roberts's dissertation no doubt had to invest much more thought into the question as to whether the coffee ritual really exists, how local it is and how detailed a description the researcher had provided. The situation is exactly the same if the research is concerned with a minority group and its way of life.

In many cases the problem of generalizability in qualitative research is resolved by referring to earlier research and to available statistics at all stages of the study. Roberts, for instance, in his explanation of the 'ceremony' surrounding coffee drinking in Finland, refers to ethnographic research which highlights the history of coffee as a rare and expensive stimulant, as well as to descriptions of how people were seated at the coffee table in a certain rank order. Further, he refers to a study which describes the structure of nineteenth-century Finnish estate society. In other words, Roberts ties the phenomenon to a broader context and in this way seeks implicitly to prove that there is reason to assume that the coffee ritual in this small village in southwestern Finland is more than just a curious exception.

Another situation where it will be necessary to prove the existence of a phenomenon is where it is not very public or part of the 'collective consciousness'. This is often the case with statistically observable patterns and regularities. The researcher who relies entirely on qualitative methods will not often be engaged in revealing or at least in empirically proving the existence of this kind of phenomena. But this does not mean that these phenomena cannot be fruitfully studied by qualitative methods.

Consider, for instance, the problem that Paul Willis set out to explore in his *Learning to Labour* (1977): 'How working class kids get working class jobs', as the subtitle of the book put it. Although the phenomenon is commonly recognized (with ample research to back it up), it is only observable as a statistical regularity, not as a determinist law. The entire research design of Willis's ethnography, based on participant observation and qualitative interviews of a small group of 'lads', relies on these statistics; the only job that Willis takes on is to provide an explanation.

Does this mean that qualitative research has nothing more than a scavenger role in the social sciences? By reading research reports based on representative samples from a population one gets questions that one sets out to answer by gathering qualitative material that sheds light on the mystery. Is this all it is capable of, living off leftovers?

Research today is hardly ever fully self-sufficient. Different methods and different research designs are mutually supportive. In many cases distributions and correlations discovered in social surveys are explained by reference to qualitative studies. Many researchers collect both qualitative and quantitative data side by side.

On the other hand, reference to statistical data or results that are empirically representative of the whole population is by no means the only strategy of generalization. The generalizability of Paul Willis's *Learning to Labour*, for example, is based primarily on logical deduction. After observations and interviews with no more than half a dozen schoolboys he shows that at least in these cases the working-class career was not due to poor school success, to the fact that they didn't have the brains or the skills. This has often been suggested as a reason for the inheritance of social positions in society. It has been argued that the living conditions of the working class lead to 'relative deprivation'; that their environment simply does not offer meaningful stimuli. It has also been argued that working-class children as such are quite clever and resourceful, but that the skills and aptitudes required at school come closer to those promoted by the family life of the middle class and the intelligentsia. Rejecting all these explanations, Willis suggests instead that the reason lies in the 'counter-school culture' that prevails among these boys, and above all in the rejection of mental work, which to them is inherently feminine. Manual work, on the other hand, is associated with masculinity.

In itself this well-documented argumentation only goes to prove that this might be one factor among many others in explaining educational inequality. Willis gives more general validity to his findings by inferring that if the prevailing ideology of education were true, if all people really tried their very best to do well at school, then society could only be stopped from falling to pieces at gunpoint. It can therefore be assumed that the reluctant schoolboys he is studying are by no means marginal exceptions, but that the aversion towards mental work that forms part of the working-class culture produces a counter-school culture that results in working-class children voluntarily and unknowingly submitting to the prevailing social order.

To prove the broader relevance of one's findings may require a demonstration of the generality or significance of the discourses discovered; but it may also consist in something else. In their analysis of barbecues in Mediterranean tourist resorts, Eeva Jokinen and Soile Veijola (1987) present the empirical argument that 'in spite of their local features the structure of these barbecues is fundamentally the same in all resorts', but the main thrust of the analysis is completely different: the chief concern is to demonstrate that the barbecue is a modern *carnival*, a specific type of ritual. In other words the objective is not to do an empirically generalizable study of barbecues, but to explore the partying as an example of carnival.

The Research Process and Generalizability

The treatment of the problem of generalizability does not constitute a separate phase in the research process; the whole process of qualitative research unfolds and takes shape with a view to a certain type of 'generalizability'. As far as generalizability is concerned, the qualitative research process applies a sort of hourglass model.

Consider, for example, our study *The Realm of Male Freedom* (Alasuutari and Siltari 1983) and the follow-up to this study, *The Local Tavern* (Sulkunen et al. 1985). These projects were grounded in the view that the consequences of the massive movement of people during the 1970s into the cities and towns of Finland were *crystallized* in the suburbs and most particularly (and even exceptionally) so in the local pubs. Within the local pubs, we focused on one *exceptional group*, a male community consisting of regulars. The ethnographic analysis of this group was used as a prism for studying the changing living conditions in the surrounding community.

So the concern was with rather broad, structural issues. After several operations to narrow down the focus, we proceeded to the epicentre of the hourglass, to analyze in detail a very specific, closely defined object of study.

Later on in the *Local Tavern* project we had additional case-analyses to fill in the picture of local pubs and their cultures of drinking. A second ethnographic study was carried out to explore the clientele of one local tavern. This time we focused on a group where drinking was heavier and where many had been through a divorce. We studied the names of local taverns, the semiotics of their interior decor, the music that was played on the jukebox. We interviewed the local women of the suburbs, including the wives of some darts players studied in the first case-study.

It is important to note that the 'sample logic' of surveys does not come into play in the selection of the objects of study at any level: the local tavern does not 'represent' the problems that were caused by the influx of people from the countryside, nor do the regulars of the local taverns 'represent' the drinking habits in the suburbs or among the regulars of local taverns in general. Strauss (1987, 16–21) describes this strategy for the selection of research objects as *theoretical sampling*.

Ethnographic research of this kind is not so much generalization as extrapolation: in certain, explicated respects the results are *related* to broader entities. For instance, in the case-study dealing with the darts players an analysis is carried out on the attitudes and life-styles of the men concerned to see how their views of life serve as solutions to the tensions and contradictions flowing from suburbanization and other changes in living conditions. On the basis of this analysis the aim is then to find out what is specific and particular about the solutions adopted by *these men* compared with the solutions that the more 'ordinary' suburban residents may be imagined as adopting. In other words, the case-analysis is *related* to the broader population. Although the solutions adopted by the men included in the study may be regarded as isolated individual cases and as such as exceptional, the living conditions and the conflicts addressed by the life-styles of these men are very much the same for large numbers of Finnish people. This means it is possible indirectly (for example, by referring to other research) to conclude in which respects and to what extent the life-style of these men really is exceptional, in which respects it is comparable to other solutions or population groups, and what sorts of *different* solutions exist.

In short, then, a narrow case-analysis is broadened, at the stage of resolving the mystery, through the search for contrary and parallel cases, into an example of a broader entity. Thus the research process advances, in its final stages, towards a discussion of broad entities.[4] We end up on the bottom of the hourglass.

In the process of pointing out the wider meaning of the study results, generalization to the population level is not the only option. One of the concluding chapters of *The Realm of Male Freedom*, for instance, discusses Finnish drinking habits, working-class culture and the heavy-drinking baby-boom generation; another discusses activity and consciousness in semiotic culture theory; and the third proceeds to present alcohol policy conclusions.

So in qualitative research the object is always to discuss *in what regard* the researcher assumes or argues that the study has general validity beyond the individual case explored. Some commentators reviewing our darts players case-study, for instance, approached the work as if it had been intended as a generalizable description of *darts players*. In this sort of commentary the purpose and meaning of the case-study was misunderstood in accordance with the 'sample logic' of the social survey.

This line of generalization would theoretically be possible. We could discuss how darts playing as a leisure activity or as a form of sports compares with other leisure activities and what is distinctive about darts. Although the case-analysis would remain unchanged, a different direction of generalization would require a somewhat different theoretical frame of reference and, above all, reference to different kinds of other studies.

Generalization is in fact the wrong word in this connection. That should be reserved for surveys only. What can be analyzed instead is how the researcher demonstrates that the analysis *relates* to things *beyond* the material at hand. In this sense *relating* could be a more suitable term, but

---

[4] It should be noted, however, that research is an altogether different matter from the literary outcome of the research process, the presentation. At the level of the presentation, the broad deliberations involved in the planning stage will rarely be presented at the beginning of the qualitative study, but the text often begins to unfold inductively directly from empirical observations, so that all that remains of the hourglass model is its bottom part.

as a whole we are dealing with such a broad issue that no single term will cover the problematic. As far as generalization to a population is concerned, *extrapolation* better captures the typical procedure in qualitative research. On the other hand, no extrapolation may be required of a study analyzing a phenomenon or case regarded important in a culture. Consider, for instance, research dealing with Jesus as a historical figure. The broader issue at stake is the *relevance* of the research one undertakes. No matter what science or discipline we are dealing with, that is never just a technical question, handled as a distinct part of the investigation. It is an integral element of the whole research design, and ultimately it is a social and cultural question.

13

The Research Process

For some reason I have always found it difficult to relate to textbook descriptions of the research process; somehow they seem to be far removed from my own experiences. I cannot honestly say that the rules they provide have been of very much help to me.

It is hard to believe that this is due entirely to the differences between qualitative and quantitative research (with the latter of course typically serving as the model for textbook accounts). It would seem that the same applies throughout the field of social science. The flow charts you find in textbooks to describe the research process seem to portray and retrace the history of the greatest success stories of social science, leaving aside all false starts, all problems and culs-de-sac – probably because no one really wants to report on their failures. However, it is precisely in these situations that the researcher most desperately needs help and advice, rather than where everything is going smoothly and according to plan. Another difficulty is that the research process is traditionally defined in very strict and narrow terms. The work that goes on before the 'empirical stage' is given only scant attention. The different stages of the research process – defining the problem, collecting the data, reporting, etc. – are described as coherent steps that follow each other neatly in a set order, even though in reality (at least in the case of qualitative research) there is always considerable overlap.

One (partial) explanation for the obvious lack of correlation between the flow charts and reality is that the descriptions of how the research process advances in reality seem to be confused with implicit normative demands as to how the research *should* advance. Jukka Mäkelä (1991, 40–44) lists a number of examples to show how textbook descriptions of the research process are still grounded in the model of hypothesis-testing which was first introduced in the late 1920s and early 1930s by British statisticians and subsequently adopted as the textbook paradigm of social research. The basic requirement is that the research is always carried out in a set order (see Mäkelä 1991, 44–52):

1 A model is chosen, that is, the assumption is made that a random sample is available from a certain distribution.
2 Hypothesis H_0 (the prevailing view) and hypothesis H_1 (the alternative view that the researcher favours) are inserted into the model.
3 The significance level α is set at 0.05, 0.01 or 0.001. The more important the null hypothesis, the lower the figure for α.

4 The observations are collected and the value for the test parameter is calculated.
5 The final decision is made. If the test parameter falls within the critical range as defined by the selected significance level α, then H_0 is rejected; otherwise it is accepted.

Within this statistical paradigm it is thus required that the hypotheses be set before collecting the data. 'Data-snooping' is also strictly forbidden: the researcher must not try to learn anything from the material that might inspire new ideas (Mäkelä 1991, 52).

In practice, however, this model is hardly ever followed even in purely quantitative sociological research. It is even less applicable to qualitative research.

Quite frankly I do not believe that very much can be done to improve existing descriptions of the research process simply by adding new 'feedback' arrows between the blocks representing different research phases: 'defining the problem', 'collecting the data', 'reviewing earlier research', 'developing the theoretical frame of reference', 'data analysis', 'reporting', etc. These sorts of flow charts which cover all possible relations of interaction do not, I am afraid, really help to explain anything (even though the diagrams as such can be quite impressive). Therefore, in the following discussion of the research process I have opted instead to write about my own experiences and to look at some of my own earlier studies.

Where Does the Research Process Begin?

Qualitative methods are often said to be ideally suited for purposes of pilot research. After the initial overview produced with those methods, you can generate hypotheses for testing with quantitative methods. Implicit in this line of thinking is the assumption that the research proper *begins* once the hypotheses have been laid down. In qualitative research, however, a different rationale applies; here it is thought that the most difficult phase has already been completed when the questions have been formulated and even the alternative answers are known. So what is the point that marks the 'real' beginning of research? Does it begin with data collection, or with the completion of the research plan? It is clearly no easy task to pinpoint the exact starting point for the research process. Every study is based, to a greater or lesser degree, on earlier research and on the researcher's earlier experiences.

An example is provided by a study previously mentioned several times in this book *The Realm of Male Freedom*, which I wrote in collaboration with Jorma Siltari (Alasuutari and Siltari 1983). For my part, the roots of that study trace back to the village of Båtsfjord in northern Norway, where I worked (with countless other Finnish and Norwegian youths) at a fish-packing factory in the summer of 1979. There were several factories in this one small village, and to house the seasonal workforce there were also a number of hostels. Especially during weekends life was quite raucous in the village and in the hostels, which were full of young people who were a long way from home and who scarcely spoke the language. In addition to the legitimate drink that you had to order from the state via the post, there was also plenty of the local illicit beverage.

Afterwards, looking back at the months I spent in Båtsfjord, I thought about this small village as a sort of laboratory for all the changes that had resulted from the changing industrial structure in Finland and the massive movement of people into the urban south. This was a place where the social consequences of these processes were even more clearly visible than they were in Gothenburg, Sweden, which attracted large numbers of immigrant workers into the local auto factories. In Båtsfjord, the young immigrant workers lived virtually in a social vacuum; in a place where, if you did not speak the language, there was really nothing to do during your leisure time – except drink.

At first I thought of writing a newspaper article about Båtsfjord, and even spoke to the factory owner about this. Then, upon my return to Tampere to continue my studies in sociology, I seriously thought of Båtsfjord as a subject for my thesis – but soon dropped the idea because the village was just too far away. Instead I became interested in aspects of the Finnish alcohol culture within the broader framework of the Great Migration, the massive process of rural depopulation. I decided to begin to study local (that is, suburban) pubs or taverns within this context. After all, the Finnish high-rise suburbs are monuments to the Great Migration; working-class villages built in a social vacuum. And life in these local taverns (I presumed) corresponded to the social problems that followed with these profound changes in life. I also managed to interest my good friend Jorma Siltari in this subject and so we set out to write the thesis together.

During the summer of 1981 I went to see Pekka Sulkunen at the Social Research Institute of Alcohol Studies. I was familiar with his writings on the 'wet generation', the Finnish baby-boom generation which drank more heavily than those born before or after them. I thought he would be interested in our plans. Sulkunen told me that they had in fact been working on some very similar ideas at the Institute, and that a project had been carried out in local pubs in Helsinki within the framework of an in-house training course in qualitative research methods. However, no report had been written from the fieldnotes of these passive observations. Sulkunen agreed that Siltari and I would prepare our own report from the existing fieldnotes and our observations in Helsinki pubs and have our expenses covered by presenting that report to the Institute. This would then serve as the basis for the research proper that would be carried out in Tampere.

The report we prepared and the experiences we gathered in the course of the observations were quite useful; and at once not so useful. The fieldnotes consisted mostly of more or less sketchy observations that left the reader wondering whether they merely reflected the researchers' own prejudices rather than the world of the people whom we were supposed to be studying. During an observation session that lasts a couple of hours at most it is impossible to gain any relevant insights simply by watching other clients. So one would end up recording more or less enlightened guesses as to who this or that client was or one would (to justify the work one was doing as a serious scientific project) begin to count the number of beers that the clients were drinking. The only real benefit of the report and the whole operation was that they gave a more concrete form and shape to the problems that needed to be solved in a field study.

We decided to focus our attention on just one local tavern and within that tavern on one particular group, that is, the regulars. This would make it much easier to get to know the people we were supposed to be studying. Secondly, we also decided that the project would be based on participant observation; we wanted to tell the people concerned that we were intending to do a research project, that we wanted to get to know the regular clientele and that we also intended to interview them. Thirdly, we decided that we would not count the number of drinks people were having; we did not want to have any strict patterns in recording our observations.

The following winter we picked out a local tavern in Tampere and the regulars of that tavern as the subjects of our study. But this was by no means the beginning of the research process. A lot of work had preceded this during which the very object of study had been changed once (within the frame of a broader theme) and then, as a result of our pilot study, redefined in more specific terms.

This process, in which we chewed over the main problems of our project and made false starts and rethought it all over again, is hardly an exceptional beginning for a research project. It is just that researchers very rarely report on all of this. However, an early failure to choose the right road does not have to mean you are ultimately trapped in a dead-end. Nor should you just sit back and complain if the project does not seem to produce very interesting results. If you find that something does not work as you expect it to, then you have already made a discovery, learned something that you did not know before the project commenced. The project has by now produced at least one result. Revise your strategy on the basis of that result and you might be able to move on to other results.

In our case the false starts we made and the research ideas we had to discard as unrealistic in view of existing resources led to a better plan and a clearer view of how the project should be carried out. However, there is no reason why these false clues and false starts should not be included in the final report; not in the past tense as an account of what the project team did before it got the research design and the problems right, but as an account in which the reader, in the present tense, is guided via these false clues onto a completely new track.

From Theoretical Framework to Local Explanation

We made even more changes and more readjustments in the work to develop the theoretical framework for our study. Initially we set out with what is perhaps best described as a late-Marxian model which was heavily influenced by the 'logic of capital' perspective and the related critique of civilization. However, by that time the economic determinism and macro-sociological approach inherent in the 'logic of capital' perspective had been challenged or balanced out by the concept of 'way of life'. A new generation of Finnish sociologists was enthusiastic about studying ordinary people's way of life with the means of qualitative methods and participant observation. The way of life was then to be explained in the larger framework of political economy. We familiarized ourselves with, for instance, the German social psychologist Klaus Ottomeyer's (1977) scheme of the 'form-determinants' of the way of life in capitalism, which seemed to provide a promising theoretical framework. This provided a useful backdrop for reading studies dealing with the ecomomic background for the development of the Finnish restaurant institution and the founding of local taverns. Further, this frame of reference provided a useful setting for a thematization of issues concerning way of life and culture in terms of differences between the exchange-value and use-value of commodities. We therefore also studied the writings by Wolfgang Fritz Haug (1971; English translation 1986) on commodity aesthetics and the debate that unfolded on that subject. Underlying the Marxist line of everyday life research was the Frankfurt School critique of civilization, which criticizes capitalism by showing how the living conditions it produces and the form-determinants of way of life generate social problems and impoverish people's everyday life. From this point of view it may be postulated that the success of the restaurant business is based on the sale of alcohol to the working class and the marketing of the company of other clients in order to alleviate their alienation.

However, by the time the fieldwork commenced in early 1982, we had also read the studies by the Birmingham School scholars on youth subcultures, including Paul Willis's *Profane Culture* (1978) and *Learning to Labour* (1977). These had a profound impact on our way of thinking. The thinking that we adopted from the Birmingham School departed from a different point of view, that is, that of people's everyday life and cultural forms. The starting point was no longer provided by research on impover-ishment; instead the idea was to study how people organize their lives in such a way that they can retain their self-respect and feel that theirs is a meaningful existence. The attempt to organize one's own life and living conditions may lead to greater or lesser difficulties, such as problems in family life, disagreements with the boss at work, problems with one's own drinking habits – which of course was what our study was really about. In this sense we were not out to deny the existence of problems or the general misery of life. However, the perspective was different from that adopted in

Marxist way-of-life research, where the current way of life is *deduced* from the system and the form-determinants it has produced. Our baseline assumption was that people's way of life is determined by the way in which they perceive their own living conditions and how, within this general framework, they *take into account* those conditions for their everyday life. This means that culture – collective notions of how the world is organized and collective images of the good life – takes on a central and relatively independent status. As an indication of this theoretical shift we no longer spoke about way-of-life research; we now identified ourselves with *cultural studies*.

With this change we also adopted new theoretical concepts; the key terms now were meaning and meaning structures (in a semiotic sense). As far as methodology was concerned, the focus shifted to the distinctions that people made in their speech as well as to the broader systems of distinction that provided the general structure and organization of their everyday life. A further concern was with the homological relationship between the meanings of different aspects of everyday life. Before we proceeded to the stage of fieldwork, I wrote the following lines in my field diary:

> I guess the most important function of subculture is to create a sense of group cohesion, or to protest against mainstream culture and its lifestyle. As the name implies, a counterculture is a 'denial' of mainstream culture; it is not independent. Its meanings lie within mainstream culture.
>
> Subculture gives its meanings to the objects and to the environment in which it appears. The clothes of young people, motorbikes, etc. Shared experiences, shared objects are what ties the group together.
>
> Could we assume that the interior decor of a restaurant and the 'societal' relation that determines the relationship between doormen and clients also finds its expression in the subculture of the regulars?

On the other hand, after reading the subculture studies by Willis and other Birmingham scholars, I observed (in another memo that I wrote at the time) that subculture reflects an intergenerational conflict:

> In a subculture the internal conflicts of the parent culture (which in the final analysis are of course due to changes in the real life process, i.e. to the development of capitalism) find expression in the form of intergenerational conflicts. The latent function of a subculture is to manifest and resolve, albeit 'magically', the conflicts of the parent culture. Conflicts are the ideological themes that youth culture deals with in the discourse it has created.
>
> What this means is that in our studies of the regulars of a local tavern as a subculture, we are in effect trying to uncover the conflicts of the parent culture – parent culture in this case being something like the 'new urban working class', which leads a family-centred way of life in suburbia.
>
> It would be extremely useful in view of the advance planning of participant observation to try to 'guess' what kind of conflicts there are within the parent culture. This would make it easier to interpret the discourses that appear non-verbally, for instance.

In early 1982 we proceeded to the field stage of our project, picking out for our case-analysis a tavern that we called 'Vapaavuoro' ('The Off

Duty'). One of the main reasons we selected this particular tavern was that there was a group of darts players among the regulars whom we thought we could approach relatively easily. After just two visits to the pub we told the darts players that we were doing a study about them. One of the players made some crack about learned men joining their ranks; someone else said, well why don't you just go ahead and ask your questions. We said we were in no hurry; could you begin instead by teaching us the rules of darts . . .

We went down to the pub quite regularly, perhaps three times a week, spending two to four hours there each evening. We tried (honestly) not to overdo the drinking, but it was quite clear from the outset that if we wanted to talk with our subjects in any atmosphere of frankness and openness we could not go around drinking club soda. To a great extent the research process consisted simply in spending time with the darts players. We played darts with them, we listened to them, we talked to them. Every now and then we conducted interviews with individual men, and some-times arranged tape-recorded group conversations. During the next day we both wrote our own observation reports. The daily discussions I had with Jorma Siltari were an important part of the research method. In these discussions we tried to figure out what we had actually seen and what we had experienced. We worked out new questions for our study, generated new hypotheses and interpretations that we could then 'test' against new observations, taking our observations and ideas back to our group conversations or interviews.[1]

The fieldwork was completed later that spring, and we wrote our final report during the summer and autumn. Our explanations of the subculture rested to a great extent on the homological relationships between the meanings taken on by the darts players' different spheres of life. On the basis of our analyses of the speech of these men, we showed how the local tavern represented a 'realm of male freedom'; a closed milieu with its symbolic counterparts in other domains of everyday life. Darts playing had its parallel in labouring; and the doorman in the boss down at works. However, an important difference which makes the tavern a far more exciting place than the rest of the everyday world is that within this 'miniature society' of leisure, our darts players were much better placed to mould and shape their lives, to actually have some control over matters. Through their activities they could highlight and develop their relationship to wage labour as well as a life-orientation to which they could anchor their self-esteem and their identity. Darts playing, for instance, served as a means for highlighting one's skills and common sense as a skilled worker, but without the seriousness that is necessarily involved on the job; it was just a pastime, an amusement they could enjoy whenever they wanted to.

---

[1] In its later stages the *Local Tavern* project involved four researchers. We had several seminars which lasted two to three days, working through different versions of the manuscript.

Our attention was also drawn to the differences between the life-orientation of the generation they and their parents represented and, on the other hand, the life-orientation of the regulars and other people living in the suburb. Another important theme in our analyses was the tension between the local tavern and the home.

Were we applying a deductive approach in this study, testing hypotheses generated on the basis of the theoretical literature? This was hardly the case, even though it was the Birmingham theory of subculture and the semiotic approach that drew our attention to certain key aspects. These served as a theoretical frame of reference; they were not the hypotheses we were testing.

A theoretical frame of reference (which can be elaborated by reading earlier research and the theoretical literature) must be distinguished from the *local explanation* of matters, from the work to make intelligible phenomena and paradoxes observed in the empirical material. There were no sources that would have told us that darts playing symbolizes the craftsman's relationship to his job, or that the management of the local pub has its parallel in management at the workplace. Of course, it may be possible to extract such clues from earlier research and in this way to get support for the task of local explanation. A good example is provided by the interpretation that Willis suggested in his studies, and Corrigan and Willis (1980) repeated in an article, that the 'rejection of mental work' was a distinctive characteristic of (male) working-class culture. This characteristic was clearly evident in our darts study, and having read about it we were perhaps even more keenly aware of it. But even here we are still talking about a comparatively general idea; how it was concretely reflected in the life-orientation and discourses of the darts players, how it made the cultural forms of the darts club understandable – this required local explanation, not a deduction from explanations.

Local explanation of the empirical material always forms the hard core of research. Its role is perhaps least significant in a study where, for example, an empirical result obtained in earlier research is tested as a hypothesis against survey data. However, even in this case the hypothesis will normally be tested in a setting which in one way or another differs from the original one, or the aim will be to establish whether the explanation applies to some other sphere of life or to a related phenomenon. The only (rare) situation in social research where local explanation is not needed at all is in a repeat study to verify a dubious set of results.

As Malinowski stressed, it is particularly important in ethnographic research to approach your object of study with an open mind and on its own terms, that during the stage of fieldwork you forget all theories and hypotheses. In practice this is of course impossible, but what Malinowski probably meant here was that you have to try to make observations about everything that is observable, not just about things whose utility can be deduced from the theory you have. The more open-minded you are in gathering observations, the less you exclude, the richer your material will be, and, accordingly, the better your chances of inventing completely new (theoretical) ideas on the basis of the material. The paradox here is that one of the best ways to teach yourself that crucial skill of open-mindedness is to read and study as many different theories as possible.

So local explanation forms the hard core of research; but it is by no means the end-point of the study. Referring back to the theoretical frame of reference you have adopted, you still need to identify the broader conclusions that can be drawn from the results. For instance, you can put forward your assumptions as to how far a certain local explanation applies to other aspects of everyday life. You also need to make clear in which respects you assume the results are generalizable. For example, in our darts study we concluded that the results cannot be generalized as an analysis of Finnish restaurant culture or darts playing, but that they reflect the life-orientation and the contradictions that the working class encounters in adapting to a suburban way of life and the changes in the gendered division of labour.

From Local Explanation to Theoretical Ideas

Local explanation often throws up new topics for research, or new theoretical ideas. For instance, while we were still working on our darts study we gave a lot of thought to the contradictory relationship that our darts players appeared to have to their drinking habits. This is what I wrote in my diary during our fieldwork:

> These men have a contradictory relationship to alcohol: on the one hand they say that drinking beer is not at all important when they are playing, that the most important thing is meeting their mates; on the other hand they admit that beer is the most important thing after all, that darts is just a good excuse to get away from home and the wife. There are different views among the men as to how far frequenting the pub is a symptom of an alcohol problem.

In this entry I discussed at some length the 'double hermeneutics' of alcoholism or – as I phrased the idea many years later (Alasuutari 1992a) – the 'double epistemological status' of alcoholism:

> Even though it seems that, at an informal cultural level, these men are well aware that they are not alcoholics, the pressure of the ideology is nevertheless there. Deep down inside, the other half of them admits that alcohol is a problem. This of course implies the admission that they are keeping bad company and (by the same token) that they themselves are bad people . . . . It could be argued that insofar as these men admit that their circle of friends is just an association of alcoholics, they themselves *become* alcoholics; after all alcoholism is largely a psychological condition in which the lack of self-esteem is one of the most important factors.

In the darts study and during the interviews we did with the darts players, we were not yet seriously interested in the theme of alcoholism. We were doing a study of the role of the local tavern in the way of life and life-orientation of working-class men, not a study of alcoholism. When one of our interviewees raised the possibility that he might in fact be an alcoholic, we immediately veered to other topics; to themes that we thought formed the object proper of our study. Implicitly, we thought our chief concern was with the darts players as a cultural group that had its own collective distinctions and ways of thinking; that any deliberation at the individual level was wholly irrelevant. This was an obvious mistake in view of the fundamental principle of open-mindedness in fieldwork.

This single mistake did not by any means affect the reliability of the study. On the contrary, looking back at the technical error we had made, I began to give more serious thought to the question of how alcoholism should be approached and studied. In the study we eventually wrote we already discussed the ambivalent attitudes of men towards alcoholism. In my later studies, this theme that first emerged in the darts project as a sideline became the key subject, the focal concern of my work. With the empirical observations and analyses of the dual role of alcoholism – on the one hand as a more or less correct diagnosis of a person's relationship to alcohol, on the other hand as a social construct which, as it is used, also changes the nature of the phenomenon it describes – I was drawn into studying many new theories and questions.

In much the same way I got a new theoretical idea from empirical analysis when I was conducting an ethnographic study of a genuinely Finnish self-help group for alcoholics. Reading through my fieldnotes and the tape-recorded group discussions, my attention was drawn to the way in which certain members of the local A-Guild (and particularly the Chairman) repeatedly reproached certain behaviour in other members. For instance, when someone belittled the alcohol problem of another group member, the Chairman would make the emphatic point that it is enough if the person himself thinks that he has an alcohol problem, no matter how small the quantities he used to consume. Similarly, it was commonplace for members to complain that they were a hopelessly lazy bunch. If there was any project that had to be done at the group's summer place, for instance, it was best not to tell anyone in advance because otherwise no one would turn up. Nonetheless, many group members had all sorts of excuses for avoiding work.

These sorts of reproaches are characteristics that in sociology are traditionally attached to social norms. Norm theory assumes that society or any community is held together precisely by a unanimity about norms that all should follow. In cultural studies, on the other hand, where the key concept is that of meaning, the theory is that, for group cohesion, all members share the same view and understanding of reality and of what makes for a meaningful life and existence. Normative statements will here often pass unnoticed. At best they will be associated with the relationships between different subcultures and social groups.

But what I had here in the self-help group were norms; there were no two ways about it. The interesting thing about these norms was that even though they were repeated time and time again, they seemed to have little real effect. No matter how often the Chairman said that the group should not belittle the drinking of other members, they still did. And even though all the members complained that they were a lazy bunch, the same people could not help boasting about how they had escaped a certain job without even lending a hand. However, from an outsider's point of view, one would have been very hard put indeed to describe these people as lazy: they were always arranging all sorts of fêtes and lotteries and bazaars.

I eventually realized that when you encounter a normative statement you have to ask: what is the social meaning of each social norm? I discovered that the seemingly paradoxical way in which the self-help group members described (or bragged about) their earlier drinking habits was closely linked to the firm views these people had that a former alcoholic is much better placed to help a person who is trying to stop drinking than a professional helper with no 'field experience'. From this it follows that the person who has a longer and heavier drinking history is more competent in counselling than someone who has less 'field experience'. The contradictory emphasis on laziness, then, was related to the shared view that the first thing you need to do when you quit drinking, or when you try to quit drinking, is to clear your head, that is change your attitude to life and to wage labour. In our discussions many group members referred to getting out of the rat race, where heavy working is followed, at regular intervals, by heavy drinking. When you become trapped in a serious drinking bout and when you lose your job as a consequence, you get another job as soon as you are off the bottle, try to get your life organized, pay your bills and so on – only to fall into the same trap again. According to the group members, the best way to break this vicious circle is not to go back to work for six months or a whole year, to change your whole attitude to life. You have to learn to take things easy, to be a bit lazy. That is why when members complain that they are such a lazy lot, they are making a secret confession that these lazy sods have understood what the group's 'treatment philosophy' is all about: that they have managed to get out of the rat race.

These are both examples of the meaning or function of normative statements in the interaction among A-Guild members. In these cases the life-philosophy that has taken shape at an informal level among the group members is at sharp variance with the values or rational logic of the rest of society. Even though it makes sense from the point of view of the group's world of meanings to brag about one's drinking, it seems utterly pointless and meaningless from the point of view of 'normal thinking'. In this way the explicit normative statement can serve as a sign of contradiction (Alasuutari 1992a, 178–180). The appearance of a normative statement is an indication that some model of activity or thinking has been taken under reflective consideration; it is no longer a matter of course simply to act or think in a certain manner, instead other options are also recognized and they are given partial recognition with some normative statement.

Qualitative Research as Hypothesis-Testing

Textbooks in statistical social research say that the research process consists typically of testing hypotheses that have been formulated within the research plan; the testing is supposed to take place against material collected specifically for that purpose. Qualitative research (and indeed most of quantitative research which uses questionnaire materials) differs in certain essential respects from this textbook model. The whole effort is grounded in a single theoretical frame of reference, and even that may be changed or modified as the project unfolds. The themes of the study are formulated in terms of general questions. In the case of the above study on the A-Guild, for instance, the questions I had were along the following lines: What sort of treatment philosophy does the group have? Why is this philosophy what it is? In order to present hypotheses in the research plan, you need to have a fairly close familiarity with the object of study. Hypotheses belong to local explanation, and that is why they can be presented in the research plan mainly in the context of follow-up studies.

However, the qualitative research process also consists of the testing of hypotheses. The difference is that these hypotheses are not formulated in advance; they evolve as the research project and the analysis unfold, as you learn more about the object of study and as you learn what sort of questions to ask and hypotheses to formulate.

This distinctive characteristic of the qualitative research process is most clearly visible in ethnographic research, where the analysis of the material and the phenomenon proceeds side by side with data collection so that the testing of the hypotheses provides important clues for the collection of new material. At first you simply make observations and record impressions, look at the observations and the materials with an open mind, from as many different angles as possible. It might be useful to do some preliminary analyses with the material collected, focusing for instance on systems of distinction, plot structures or rules of conversation. You can also apply the methods that were discussed in chapter 11, using these tools to actively produce useful why-questions. When you then have your questions and preliminary hypotheses formulated on the basis of those questions, you move on to answer them by collecting materials that throw light on the questions and to test the hypotheses against the new material.

In fieldwork this sort of hypothesis-testing often consists of asking questions of informants; the answers are then used as material in the evaluation of the validity of the hypothesis. It is particularly important not to confuse two separate things here: the question presented in the interview and the question you have set for the study. A research hypothesis cannot be tested simply by asking the informants whether your interpretation is right. This is not to say that you cannot *ask* the question; sometimes it might be very interesting to do so. But the answer to your question (whether affirmative or negative) cannot, in itself, confirm or refute the hypothesis.

The reason for this is that social scientific explanation always operates at a higher level of abstraction than the everyday understanding of things. One needs distance from the everyday mundane matters, approaching them as 'objects' that need to be explained. Explanation may be based, among other things, on the explication of those meaning structures within which matters become intelligible at a practical level, and which also make intelligible the frontier lines of conflicts and disagreements. So the discourses and the deliberations of the researcher and his or her informants are concerned with different sorts of questions: the informants will tell you what they mean, or interpret the intentions of others, whereas the researcher's job is to analyze these discourses, situations and interpretations in order to explicate the societal or cultural conditions within which practical activity is possible.

Hypotheses can, however, be tested by presenting questions to the informants. The trick is to word these questions indirectly, to *operationalize* the hypothesis. What you want to do is have questions that can help to shed light on the issue at hand. Often researchers will simply ask their informants to provide further details on a certain subject, to give more examples. The specific value and importance of the informants' discourse lies in their familiarity with the phenomenon studied in practice; as Clifford Geertz (1983) says, they have abundant 'local knowledge'. The informants' discourses both complement and enrich the picture of the phenomenon that is being studied and are themselves part of that phenomenon; they bring out the concepts, explanations and interpretations within which the phenomenon is understood.

In some cases the informants will offer their own interpretations of the matter in hand. It is important to take these interpretations into account as potential explanations, to take a hard look at how well they explain the related factors. However, these attempts do not, or should not, enjoy any most-favoured status vis-à-vis the researchers simply because they have come from the informants. The researcher can never obtain full explanations directly from the interviewees; in this sense the informants are not experts on the subject they are talking about. The interpretations suggested by the informants have special value only because these kinds of explanations form part of the phenomenon studied.

Let us revert to the A-Guild study. During the fieldwork stage of this project I took part in the group's daily sessions. In addition to these observations, there were also group discussions that were tape-recorded. The themes that were covered in these meetings were usually inspired by the hypotheses I submitted to the participants. In one particular conversation I raised the issue of why members were always so eager to compete for the title of heaviest drinker and at the same time to belittle the drinking of other members:

PA: Somehow I feel that there's this feeling in this group that there's
       someone here who hasn't drunk as much as the others or who's been
       down and out for a shorter while than others, that you tend to belittle

that person's drinking, that, you know, that's nothing really, I drank a lot more than he did.

A: Where've you heard that?

PA: I have you know.

B: I see.

PA: Even during these sessions right here.

C: It's always better the sooner you have the sense to go and get help isn't it.

A: That's right.

C: The longer you drink the more stupid you are, there's no doubt about that.

PA: But do you brag about being more stupid?

C: You tend to colour things a bit, like I've been drinking longer than you have. You've only been drinking for a year but I've been there two years. So the one who's been drinking for a year realizes that this is the point where I need to go and get help for myself. I'm so stupid that I didn't have the sense to come and get help, I had to carry on. So this is how I describe the situation so that there you are, I'm a bit better, *I know these things*, a bit better.

When I raised this question the members of the group first wanted to deny my interpretation, even though I had clear examples of these sorts of situations in my fieldnotes. When at long last it is admitted that the phenomenon really exists, member C (in the italicized section of his speech) renders further support to my interpretation that the emphasis on the seriousness of one's earlier alcohol problems is associated with the respect that the members show for practical experience. Later on in the same conversation I raise the issue in even more straightforward terms:

PA: Is it so that he who's been a heavier drinker has more experience? And the least experienced of all is the social worker who's never had any problem with alcohol?

C: Well that's it, that we don't trust these therapists at all, do we. What can they do to help? Absolutely nothing. They've no experience at all. How could they help anyone? They could just as well join up with the people from the temperance committee and provide advice to each other as far as we're concerned.

The fact that the respondent here seems to lend support to my interpretation does not mean that the hypothesis has simply and plainly been verified as correct. What it proves, in the first instance, is that one distinctive characteristic of the manner of speaking of AA group members is a critical attitude towards the A-Clinic Foundation and in general towards professional helpers, and that the critique is motivated by the lack of personal experience. However, in my study of the A-Guild (Alasuutari 1992a, 107–148) I show that the relationship of these people to the A-Clinic is fundamentally contradictory. On the one hand, there is a notable lack of trust and confidence in professional helpers, but on the other hand many members have joined the group through the A-Guild. The role and significance of the critical attitude towards professional help depends in the final analysis on the extent to which it permeates the whole material. This, after all, was what the testing of this particular hypothesis was all about. It seemed that giving priority to practical experience at the expense of theoretical knowledge was a thoroughgoing theme in the life-philosophy of the Guild members. This was reflected, among other things, in the emphasis on one's own experience, but also in many other aspects.

So field research consists of a continuous testing of hypotheses. The analysis of the material collected so far, and preliminary interpretations made on the basis of that analysis, provides directions for the further collection of data. If, for instance, a hypothesis related to local explanation proves false in light of new material, then you should retrace your tracks, reconsider different interpretations and test them against the new material. On the other hand, if some hypothesis does receive support, then that will often lead to different further hypotheses.

In ethnographic research the testing of hypotheses may have to do with more than just the kinds of thing you are making observations about or the kinds of subject that you raise with the informants. On the basis of your results you may decide to move on and collect a new data set, as I did in the AA group project. When I learned that A-Guilds in Finland had their own journal, it seemed a good idea to go through all its back volumes to determine whether the 'treatment philosophy' I had discovered in Tampere was a local or a more national phenomenon. In many cases the analysis of phenomena emerging in the fieldwork will also lead you to reading related research or theoretical literature. Further, you may decide on the basis of the preliminary results of the fieldwork that a comparative setting might be useful. No doubt it is at least equally common that the original plans for data collection turn out to be far too comprehensive in view of the revised research problem.

Even though there is an element of self-direction and unpredictability in the process of field research, you should nonetheless always give serious thought to how far you want your clues to lead the way and how far you want to continue collecting data according to the original plan, just to be on the safe side. First of all you should never rely on just one or two pieces of evidence that a certain hypothesis at a local level is valid. Secondly, it is always useful to collect as broad and comprehensive a body of material as possible; to cover (within reasonable limits) such themes and phenomena that during the fieldwork might not seem very interesting or important. That is, qualitative material is such a rich corpus that new hypotheses can even be generated and tested afterwards, without necessarily having to collect any additional data. Qualitative research is in fact often carried out in precisely this way: you collect material according to a set plan and make only minor adjustments in the course of the research process. Then, you go ahead with the process of testing hypotheses (as described above) by analyzing this material. This sort of procedure, of course, requires a fairly comprehensive data set compiled from a very loosely structured setting.

It was this sort of comprehensive, multi-purpose material that I acquired in my study on television viewing, which was based on qualitative interviews. The research plan I submitted to the Finnish broadcasting company YLE for collecting this extensive interview material was titled: 'The Reception of TV Fiction and Video Films: A Study of the Relationship of Finnish Programme Preferences to Ways of Life'. In my plan I suggested that the project

> concentrate on the connections between way of life and electronic mass media as an explanatory factor of the reception of television films, video films, and serials. The underlying idea is that the direction and nature of the audience's preferences must be uncovered in the changes in Finnish society that have forced people to change their life-values.

Further, I noted that

> the basic methodological idea is to combine narrative analysis of TV films with interviews, analyzing their reception by asking viewers to explain the plot of the film they have seen. The plot structures that are characteristic of different viewer groups and their distinctive attitudes to television programming are linked to their world-views and attitudes to life in general by asking them to tell their life-stories. A wide range of research problems related to people's way of life, programme preferences and social differences of perception can be incorporated into this basic setting.

In principle it would have been possible to incorporate all this into the research project but the interview material began to interest me in a completely different way. I started to look into television as a moral issue:

> When you listen to people talking about their viewing habits and about their favourite TV programmes, their discourses on the subject of television, it immediately strikes you how profoundly *moral* this issue is. There are very few programmes that people will freely and plainly admit they like to watch; with the exception of perhaps the evening news, people seem to feel a compelling need to explain, defend and justify their viewing habits. (Alasuutari 1992b, 561)

I now had a completely different theme for my study than was originally intended. Instead of exploring people's life-stories or their accounts of serials or films they had recently seen, I found myself operationalizing television as a moral topic by compiling a typology of all the different ways in which people refer to a certain type of television programme. The greater the share of purely laconic statements in the total number of references to a certain type of programme, the more respected and valued the programme type.

This was the first stage of the analysis, which resulted in the discovery that, overall, fiction is lower in the value hierarchy than non-fiction programmes, and likewise that romantic serials are less valued than intellectual or humorous programmes. This finding led to the question: what makes a 'good' programme, and what makes a 'bad' programme? As the analysis moved ahead, new ways of approaching the material were brought in to answer the questions that kept cropping up, allowing for the testing of the developed hypotheses.

So the chain of argumentation runs from one observation and one conclusion to another. The process of reading the material, posing the questions, formulating the hypotheses, operationalizing and testing leads to an interpretation, which in turn leads to new questions and new hypotheses that are tested against the material.

Research Designs and Reality

Although the process of field research and qualitative research in general can be described as a testing of hypotheses, the research process does not by any means advance in a straightforward fashion as a set model of hypothesis-testing. For instance, during the course of field research the informants – the people who are observed or interviewed – often become quite close friends with the researcher. The conversation that goes on with the informants is not, and should not be, a closely planned process of 'data collection' or a testing of hypotheses. You do various things together with informants, you exchange views on all sorts of things, not just on issues directly related to the research. You will also often be disappointed during the first reading of different qualitative data sets. Attempts to unravel the material will often lead to complete dead-ends. I have started to collect a number of data sets, on the basis of various theoretical or methodological ideas, that in the end have led me nowhere. The planned project ended before it was ever really launched and the only benefit I gained from it was more experience, which in itself is a valuable lesson. Given the inherent tendency of qualitative research towards self-direction, you simply have to get used to the idea that, more often than not, things will not go according to plan. For technical or other reasons, you might not get the sort of data you were looking for. The data set might not highlight the aspects you were hoping to highlight. Your advance hypotheses or research questions pale into insignificant trivialities in the light of the data, or it turns out that they are all wrong or simply impossible to study on the basis of the material collected. There might be some wholly unpredictable, surprising observation that catches all your attention. The scope of possibilities is endless. The qualitative research process is such that sometimes you have to look back and revise your premises several times over.

What do you do in this sort of situation? All you can do is admit you are heading in the wrong direction, turn around and head back. Instead of desperately trying to answer the question you originally had when the material collected clearly does not give the answer you were looking for, you need to consider which questions it *does* answer and pick out the most exciting one.

The problem, of course, is how to prepare a research plan which allows for this. You can always prepare yourself for surprises, but in most cases the research plan is written for someone else to read and evaluate. More often than not you will be submitting the plan to an outside source from whom you are expecting to get funding for the project; therefore you will be committing yourself to a certain extent and to preparing a final report in which you fulfil your promises.

It might be helpful to carry out some sort of pilot survey to make sure that the setting you have is possible at least in principle. It might also be useful to phrase your research questions in such a way that, even with the self-direction of the research process, you know you can confidently remain with the plan outlined.

The End of the Process is the Beginning of Another One

The research process never ends with the resolution of the research problem; every answer is always a partial answer, just part of the truth. Research never ends, but it has to be ended by writing a report on the results, by putting a period at the end of it all. On the other hand, the answers you obtain in the research to certain questions will usually inspire new questions and theoretical problems. The end of one research, or the idea it has inspired, may be the beginning of a new project.

It is very difficult therefore to say exactly where one research process ends and where another one begins. For instance, in my A-Guild project the idea that whenever you find a normative statement you have discovered a contradiction led me to an analysis of the motivations and excuses that people had for their television viewing. In addition, underlying this was the theme of desire and self-discipline that I had first discovered in the darts study. Even though the subject was different now, the theme was still there; I was looking at television viewing as a 'vice' or 'addiction'.

Ideas that surface with empirical data cannot be separated from insights that are gained while reading theories and earlier research. For example, the empirical analysis I did of alcoholism and the related themes of desire and self-restraint led me to read the texts of Norbert Elias and Michel Foucault from this particular angle, and this reading helped me to elaborate on those ideas. But it may work the other way around as well: a reading of theories or methods may lead to empirical questions and ideas for empirical analysis.

It is very difficult, then, to make a clear distinction between the 'empirical' and 'theoretical' parts of a study. This is most plainly the case in research which is based entirely on the theoretical literature or on research done by others. In this situation, different theoretical models and ideas are the empirical material for the researcher which he or she analyzes and interprets in one way or another, for instance in order to build a new theoretical frame. Even the methods of working are very similar to those employed in the analysis of qualitative material: in the analysis of theories and the theoretical literature you can use practically all the methods we have discussed. Theoretical articles or studies by other researchers are texts in precisely the same way as qualitative materials. As far as the researcher is concerned they also have exactly the same function: the aim is to analyze and to better understand the phenomenon at hand.

The practical methods are also largely the same regardless of whether the object is a community of people or a theoretical text. It is useful all the time to make two sorts of notes: observation reports and interpretation reports. On the one hand, you need to write down what you have seen or read. On the other hand, you need to write down your own ideas and hypotheses, and do so as they unfold, because it might be difficult to retrace them later on. The research process is also a writing process.

14

The Writing Process

Social research is, in fact, a form of literature. Of course researchers gather empirical material and analyze it, but so do fiction writers. The end-product of an investigation is in any case a literary work, and social research is to a great extent a literary process. I am not only talking about the final stage of a study, about writing the 'research report'. Instead, writing is part of the continuous process that ends up with the completed study, a literary work. In that sense writing is the most important part of research: when all is said and done, the world is left with nothing else but the text. Therefore it is worth paying careful attention to writing.

To regard social science as a literary genre, a viewpoint which has gained popularity during recent years, has been considered as a new, radical approach. For instance, Hayden White's (1975, 1987) studies have been read in a somewhat scandalous atmosphere as analyses of how behind the theoretical models of great thinkers one finds 'only' rhetorical tricks. Because of an underlying concept of science and language, the writing process, and the rhetorical and stylistic choices of scientific presentation, have been left untouched and deliberately in peace. The dominant concept of science – also social science – separates scientific research and a research report. Accordingly, writing simply amounts to reporting on the acquired results. Language and the forms of presentation are reduced to a transparent medium of communication. Science is regarded as the meta-language, as *the* language in terms of which other forms of presentation are assessed, and therefore a rhetorical analysis of science would show disrespect, and deprive science of its special position. The dominant conception separates science from art and literature, and emphasizes that only facts and results count, not 'mere' rhetoric.

The idea that writing is just a means of reporting on the results is also a carefully treasured myth. The fact that teachers and researchers have written their published works many times over, polished the texts, asked for comments and edited again is not much talked about. Just about the only advice one has been offered is the worn-out aphorism that clear thinking produces articulate texts. It assumes that formal logic is prior to writing, which is just a way to express one's ideas. There is basically nothing wrong with the idea of a link between clear thinking and a well-organized text, but we could add that clearing one's text also helps in clearing one's thinking. Talking and writing are tools of thinking not just ways for expressing one's thoughts.

Writing resembles riding a bicycle. Not in that once you have learned it you'll master it, but because riding a bike is based on consecutive repairments of balance. The staggerings or whole detours of the text have to be repaired over and over again so that they do not lead the story-line in the wrong direction; and the rambling of the first draft cannot be seen in the final product.

Writing is first and foremost analyzing, revising and polishing the text. The idea that one can produce ready-made text right away is just about as senseless as the image of a cyclist who has never had to restore his or her balance.

Like riding a bike, writing cannot be learned just by reading guidebooks. The art of writing can only be developed in practice, through trial and error. So, does one really need any other advice than that one has to write and revise?

I think so. The work of writing is a technical trade. Although we do not know the final structure and layout before the work is completed, good planning saves time and labour. It is also vain to reinvent the wheel when consulting other's texts may solve the presentational problems and impasses that one encounters. One needs conceptual tools and methods with which to analyze one's own and other's texts, so that one can identify the stylistic and structural choices of a text.

In the following pages I discuss qualitative research as a literary process. I will consider it from three viewpoints: the writing that takes place during 'fieldwork', and the macro- and microtextual levels of the research.

'Fieldwork' as a Textual Process

Fieldnotes are part of the writing process especially in qualitative research and participant observation. However, ethnographic and qualitative research are not the only types of investigation where they are needed. It is always useful to keep some kind of field diary during the research process – that is, to take notes of one's own ideas, initial hypotheses, observations, and questions which arise.

Participant observation is the classic type of research where fieldnotes are a self-evident part of the study. There is no scarcity of literature dealing with the techniques of taking notes and that is why I am not going to deal with the technical details here. Suffice it to say that usually researchers write down something at the site of participant observation, for instance direct quotations of what was said, or just some key words that will help to remember the events. After returning home from, say, an evening of participant observation, one then types a report of the night, using the notepad markings as an *aide-mémoire*. To put it briefly, keeping a field diary means that one scrupulously reports on events and impressions. One has to bear in mind that they can also be used in the published study as direct quotations. After reporting on an event, and on one's feelings associated with it, one can write a separate section about the hypotheses and interpretations that come to mind at the time.

In a similar way any kind and phase of a research process can be treated as 'fieldwork': one can, for instance, take notes of the literature one goes through. While reading other studies dealing with the same research topic, or literature that has to do with the theoretical framework, it is worthwhile to make summaries and take notes of one's own thoughts and insights.

There are several reasons for keeping a diary about one's remarks, ideas and initial hypotheses during the research process. For one thing, such notes can later be expanded into sections of the final product. Secondly, although many of the ideas will turn out to be not that thrilling on a later reading, the first impression one gets of a social environment, incident or text is often insightful. Without the help of a diary it is very difficult to bring it to mind after one has become used to it, 'gone native' as the anthropologists say. Thirdly, the misinterpretations and false leads are valuable to remember when writing the final text, because the readers might also be tempted to reach the same conclusions.

Sometimes the research entails tape-recorded or video-taped interviews, group discussions or naturally occurring situations, which are often transcribed so that the text can be analyzed, for instance, with the help of a computer program. Of course the recordings can also be used as direct quotations. It is advisable to transcribe and read the recordings along with gathering more data. Here, again, it is useful to take notes of the first impressions one gets of the transcripts.

The Macrostructure in Writing

When dealing with the problems related to writing a study it is useful to distinguish two textual levels which can be called the macro- and microstructures of a text. The difference between the two could be compared to different dimensions of the architecture of a house. At the macrolevel one thinks how the rooms and different activities are placed in relation to each other, whereas at the microlevel one considers the furnishing and interior decoration of different rooms.

Figuring out the macrostructure of a study is probably the most difficult part of writing. The macrostructure is how the investigation proceeds from one chapter to another so that it forms a logical and sound whole.

The difficulty of this aspect is certainly partly related to the soundness of the research design. If the study is designed to answer a clear question and if the object of research is well defined, it is easier to find a good order and form of presentation. Instead, an unclear research design and a blurry theme lead to – or can be seen in – a presentation that roams wildly from one theme to another. Unsurmountable problems in finding a sound macrostructure may be a sign of weaknesses in the research design; problems which have to be sorted out first.

The macrostructure is, however, a problematic in its own right, and the difficulties related to it may be because many thesis writers do not have previous experience in writing an essay or article longer than a few dozen pages. When a treatise exceeds a certain critical length, it cannot be held together with presentational and logico-chronological means that work perfectly well in a school essay or an article. For instance, a good thesis or monograph should have a 'story-line' that runs from the beginning to the end and which links different chapters together. Yet in a presentation longer than, say, 30 or 40 pages one cannot assume that the reader remembers all that was said before. That is why longer treatises consist of *chapters*, not just of *sections* as in an essay or an article. The beginnings and sometimes endings of a chapter are the places where the reader is oriented and reoriented to where he or she is; the reader may be reminded of where he or she has been before and where the tour is going to proceed next. Such signposting is to some extent needed, but there are, of course, several styles and ways of doing it. If, for instance, the reader is continuously reminded of the contents of previous chapters and told what will be discussed in the present one, it may sound paternalistic or it may be a sign of poor organization perhaps caused by an unclear question addressed in the thesis. The longer the writing, the more difficult it becomes to find a working macrostructure.

Several social research methodology textbooks advise that one should follow what could be called the 'IMRD' or journal format. By that I refer to the order of presentation followed in most American social research (Dooley 1990, 53–60; Sociology Writing Group 1994, 22–23), where a research report is divided into four parts: Introduction, Methods, Results and Discussion. The introduction leads the reader to the subject, tells about previous research, and presents the theory and hypotheses which predict what the results of the research are going to be. The section on methods tells how the study was conducted, so that the reader can assess the validity of the research, or can even repeat the research design. After that, the results are presented. The last section discusses the implications and validity of the results and perhaps suggests what follow-up studies could be made.

The textbook writers do not recommend this presentational structure because they necessarily think that it is a good, captivating rhetorical solution. On the contrary, its possible advantages are precisely in its standardized nature: when browsing through previous research reports written in the journal format, one does not have to read them from beginning to end to get the information one is looking for (Dooley 1990, 53–58). Abiding by that format is also a necessity in order to get one's article published in a journal that subscribes to it. It is through such formats that a certain notion of (social) science reproduces itself at the level of rhetoric.[1]

---

[1] For further discussion of the rhetoric of inquiry, see chapter 8.

The journal format – or the APA standard (Bazerman 1987; Budge and Katz 1995) – resembles the form which journalism students are advised to use to write a news story. In the journalism guidebooks it is compared to an inverted pyramid. In a news story the headline itself breaks the news, the 'ingress' repeats it with some more words, and the ordinary text tells details about it. The order of paragraphs is such that the more unessential a detail is, the farther away it is placed from the story headline and the ingress.

The functions of the technique are two-fold. First, by just browsing through the headlines, busy readers of a newspaper can get an idea of what has happened in the world; they can then read more details only on the events that interest them, and to the length that they like. Secondly, it is useful for those who make the layout of a newspaper page: news stories written that way can be fitted in the space allotted to them by cutting them at almost any spot without destroying the story or leaving off anything very essential.

Social research reports are similar in the sense that a busy reader does not have to read through them. An abstract at the beginning explains the essential content of an article following the format. A person interested in other research in the area, for instance to list it in his or her own article, only needs to read the introductory section. If one is interested in methods, the description is easy to find in its own section. A student looking for a research topic might want to consult the discussion sections, where implications for future research are dealt with.

The journal format, with the hypotheses first presented and then 'tested' and discussed, makes one believe that the research process actually proceeded in that order. Whether it actually did or not is not the issue, but it is important to note that it is a rhetorical format. The actual research process and the form of presentation are two different things; to present the results in the form of a – more or less truthful – story about the way in which one proceeded is a rhetorical choice. From this perspective, all forms of presentation in social science research reports can be seen as rhetorical gadgets one chooses to use.

Consider, for instance, the functions of the 'initial hypotheses' presented at the beginning. Since they are obviously written after the research has been conducted, and to find interesting results various cross-tabulations have been run over the data, one can choose how well they will turn out to 'predict' the 'empirical results'.

One function is obviously confirming. On the basis of previous research and a theory applied to the area, the writer presents hypotheses that turn out to be correct. This reaffirms that the researcher thinks clearly and knows what he or she is doing.

> The findings confirm earlier expectations that elderly parents with more resources receive less help, while older parents and parents in poor health give less aid to their children. (Mutran and Reitzes 1984, 127)

On the other hand, just reaffirming expectations and hypotheses obviously only based upon previous research (one is not supposed to know one's own results when writing the introduction section) can sound too dull and predictable. The findings, in contrast with the hypotheses, also can serve a surprise function: 'Look what I found.' Although it might appear to be embarrassing to admit that the initial hypotheses turned out to be wrong, one was led into them by the line of thought followed in previous research and theorizing. Thus, actually it was not the writer's fault. Besides, the writer can present him- or herself as the hero/ine who points out earlier fallacies and leads the research back onto the right track. The shared guilt for earlier errors can even be emphasized by writing in first person plural.

> We found little support for our hypothesis that, under conditions of uncertainty, proximity is a function of two actors having similar characteristics (H1). . . . Nor did we find that the effects proposed in H1 were suppressed by the associational memberships of giving officers (H2). . . . Clearly we erred in anticipating what happens under conditions of environmental uncertainty. Rather than turning to someone like themselves, giving officers turned to those in the network who had better knowledge or a higher status. This was the way they solved their problems. (Galaskiewicz 1985, 655)

What are the origins of this rhetorical standard of the social science research report? Why does it appear to give, at least in American quantitative social research, a label of science to a piece of research presented in that format? In the background one finds the old theory of hypotheses-testing, according to which objectivity of research is secured by following the procedure of first defining the hypotheses, then collecting the data, and finally testing them. Although hardly anyone takes the original norms seriously, they have nevertheless preserved their place in methodology classes and textbooks as a description of the research process and as a model of the structure of a research report. Those dedicated to the profession of the researcher know that research does not really proceed according to that formula, but that is how it is, nevertheless, described to the students. For instance, Rose (1982, 20) notes that although the actual process often differs from the exemplary formula, in writing the research report it is advisable to follow it because it makes it more convincing.

In practice it often turns out that the original hypotheses are simply wrong or impossible to test. That is, the core of the original research design has to be abandoned for substantive or technical reasons. Or it might be that the initial hypotheses are confirmed, but that the researcher finds them too dull and obvious. In any case, the investigator runs all kinds of cross-tabulations and other statistical analyses with the variables included, with the aim of coming across an interesting and not trivial finding. If such a finding can be 'staged' by giving it a plausible interpretation that goes against prevalent expectations or previous findings, the researcher will write a research report following the narrative form outlined above.

Since the research as an evolving process and the presentation with its 'story-line' or sequential order are two different things, it makes more sense to think about the presentation as an independent artefact. The journal format of empirical social research is dull because it is so predictable. By following the norms of 'scientific' presentation derived from early British statistics, its main function is to legitimize social research. However, the format fits so badly with the characteristics of qualitative research and the nature of its logic of argumentation that it hardly makes a study more convincing. Besides, the journals that publish articles reporting on qualitative research do not require its use.

Rather than the journal format, it is more advisable to apply an approach that, instead of hypothesis-listing in the beginning, proceeds by pointing out mysteries and by gradually developing questions and answers. Such a presentational format, often referred to as the 'essay format' (Sociology Writing Group 1994, 21–22), does not start out with a heavy dose of theory and previous research, to be followed by a separate 'empirical section' near the end. Instead of an inverted pyramid, it resembles a normal pyramid or an iceberg. One preferably starts directly from empirical examples, develops the questions by discussing them, and gradually leads the reader into interpretations of the material and to more general implications of the results. If one feels like discussing and constructing them, the best position for grand theoretical models is in the final pages.

Many classics of sociology apply this kind of 'mystery' format in their works. For instance, in his study *Suicide* (1951) Émile Durkheim leads his readers little by little to his proposed solution about the mystery of the suicide. He starts out by wondering how one should define the suicide. After arriving at a satisfactory definition, he already, by presenting a table about suicide rates in three periods in different European countries, 'reveals' to the reader that, at each moment of its history, each society has a definite aptitude for suicide: 'During the three periods there compared, suicide has everywhere increased, but in this advance the various peoples have retained their respective distances from one another. Each one has its own peculiar coefficient of acceleration' (Durkheim 1951, 50–51). Thus suicide – although an individual's act affecting the individual only – does not only belong to the field of psychology. Instead, it is possible to identify a particular 'suicidal tendency with which each society is collectively afflicted'. After these initial observations Durkheim specifies his problem: 'We do not accordingly intend to as nearly complete an inventory as possible of all the conditions affecting the origin of individual suicides, but merely to examine those on which the definite fact that we have called the social suicide-rate depends' (1951, 51).

In the next chapter Durkheim begins to deal with different attempts to explain the social suicide rate. First he discusses psychopathic states:

The annual rate of certain diseases is relatively stable for a given society though varying perceptibly from one people to another. Among these is insanity. Accordingly, if a manifestation of insanity were reasonably to be supposed in every voluntary death, our problem would be solved; suicide would be a purely individual affliction.

This thesis is supported by a considerable number of alienists . . . . (1951, 57–58)

In discussing the issue Durkheim proceeds by showing that there does not exist any particular suicidal mania *sui generis*, although some suicides are committed by insane persons. Next, by studying and relying on statistics he ends up inferring that the social suicide-rate does not have a relation to the prevalence of psychopathic states. Accordingly, he can end the chapter dealing with the mutual relation between psychopathic states and suicide with the following remarks:

> Thus no psychopathic state bears a regular and indisputable relation to suicide. A society does not depend for its number of suicides on having more or fewer neuropaths or alcoholics. Although the different forms of degeneration are an eminently suitable psychological field for the action of the courses which may lead a man to suicide, degeneration itself is not one of these causes. Admittedly, under similar circumstances, the degenerate is more apt to commit suicide than the well man; but he does not necessarily do so because of his condition. This potentiality of his becomes effective only through the action of other factors which we must discover. (1951, 15)

Although in this essay or 'mystery' genre the solution of the research problem is only gradually revealed to the reader, the secret can and often has to be partly unveiled earlier. This is often done in the introduction, where the content and structure of the study is described. However, to avoid revealing too much too early, the solutions are often described at a fairly general level. For instance, at the end of the introduction of *Suicide* Durkheim writes:

> Such is the subject of the present work, to contain three parts.
> The phenomenon to be explained can depend only on extra-social causes of broad generality or on causes expressly social. We shall search first for the influence of the former and shall find it non-existent or very inconsiderable. (1951, 52)

It would be too simple to say that, compared to the journal format or 'research report' genre, the order of presentation is reversed in the essay or 'mystery' format. In practice, it is hard to write an introduction where one totally leaves out a description of the methodological approach, or what the empirical data are used for. Similarly, to amalgamate all theoretical sections into a single large conclusion is not necessarily a user-friendly solution either. It is often a good choice to start out with an extract from empirical observations and to lead the reader to the questions studied from there. More general or theoretical observations and remarks can be discussed at the ends or beginnings of respective chapters. There are an unlimited number of choices, and that's the whole problem.

When planning the macrostructure of one's study it is always useful to consult other studies as examples and exemplars. Consider, for instance, the opening sentences and chapters in different studies. Nothing is probably more important than the beginning, because it is crucial in either turning off or capturing a reader, and because it more or less determines or sets the stage for the whole writing.

There are several kinds of openings. Michel Foucault, for instance, is famous for his introductions which start with case-examples. *Discipline and Punish* (1979) starts with a description of the public execution of Damiens the regicide on 2 March 1757 in Paris. This detailed description of a very cruel execution, based on historical records, takes three whole pages. After that, separated by a line of space, there is a second case-example:

> Eighty years later, Léon Faucher drew up his rules 'for the house of young prisoners in Paris':
> 'Art. 17. The prisoners' day will begin at six in the morning . . .' . (1979, 6)

This extract, listing articles 17 to 28, takes a page and a half, and only after that does Foucault begin to develop the theme of his study by contrasting the two cases:

> We have, then, a public execution and a time-table. They do not punish the same crimes or the same type of delinquent. But they each define a certain penal style. Less than a century separates them. (1979, 7)

David Rothman's work *The Discovery of the Asylum* (1971), dealing with a similar topic, is an example of a more straightforward opening. He starts by presenting the main research problem right away:

> The question this book addresses can be put very succinctly: why did the Americans in the Jacksonian era suddenly begin to construct and support institutions for deviant and dependent members of the community? Why in the decades after 1820 did they all at once erect penitentiaries for the criminal, asylums for the insane, almshouses for the poor, orphan asylums for homeless children, and reformatories for delinquents? (1971, xiii)

Thus, the theme of the study can be introduced by giving concrete examples which illustrate it, or it can be presented right at the beginning. But how does one proceed to discussing the approach, the materials analyzed, or whatever seems relevant at the beginning? Again, the possibilities are unlimited, and other writers can be consulted.

Consider, for instance, the way Ien Ang has organized the introductory chapter of her work *Watching Dallas* (1985). She starts by telling us about the phenomenon and discussing its dimensions:

> If we are to believe the plethora of studies, commentaries and warnings from journalists, critics and even politicians, the beginning of the 1980s was marked by the world's television viewing public by a new, spectacular phenomenon: *Dallas*. This unique status . . . (1995, 1)

After this section, addressing *Dallas*'s popularity, she starts a new section which describes the series: that it is a continuous serial; who the main characters are; what has happened in the story this far, etc. Then, the last section introduces the research design: first the main question asked and then the material used in addressing it and the way that material is approached:

Why do people watch *Dallas*? Clearly because they find it enjoyable. Nobody is forced to watch television; at most, people can be led to it by effective advertising. What then are the determining factors of this enjoyment, this pleasure? . . .

In order to obtain information on the way in which people experience watching *Dallas*, I placed a small advertisement in a Dutch women's magazine called *Viva* . . . . I had forty-two replies to this advertisement. Letters, all addressed personally to me, varying in length from a few lines to around ten pages. (1985, 9–10)

Although well-written studies can be used as exemplars, studies with their different questions are always unique to some extent. Often one has to search and develop a working macrostructure throughout the writing and research process. One has to plan, try and revise. One way to go about it is to write a plan about the contents and then to extend it into an abstract of the whole study. When one then starts writing the study to its final length, one can see how well the structure works. The plan is then changed if needed.

A plan of the structure, and structural analysis of one's text, is useful also because it reveals what does or does not belong to the thesis. A good investigation is indeed like a murder mystery in that it does not contain much irrelevant text: themes or details that have nothing to do with the solution revealed in the end. There is, for instance, no reason for dwelling on descriptions of such other research in the area which does not either support (or challenge) one's own conclusions, or clarify one's own approach in relation to previous studies. One could talk about the economy principle of a study: everything included must be related and tied in with the argumentation developed and presented in the investigation.

The Microstructure

By microstructure, I mean the way in which the text flows from sentence to sentence and paragraph to paragraph. In this instance, it is naturally also true that clear argumentation more easily produces a clear text, but these two are interrelated. When one thinks how the text could be clarified and how it would flow better, one in effect also reflects on one's argumentation, and how it could be clarified.

Before writing a chapter, one usually makes a plan about its contents and logic. Then, when the first draft is written, it is useful to go through it and analyze its contents by listing them into a summary. This often reveals quite well whether the organization is good. For instance, are the same themes discussed in more than one place? Are the themes discussed in the right order? Do all the details belong to this particular chapter? After such an analysis, the place and order of the parts of the chapter can be changed by first editing the summary and then realizing them in the text itself.

In qualitative research one often uses quotations: extracts from transcribed spoken language or from other sources. This requires that one finds a good style and rhythm. If the extracts are spoken language, they differ from the written language the researcher uses. This has its advantages in that, with the quotations, one can increase textual diversity in a similar manner to the way in which television journalists use interviews. The news stories typically alternate between extracts from the interviews and parts where the journalist tells about the topic discussed.

The danger lies in the fact that spoken language may strike us as very naïve in contrast to the scientific text surrounding it. Therefore the writer should try to adjust the style of his or her written language so that it is closer to spoken language. It gives a particularly dumb impression of the respondents if the writer first describes what the respondent is going to say, then inserts a direct quotation, and after that repeats in written language what the interviewee tried to say. Of course the writer can and must lead the reader to the point of the next extract, but one should not tell what it says or just repeat the same by using 'scientific' language. It is better to use quotations in the same way that novelists use dialogue: as part of the story. Of course the writer often comments on the extract afterwards, and in that sense leads the argument onward, but that is not the same as repeating it. In this instance, we are also dealing with method: it does not pass as analysis to simply translate spoken language into another, 'scientific' language.

Often extracts from spoken language are much more lively and interesting than the dry language of science, but one should not get too excited about it. If there are too many or too long quotations, it may be that the reader skips them (or the writer's text). One has to find the right rhythm, in which these two types of text are alternated, so that the reader does not get too bored with either of them.

The tense of the text is also an important choice, as minor as it might seem. Tense is actually one of the central features of a social science text to inform, determine and reflect the writer's relation to his or her material.

By using the past tense when discussing one's data, the writer in effect underlines that he or she is reporting on research already conducted. Consider, for instance, the part of a study or article that reports on how the data 'were collected' and what methods 'were used'. The use of the past tense is also more merciful when one is reporting on findings that are not used as evidence in an explanation for a research problem. When reporting on the data and results of one's research the researcher can more easily use the past tense to tell about findings and statistically significant relations whose overall meaning is not assessed in any way. Such a reporting style is based on the implicit assumption that, since the findings of a social survey represent the population, they have news and information value as such. In that sense, the past tense is the tense of a descriptive survey.

The present tense is a more demanding choice, but as such it is also an advisable choice when discussing the research material. Whereas the past tense is used to tell a story, a monologue about gathering data and finding different things in it, the present tense simulates a dialogue, where the researcher presents pieces of evidence and discusses their meaning with the reader. When presenting a qualitative analysis, it is a natural choice. In qualitative research it is usually obvious to everybody that the observations themselves are not results; they do not, for instance, represent a 'typical' case in a 'population'. Their only meaning is in the inferences one draws from them, in the way they are used as clues. What this or that means or represents cannot just be assumed; it has to be argued.

In qualitative research it is often the case that the material consists of observational fieldnotes, transcribed qualitative interviews or group discussions. The object of analysis is a limited number of people, sometimes a cultural group or community. By the time the research is completed, it may be that the observations and interviews were conducted several years before. People have changed since then, their life situations have altered. How is it possible, in such a case, to talk about the material in the present tense?

In a qualitative study the analysis is presented *here and now*, because the present tense refers to the research *material* and to the time of writing, not to the events 'back then'. The material is for the writer (and reader) always here and now. In anthropology this form of presentation is known as the 'ethnographic present'. By presenting the observations in the present tense one also implies that, although the researcher is attempting to find explanatory models for observations about events that took place long ago, the models should apply more generally. The present tense is the tense of theory.

Consider Paul Willis's ethnographic study, *Learning to Labour* (1977). He reports on the results of participant observation focused on a small group of schoolboys, the 'lads'. Although a considerable time has passed since the fieldwork, his discussion is almost totally in the present tense. This is how he starts the ethnography in chapter 2:

> The most basic, obvious and explicit dimension of counter-school culture is entrenched general and personalised opposition to 'authority'. (1977, 11)

The primary object of analysis, reflected in the particular group studied and in the qualitative materials to be analyzed, is referred to in the present tense. It is only in the very first pages that he temporarily uses the past tense. Here is an example, where a paragraph starts out in the past tense for one sentence, to be continued in the present tense:

> Joey was an acknowledged group leader, and inclined at times to act the old experienced man of the world. As is clear here, and elsewhere, he is also a lad of considerable insight and expressive power. In one way this might seem to disqualify him as typical of school non-conformist working class lads. However, although Joey may not be *typical* of working class lads, he is certainly representative of them. He lives in a working class neighbourhood, is from a large family known as a fighting family whose head is a foundryman. He is to leave school without qualifications and is universally identified by teachers as a troublemaker – the more so that 'he has something about him'. (1977, 16)

The first sentence reminds the reader that the group existed at a school at one particular time when the fieldwork was conducted. It underlines the temporary character of the concrete object of research, the group of these 'lads'. The shift to the present tense implies at least two things. In the second sentence the word 'here' refers to an extract from an individual interview with Joey right above the paragraph quoted. 'Elsewhere' refers to other quotations in the book, and the validity of the writer's claim that Joey is a 'lad of considerable insight and expressive power' can be assessed by the reader here and now, in the act of reading the study. Secondly, Willis constructs a picture of Joey as 'representative' of working-class lads. As an individual he may be atypical, but, as Willis puts it, 'the cultural system he reports on is representative and central, even if he is related to it in a special way' (1977, 16). Thus, when framed this way, what Joey says or does can be seen as clues about a cultural system that is not restricted only to the time and place of the fieldwork.

The choice of tense affects the contact that the writer establishes with the reader. The past tense underlines that we are dealing with a 'research report', that the writer already knows what the results are. This is, of course, true: the writer always does know the solution. This is why the description of how one came to the conclusion can be presented in the past tense. However, the past tense tends to slacken the reader's interest. When using the present tense, the writer does not continuously underscore the fact that it is all worked out already. The present tense creates the illusion that the writer is struggling towards the solution of the case side by side with the reader. In that sense such a presentation resembles a murder mystery. The reader is led to the track of right and wrong questions and answers; the tension is preserved for as long as possible, and the clues that lead to the solution of the case are disclosed only gradually.

The choice of voice is also worth considering. Often scientific text is criticized for its prevalent use of the passive voice: 'the data were collected' or the 'hypotheses selected', as if there were no individual researchers or writers. Diminishing the subjects is a questionable means of intensifying the impression of objective research, although it may be that the writer chooses to use the passive voice because of modesty. Especially in the parts where the writer or writers tell how they conducted the study, it is advisable to use the appropriate voice, first person singular or plural.

On the other hand, to overemphasize 'I' or 'we' can easily appear as self-assertion and be irritating as such. To emphasize the self ('In my opinion' or 'I think') goes against the principle of rational argumentation that the arguments and the evidence are decisive, not the fact that this or that person presents it. Sometimes social scientists use the first person to emphasize that their interpretations do not represent a final objective truth. However, as a stylistic technique this contains the danger that the reader may conceive of it differently. The reader may think that the writer considers him- or herself as such a great authority or specialist that 'in my opinion' is used as an additional argument for the interpretation presented.

By pointing out these problems I do not intend to argue that the first person singular is not an appropriate voice in writing social science. It certainly has been uncommon, but the situation is changing. For instance, along with increasing reflexivity about ethnographic writing (Atkinson 1990; Clifford and Marcus 1986; Geertz 1988; Marcus and Fischer 1986), 'objective' cultural description has been challenged. Adopting elements of a more 'postmodernist' style does not necessarily mean that one gives up rational argumentation and retreats all the way to fiction. For instance, the usage of the first person singular voice has to have a function; it has to make a point.

And there are points it can make. Consider John O. Stewart's study *Drinkers, Drummers, and Decent Folk* (1989). He starts out by discussing the recent critique of written ethnography and anthropology's tendency to regard people in the field mainly as 'strangers,' 'others' or 'natives', as 'severely edited and generalized versions of themselves, which may be manipulated for intellectual purposes' (1989, 9). As a way of addressing these challenges, he then suggests more innovative means of presentation:

> What I want simply to say is that I see most current ethnographic writing – traditional and experimental – as deficient in dealing with the inner lives of people: that ethnography would be a more complete and productive artifact if it undertook to present this interior universe. Such presentation cannot be done through abstract chatter, or any series of direct expository statements. Indirection has to be the mode. (1989, 12)

After these introductory sections he makes a stylistic shift and starts the new section by telling personal, subjective anecdotes about his college years and about his feelings when returning to his country of origin, Trinidad, to do fieldwork:

> When I first entered college many years ago, I signed myself up to major in anthropology as we went through the gymnasium during registration. It was what I wanted to do. I had never met an anthropologist before. I had read and heard a little about Egypt, and I was egotistical enough to believe I deserved to undertake 'the study of man'. In my first class, however, a clear-sighted professor in the discipline kindly suggested that anthropology was not for people like me. Why not try P.E., he said. I didn't know what P.E. was. We had no such thing in my school in Trinidad, and I had never heard of it. I ended up as an English major instead. (1989, 13)

Although the personal experiences Stewart tells about are not 'representative', they make a point by giving a very powerful, almost palpable example of the problematic of the 'other' in present-day anthropology. The 'other' gets a voice.

> The 'other' in my field was heavily constituted out of a tension between my own memory of an earlier time, and the recognizable changes of my return: out of the memory of how I used to be, and the inadequacy of my new cultural reflexes. (1989, 15)

There are, however, pitfalls in the more subjective and artistic techniques of writing social science. Stylistic experimentation and tricks may take over from rational argumentation, which is the core of science. Another danger is that, although the writer does try to make a point, the stylistic features hinder instead of aid in getting the point. As I see it, social science is difficult enough without further obstacles.

The choice of the voice is closely related to the extent to which the speaking subject is visible in the text. In some places, particularly at the beginning of the study, it is quite pertinent to address the readers by telling them how the text will proceed. However, recurrent descriptions of what the writer is going to say next, or summaries of the contents of the previous chapters, are distracting. Imagine a novelist who announces what he or she is going to tell us next! Social science text is of course a somewhat different case, but in many instances it is needless to explain what one is going to say next. The double role of the writing self – one both tells a story and tells us about the telling – is also symptomatic of an unsatisfactory organization of the text. One should aim at a story line that carries the text forward without the need for continuous bridging.

This is also related to the question of how to address the readers, or whether they are addressed at all. One can perfectly well do without it. For instance, a question problematized in the text can be taken up in the following manner: 'To define the concept of race is not an easy matter.' On the other hand one can use a rhetorical question, one not specifically addressed to anyone else but the 'implied reader' of the text. For instance, Durkheim uses this possibility on many occasions:

First, what is a race? A definition is especially necessary because . . . . (Durkheim 1951, 82)

The use of a thinking voice that does not identify itself in any way is captivating in the sense that the reader forgets about reading a book or listening to the voice of the story-teller. This creates the illusion that the impersonal voice of the story-teller is right beside the reader, struggling with the same problems as the reader. The story-teller does not spoil the pleasure by reminding us that he or she has already worked it all out and knows the solution to the riddle. That is the experience one gets when reading a 'research report': by using the past tense, the story-teller just reports on the dead-ends and insights made during the process.

We can also use the first person plural in science writing. It addresses the readers by joining in with them, and often by proposing this or that to them. Durkheim used it often:

Yet let us agree that there are certain great types in Europe the most general characteristics of which can be roughly distinguished and among whom the peoples are distributed, and agree to give them the name of races. (Durkheim 1951, 85)

The first person plural can connote different things. The oldest is probably the way in which the royals have used it to denote a singular but powerful person: 'We, the King of Sweden.' However, usually it is thought that the writer enjoins with the readers to form a community. For instance, feminists have problematized this by asking who are the 'we'; who is included or, to put it differently, to whom is the text addressed. Often, one gets an old-fashioned, paternalistic impression by reading writers like Durkheim who use first person plural a lot. Of course, there are different ways of using it. For instance, what 'we' should think about this or that can be kindly proposed ('let me suggest that we . . .') or just assumed. Especially when a pact between the writer and the reader is stated matter-of-factly ('In the previous chapter we came to the conclusion that . . .'), one gets an intrusive impression.

Critique does Not Equal Complaint

It is important to ask others to read one's text at an early stage. Researchers always become more or less blind to their texts and thoughts, so that they do not notice that they have failed in spelling out certain premises or starting points without which an outsider has a hard time understanding the text. It is precisely for this reason that taking 'fieldnotes' about the development of one's thinking is needed. One has to bear in mind that a text does not only present certain explanatory models. The writer also has to discuss other possibilities, for instance those that he or she first invented but then rejected during the research process. They must also be discussed, and one must show the readers why they are not fruitful after all. The text can be like a detective story, where one presents these kinds of 'false leads' until they are revealed to be dead-ends.

When asking others to read one's text one should try to resist the attitude that others are stupid and malevolent, that they refuse to understand even the simplest thing, or that they 'criticize' one's text on the wrong bases. If someone criticizes the text for something for which you think you are innocent, it is a good hint that the point was not made clearly enough. Good friends and colleagues may appear to be incredibly stupid, to whom everything has to be spelled out in very simple terms. However, when realizing that, you have to remember that to those farther away from you the text would be even more cryptic. Criticism is not aimed at the person of the writer; it criticizes and analyzes a literary product. That is why it is useful to ask for outsiders' assessments already at a stage when the biggest misunderstandings can be avoided. The text starts a life of its own as soon as you let it out of your hands.

References

Acker, Joan, Kate Barry and Johanna Esseveld (1991) Objectivity and Truth: Problems in Doing Feminist Research. In Mary Margaret Fonow and Judith A. Cook (eds), *Beyond Methodology: Feminist Scholarship as Lived Experience*. Bloomington, IN: Indiana University Press, 133–153.

Alasuutari, Pertti (1986) *Työmiehen elämäntarina ja alkoholismi: Tutkimus alkoholismin suhteesta emokulttuuriin* [Blue-Collar Men's Life-Stories and Alcoholism: A study of the Relation between Alcoholism and its Parent Culture]. Research Reports, series A9. Tampere: University of Tampere, Department of Sociology and Social Psychology.

Alasuutari, Pertti (1989) *Erinomaista, rakas Watson: Johdatus yhteiskuntatutkimukseen* [Elementary, Dear Watson: An Introduction to Social Research]. Helsinki: Hanki ja Jää.

Alasuutari, Pertti (1992a) *Desire and Craving: A Cultural Theory of Alcoholism*. New York: State University of New York Press.

Alasuutari, Pertti (1992b) 'I'm Ashamed to Admit but I Have Watched *Dallas*': The Moral Hierarchy of TV Programmes. *Media, Culture and Society* 14, 561–582.

Alasuutari, Pertti (1993) *Radio suomalaisten arkielämässa* [Radio in the Everyday Life of the Finns]. Yle Research and Development Research Report 3. Helsinki: Yle.

Alasuutari, Pertti and Juha Kytömäki (1986) Pahuus on tappava bumerangi: Vanha Kettu -televisiosarjan maailmankuva ja juonirakenne [Badness is a Deadly Boomerang: The World-View and Narrative Structure of the Serial *Der Alte*]. In: Kalle Heikkinen, (ed.), *Kymmenen esseetä elämäntavasta* [Ten Essays on the Way of Life]. Lahti: Oy Yleisradio Ab, 139–150.

Alasuutari, Pertti and Jorma Siltari (1983) *Miehisen vapauden valtakunta* [The Realm of Male Freedom]. Research Reports, series B37. Tampere: University of Tampere, Research Institute of the Social Sciences.

Allardt, Erik and Yrjö Littunen (1972) *Sosiologia*. Helsinki: WSOY.

Allport, Gordon W. (1937) *Personality: A Psychological Interpretation*. New York: Holt, Rinehart & Winston.

Allport, Gordon W. (1962) The General and the Unique in Psychological Science. *Journal of Personality* 30, 405–422.

Ang, Ien (1985) *Watching Dallas: Soap Opera and the Melodramatic Imagination*. London: Methuen.

Atkinson, J. Maxwell and Paul Drew (1979) *Order in Court: The Organization of Verbal Interaction in Judicial Settings*. London: Macmillan.

Atkinson, Paul (1990) *The Ethnographic Imagination: Textual Constructions of Reality*. London: Routledge.

Austin, J.L. (1962) *How to do Things with Words*. London: Oxford University Press.

Bazerman, Charles (1987) Codifying the Social Scientific Style: The APA Publication Manual as a Behaviorist Rhetoric. In John Nelson, Allan Megill and Donald D. McCloskey (eds), *The Rhetoric of the Human Sciences: Language and Argument in Scholarship and Public Affairs*. Madison, WI: University of Wisconsin Press, 125–144.

Berg, Bruce L. (1989) *Qualitative Research Methods for the Social Sciences*. Boston: Allyn & Bacon.

Berger, Peter and Thomas Luckmann (1967) *The Social Construction of Reality: A Treatise in the Sociology of Knowledge*. Harmondsworth: Penguin Books.

Bernard, H. Russell (1988) *Research Methods in Cultural Anthropology*. Newbury Park, CA: Sage.

Bertaux, Daniel and Isabelle Bertaux-Wiame (1981) Life-Stories in the Bakers' Trade. In Daniel Bertaux (ed.), *Biography and Society: The Life History Approach in the Social Sciences*. Beverly Hills, CA: Sage, 169–190.

Bertaux, Daniel and Martin Kohli (1984) The Life Story Approach: A Continental View. *Annual Review of Sociology* 10, 215–237.

Blom, Raimo, Markku Kivinen, Harri Melin and Liisa Rantalaiho (1992) *The Scope Logic Approach to Class Analysis: A Study of the Finnish Class Structure*. Aldershot: Avebury.

Blundell, Valda, John Shepherd and Ian Taylor (eds) (1993) *Relocating Cultural Studies: Developments in Theory and Research*. London: Routledge.

Bogdan, Robert and Steven J. Taylor (1975) *Introduction to Qualitative Research Methods: A Phenomenological Approach to the Social Sciences*. New York: John Wiley & Sons.

Bourdieu, Pierre (1977) *Outline of a Theory of Practice*. Cambridge: Cambridge University Press.

Bourdieu, Pierre (1984) *Distinction: A Social Critique of the Judgement of Taste*. Cambridge, MA: Harvard University Press.

Brown, Penelope and Charles C. Levinson (1987) *Politeness: Some Universals in Language Usage*. Cambridge: Cambridge University Press.

Brown, Richard Harvey (1977) *A Poetic for Sociology: Toward a Logic of Discovery for the Human Sciences*. Cambridge: Cambridge University Press.

Brown, Richard Harvey (1987) *Society as Text: Essays on Rhetoric, Reason, and Reality*. Chicago: University of Chicago Press.

Brown, Richard Harvey (1989) *Social Science as Civic Discourse: Essays on the Invention, Legitimation, and Uses of Social Theory*. Chicago: University of Chicago Press.

Brown, Richard Harvey (ed.) (1992) *Writing the Social Text: Poetics and Politics in Social Science Discourse*. New York: Aldine de Gruyter.

Budge, G. Scott and Bernard Katz (1995) Constructing Psychological Knowledge: Reflections on Science, Scientists and Epistemology in the APA *Publication Manual. Theory and Psychology* 5, 217–231.

Caughey, John L. III (1970) Cultural Values in a Micronesian Society. PhD dissertation, University of Pennsylvania.

Chafe, Wallace L. (1977) The Recall and Verbalisation of Past Experience. In Roger W. Cole, (ed.), *Current Issues in Linguistic Theory*. Bloomington, IN: Indiana University Press, 215–246.

Clarke, John, Chas Critcher and Richard Johnson (eds) (1979) *Working Class Culture: Studies in History and Theory*. London: Hutchinson.

Clifford, James and George E. Marcus (1986) *Writing Culture: The Poetics and Politics of Ethnography*. Berkeley, CA: University of California Press.

Collins, Randall (1988) Theoretical Continuities in Goffman's Work. In Paul Drew, and Anthony Wootton (eds), *Erving Goffman: Exploring the Interaction Order*. Cambridge: Polity Press, 41–63.

Corrigan, Philip and Paul Willis (1980) Cultural Forms and Class Mediations. *Media, Culture and Society* 2, 297–312.

DeFrancisco, Victoria Leto (1991) The Sounds of Silence: How Men Silence Women in Marital Relations. *Discourse and Society* 2, 413–423.

Denzin, Norman K. (1989) *Interpretive Interactionism* Applied Social Research Methods, Vol. 16. Newbury Park, CA: Sage.

van Dijk, Teun A. (1980) *Macrostructures: An Interdisciplinary Study of Global Discourse, Interaction, and Cognition*. Hillsdale, NJ: Lawrence Erlbaum Associates.

Donald, James and Ali Rattansi (eds) (1992) *Race, Culture and Difference*. London: Sage.

Dooley, David (1990) *Social Research Methods*. 2nd edn. Englewood Cliffs, NJ: Prentice Hall.

Drew, Paul and John Heritage (1992) Analyzing Talk at Work: An Introduction. In Paul Drew and John Heritage (eds), *Talk at Work: Interaction in Institutional Settings*. Cambridge: Cambridge University Press, 3–64.

Droysen, Johann Gustav (1960) *Historik: Vorlesungen über Enzyklopädie und Methodologie der Geschichte.* Darmstadt: Wissenschaftliche Buchgesellschaft.

Durkheim, Émile (1951) *Suicide: A Study in Sociology.* New York: Free Press.

Durkheim, Émile (1965) *The Elementary Forms of the Religious Life.* New York: Free Press.

Durkheim, Émile (1974) The Determination of Moral Facts. In Émile Durkheim, *Sociology and Philosophy.* New York: Free Press, 35–62.

Durkheim, Émile (1982) *The Rules of Sociological Method.* London: Macmillan.

Edmondson, Ricca (1984) *Rhetoric in Sociology.* London: Macmillan.

Elster, Jon (1986) *The Market and the Forum: Three Varieties of Political Theory.* In Jon Elster and Aanund Hylland (ed.), *Foundations of Social Choice Theory.* Cambridge: Cambridge University Press, 103–132.

Eskola, Antti (1985) *Persoonallisuustyypeistä elämäntapaan* [From Personality Types to Way of Life]. Helsinki: WSOY.

Eskola, Antti (1988) *Blind Alleys in Social Psychology: A Search for Ways Out.* Amsterdam: North-Holland.

Eskola, Katarina and Erkki Vainikkala (1994) Nordic Cultural Studies – An Introduction. *Cultural Studies* 2, 191–197.

Falk, Pasi and Pekka Sulkunen (1983) Drinking on the Screen: An Analysis of a Mythical Male Fantasy in Finnish Films. *Social Science Information* 22, 387–410.

Feierman, Steven (1974) *The Shambaa Kingdom: A History.* Madison: University of Wisconsin Press.

Fisher, Sue (1991) A Discourse of the Social: Medical Talk/Power Talk/Oppositional Talk? *Discourse and Society* 2, 157–182.

Foucault, Michel (1979) *Discipline and Punish: The Birth of the Prison.* New York: Vintage Books.

Foucault, Michel (1980) *The History of Sexuality, Vol. I: An Introduction.* New York: Vintage Books.

Foucault, Michel (1986) *The History of Sexuality, Vol. 2: The Use of Pleasure.* New York: Viking.

Galaskiewicz, Joseph (1985) Professional Networks and the Institutionalization of a Single Mind Set. *American Sociological Review* 50, 639–658.

Garfinkel, Harold (1984) *Studies in Ethnomethodology.* Cambridge: Polity Press.

Geertz, Clifford (1973) *The Interpretation of Cultures.* New York: Basic Books.

Geertz, Clifford (1983) *Local Knowledge: Further Essays in Interpretive Anthropology.* New York: Basic Books.

Geertz, Clifford (1988) *Works and Lives: The Anthropologist as Author.* Cambridge: Polity Press.

Georges, Robert A. and Michael O. Jones (1980) *People Studying People: The Human Element in Fieldwork.* Berkeley, CA: University of California Press.

Gergen, Mary and Kenneth Gergen (1984) The Social Construction of Narrative Accounts. In Kenneth J. Gergen and Mary M. Gergen (eds), *Historical Social Psychology.* Hillsdale, NJ: Lawrence Erlbaum Associates, 173–189.

Gilroy, Paul (1987) *'There Ain't no Black in the Union Jack': The Cultural Politics of Race and Nation.* Chicago: University of Chicago Press.

Ginsburg, Gerald P. (1978) Role-Playing and Role-Performance in Social Psychological Research. In Michael Brenner, Peter Marsh and Marilyn Brenner (eds), *The Social Contexts of Method.* London: Croom Helm, 91–121.

Glaser, Barney G. and Anselm L. Strauss (1967) *The Discovery of Grounded Theory: Strategies for Qualitative Research.* Chicago: Aldine.

Goffman, Erving (1967) *Interaction Ritual: Essays on Face-to-Face Behavior.* New York: Pantheon Books.

Goffman, Erving (1974) *Frame Analysis. An Essay on the Organization of Experience.* Cambridge, MA: Harvard University Press.

Goffman, Erving (1979) Footing. *Semiotica* 25, 1–29.

Greimas, Algirdas Julien (1987) *On Meaning: Selected Writings in Semiotic Theory*. Minneapolis: University of Minnesota Press.

Griffin, Charles J.G. (1990) The Rhetoric of Forms in Conversion Narratives. *Quarterly Journal of Speech* 76, 152–163.

Gubrium, Jaber F. (1993) *Speaking of Life: Horizons of Meaning for Nursing Home Residents*. New York: Aldine de Gruyter.

Gubrium, Jaber F., James A. Holstein and David Buckholdt (1994) *Constructing the Life Course*. New York: General Hall.

Gusfield, Joseph (1976) The Literary Rhetoric of Science: Comedy and Pathos in Drinking Driver Research. *American Sociological Review* 41, 16–34.

Hagood, Margaret Jarman (1970) The Notion of a Hypothetical Universe. In Denton E. Morrison and Ramon E. Henkel (eds), *The Significance Test Controversy: A Reader*. Chicago: Aldine, 65–78.

Hall, Stuart (1990) The Emergence of Cultural Studies and the Crisis of the Humanities. *October* 53, 11–90.

Hall, Stuart and Tony Jefferson (eds) (1975) *Resistance Through Rituals*. London: Hutchinson.

Hankiss, Agnes (1981) Ontologies of the Self: On the Mythological Rearranging of One's Life-History. In Daniel Bertaux (ed.), *Biography and Society: The Life History Approach in the Social Sciences*. Beverly Hills, CA: Sage, 203–209.

Harris, Marvin (1980) *Cultural Materialism: The Struggle for a Science of Culture*. New York: Vintage Books.

Haug, Frigga (ed.) (1987) *Female Sexualization: A Collective Work of Memory*. London: Verso.

Haug, Frigga (1992) *Beyond Female Masochism: Memory-Work and Politics*. London: Verso.

Haug, Wolfgang Fritz (1971) *Kritik der Warenästhetik*. Frankfurt (am Main): Suhrkamp.

Haug, Wolfgang Fritz (1986) *Critique of Commodity Aesthetics: Appearance, Sexuality, and Advertising in Capitalist Society*. Minneapolis: University of Minnesota Press.

Heiskala, Risto (1988) An Exclusively Male Matter? Alcohol, Gender and Family in Finnish General Magazines and Women's Magazines in 1955 and 1985. Paper presented at the Annual Meeting of the Kettil Bruun Society, Berkeley, CA, 5–11 June.

Heiskala, Risto (1991) Goffmanista semioottiseen sosiologiaan [From Goffman to Semiotic Sociology]. *Sosiologia* 28, 90–107.

Heritage, John (1984) *Garfinkel and Ethnomethodology*. Cambridge: Polity Press.

Hoggart, Richard (1958) *The Uses of Literacy*. Harmondsworth: Penguin Books.

Holland, Dorothy and Naomi Quinn (1989) *Cultural Models in Language and Thought*. Cambridge: Cambridge University Press.

Holzkamp, Klaus (1976) *Sinnliche Erkenntnis: Historischer Ursprung und gesellschaftliche Funktion der Wahrnehmung*. Kronberg: Athenäum Verlag.

Hunter, Albert (ed.) (1990) *The Rhetoric of Social Research Understood and Believed*. New Brunswick, NJ: Rutgers University Press.

Hyvärinen, Matti (1994) *Viimeiset taistot* [The Last Fights]. Tampere: Vastapaino.

Hyvärinen, Matti (forthcoming) The Rhetoric of Change and Conversion: Interpreting the Life Story of a Previous Student Activist. In Terrel Carver and Matti Hyvärinen (eds), *Interpreting the Political*. London: Routledge.

Jefferson, Gail and J. Schenkein (1978) Some Sequential Negotiations in Conversation: Unexpanded and Expanded Versions of Projected Action Sequences. In J. Schenkein (ed.), *Studies in the Organization of Conversational Interaction*. New York: Academic Press, 155–172.

Jokinen, Eeva and Soile Veijola (1987) Porsasjuhlat [Pigs Abroad]. *Sosiologia* 24, 198–205.

Keller, Evelyn Fox (1985) *Reflections on Gender and Science*. New Haven, CT: Yale University Press.

Kirn, Paul (1952) *Einführung in die Geschichtswissenschaft*. (Samlung Göschen Band 270). Berlin: de Gruyter.

Kortteinen, Matti (1992) *Kunnian kenttä: Suomalainen palkkatyö kulttuurisena muotona* [The Field of Glory: Finnish Wage Labour as a Cultural Form]. Helsinki: Hanki ja Jää.

Kunelius, Risto (1994) Order and Interpretation: A Narrative Perspective on Journalistic Discourse. *European Journal of Communication* 9, 249–270.

Kytömäki, Juha (1991) 'They Probably Have Some Internal System Which Tells Them What's Good Television and What Isn't': Parental Control and Mediation of TV Viewing in Families with Schoolchildren. In Pertti Alasuutari, Karen Armstrong and Juha Kytömäki, *Reality and Fiction in Finnish TV Viewing*. Research Report 3. Helsinki: Oy Yleisradio Ab, 63–94.

Labov, William (1972) *Language in the Inner City: Studies in the Black English Vernacular*. Philadelphia: University of Pennsylvania Press.

Labov, William and Joshua Waletzky (1973) Narrative Analysis: Oral Versions of Personal Experience. In J. Helm (ed.), *Essays on the Verbal and Visual Arts*. San Francisco: American Ethnological Society.

Lejeune, Philippe (1989) *On Autobiography*. Minneapolis: University of Minnesota Press.

Lévi-Strauss, Claude (1963) *Totemism*. Boston: Beacon Press.

Lévi-Strauss, Claude (1966) *The Savage Mind*. Chicago: University of Chicago Press.

Lévi-Strauss, Claude (1969) *Structural Anthropology*. London: Allen Lane/Penguin Books.

Lévi-Strauss, Claude (1976) *Structural Anthropology, Volume 2*. Chicago: University of Chicago Press.

Lévi-Strauss, Claude (1978) *Myth and Meaning*. London: Routledge & Kegan Paul.

McIlwraith, Robert D. and John R. Schallow (1983) Adult Fantasy Life and Patterns of Media Use. *Journal of Communication* 33, 78–91.

Mäkelä, Jukka (1991) *Sunnuntaina sataa aina – Tutkimus tilastollisen ajattelun siirtymisestä osaksi empiiristä sosiaalitutkimusta* [It Always Rains on Sunday – a Study of How Statistical Thought Has Become Part of Empirical Social Research]. Publications in the Social Sciences B 13.Rovaniemi: University of Lapland.

Mäkelä, Klaus (1990) Kvalitatiivisen analyysin arviointiperusteet [The Assessment Criteria of Qualitative Analysis]. In Klaus Mäkelä (ed.), *Kvalitatiivisen aineiston analyysi ja tulkinta* [The Analysis and Interpretation of Qualitative Data]. Helsinki: Gaudeamus, 42–61.

Mäkelä, Klaus (1991) Sosiaalisen toiminnan järkevyys, norminmukaisuus ja ymmärrettävyys [Rationality, Conformity and Understandability of Social Action]. *Sosiologia* 28, 1–14.

Malinowski, Bronislaw (1948) *Magic, Science and Religion and Other Essays*. Boston, MA: Beacon Press.

Malinowski, Bronislaw (1961) *Argonauts of the Western Pacific*. New York: E.P. Dutton.

Mandler, Jean Matter (1984) *Stories, Scripts, and Scenes: Aspects of Schema Theory*. Hillsdale, NJ: Lawrence Erlbaum Associates.

Marcus, George E. and Michael M.J. Fischer (1986) *Anthropology as Cultural Critique: An Experimental Moment in the Human Sciences*. Chicago: University of Chicago Press.

Marsh, Peter, Elisabeth Rosser and Rom Harré (1978) *The Rules of Disorder*. London: Routledge.

Marshall, Mac (1979) *Weekend Warriors: Alcohol in a Micronesian Culture*. Mountain View, CA: Mayfield.

Mills, C. Wright (1973) *The Sociological Imagination*. Harmondsworth: Penguin Books.

Moerman, Michael (1988) *Talking Culture: Ethnography and Conversation Analysis*. Philadelphia: University of Pennsylvania Press.

Murray, Kevin (1989) The Construction of Identity in the Narratives of Romance and Comedy. In John Shotter, and Kenneth J. Gergen (eds), *Texts of Identity*. London: Sage, 176–205.

Mutran, Elizabeth and Donald C. Reitzes (1984) Intergenerational Support Activities and Well-Being among the Elderly: A Convergence of Exchange and Symbolic Interaction Perspectives. *American Sociological Review* 49, 117–130.

Nelson, John, Allan Megill and Donald D. McCloskey (1987) *The Rhetoric of the Human Sciences: Language and Argument in Scholarship and Public Affairs*. Madison, WI: University of Wisconsin Press.

Nofsinger, Robert E. (1991) *Everyday Conversation*. Newbury Park, CA: Sage.

Omi, Michael and Howard Winant (1986) *Racial Formation in the United States from the 1960s to the 1980s*. New York: Routledge.

Ottomeyer, Klaus (1977) *Ökonomische Zwänge und menschliche Beziehungen: Soziales Verhalten im Kapitalismus*. Reinbek bei Hamburg: Rowohlt.

Parsons, Talcott (1967) *The Structure of Social Action*. New York: Free Press.

Peräkylä, Anssi (1989) Appealing to the 'Experience' of the Patient in the Care of the Dying. *Sociology of Health and Illness* 11 (2), 117–134.

Peräkylä, Anssi (1990) *Kuoleman monet kasvot* [The Many Faces of Death]. Tampere: Vastapaino.

Peräkylä, Anssi (1991) Hope Work in the Care of Seriously Ill Patients. *Qualitative Health Research* 1, 407–433.

Peräkylä, Anssi (forthcoming) *AIDS Counselling*. Cambridge: Cambridge University Press.

Perelman, Chaim (1982) *The Realm of Rhetoric*. Notre Dame, IN: University of Notre Dame Press.

Perelman, Chaim and Lucie Olbrechts-Tyteca (1971) *The New Rhetoric: A Treatise on Argumentation*. Notre Dame, IN: University of Notre Dame Press.

Pike, Kenneth Lee (1954) *Language in Relation to a Unified Theory of the Structure of Human Behavior*. Preliminary edn. Glendale, CA: Summer Institute of Linguistics.

Potter, Jonathan and Margaret Wetherell (1987) *Discourse and Social Psychology: Beyond Attitudes and Behaviour*. London: Sage.

Prince, Gerald (1973) *A Grammar of Stories*. The Hague: Mouton.

Propp, Vladimir (1975) *Morphology of the Folktale*. Austin, TX: University of Texas Press.

Rabinow, Paul (1977) *Reflections on Fieldwork in Morocco*. Berkeley, CA: University of California Press.

Radway, Janice A. (1984) *Reading the Romance: Women, Patriarchy, and Popular Literature*. Chapel Hill, NC: University of North Carolina Press.

Ragin, Charles C. (1989) *The Comparative Method: Moving Beyond Qualitative and Quantitative Strategies*. Berkeley, CA: University of California Press.

Reason, Peter and John Rowan (eds) (1981) *Human Inquiry: A Sourcebook of New Paradigm Research*. Chichester: John Wiley.

Renvall, Pentti (1965) *Nykyajan historiantutkimus* [Modern Historical Research]. Helsinki: WSOY.

Roberts, Fredric Marc (1982) Under the North Star: Notions of Self and Community in a Finnish Village. PhD dissertation, City University of New York.

Ronkainen, Suvi (1989) Nainen ja nainen – haastattelun rajat ja mahdollisuudet [Woman and Woman – the Limits and Possibilities of the Interview]. *Sosiaalipolitiikka: Sosiaalipoliittisen yhdistyksen vuosikirja* 14, 65–77.

Roos, J.P. (1978) Piirteitä elämäntavan tutkimisesta [Aspects of Studying Way of Life]. *Sosiologia* 15, 75–81.

Roos, J.P. (1980) Elämisen laatu ja elämäntapa 1970-luvulla [The Quality and Way of Life in the 1970s]. *Sosiaalinen aikakauskirja* 17, 17–22.

Roos, J.P. (1985) Life Stories of Social Changes: Four Generations in Finland. *International Journal of Oral History* 6, 179–190.

Rose, Gerry (1982) *Deciphering Sociological Research*. London: Macmillan.

Rosenberg, Morris (1968) *The Logic of Survey Analysis*. New York: Basic Books.

Rothman, David J. (1971) *The Discovery of the Asylum: Social Order and Disorder in the New Republic*. Boston, MA: Little, Brown.

Runyan, William McKinley (1984) *Life Histories and Psychobiography: Explorations in Theory and Method*. New York: Oxford University Press.

Rüsen, Jörn (1986) *Rekonstruktion der Vergangenheit. Grundzüge einer Historik II: Die Prinzipien der historischen Forschung*. Göttingen: Vandenhoeck & Ruprecht.

Sacks, Harvey (1992a) *Lectures on Conversation, Vol. I*, Oxford: Blackwell.

Sacks, Harvey (1992b) *Lectures on Conversation, Vol. II*. Oxford: Blackwell.

Sahlins, Marshall (1976) *Culture and Practical Reason*. Chicago: University of Chicago Press.

References 199

Saussure, Ferdinand de (1966) *Course in General Linguistics*. New York: McGraw-Hill.
Schegloff, Emanuel A. (1992) Introduction. In Harvey Sacks, *Lectures on Conversation, Vol. I*: Oxford: Blackwell, pp. ix–lxii.
Searle, John R. (1976) The Classification of Illocutionary Acts. *Language in Society* 5, 1–24.
Silverman, David (1985) *Qualitative Methodology and Sociology: Describing the Social World*. Aldershot: Gower.
Silverman, David (1993) *Interpreting Qualitative Data: Methods for Analyzing Talk, Text and Interaction*. London: Sage.
Silverman, David and Anssi Peräkylä (1990) AIDS Counselling: The Interactional Organisation of Talk about 'Delicate' Issues. *Sociology of Health and Illness* 12, 293–318.
Silvo, Ismo (1988) *Valta, kenttä ja kertomus: Televisiopolitiikan tulkinnat* [Power, Field and Narratives: Interpretations in Finnish Television Politics]. Research and Development Publications 2. Helsinki: YLE.
Simons, Herbert W. (ed.) (1990) *The Rhetorical Turn: Invention and Persuasion in the Conduct of Inquiry*. Chicago: University of Chicago Press.
Simpura, Jussi (1987) About the Drinking Habits Surveys and Their History. In Jussi Simpura (ed.), *Finnish Drinking Habits: Results from Interview Surveys Held in 1968, 1976 and 1984*. Helsinki: Alkoholitutkimussäätiö, 11–16.
Smith, Dorothy (1974) Women's Perspective as a Radical Critique of Sociology. *Sociological Inquiry* 44, 7–13.
Smith, Dorothy (1977) Some Implications of a Sociology for Women. In Nona Glazer and Helen Waehrer (eds), *Women in a Man-Made World: A Socioeconomic Handbook*, 2nd edn. Chicago: Rand McNally.
Sociology Writing Group (1994) *A Guide to Writing Sociology Papers*. 3rd edn. New York: St Martin's Press.
Stanley, Liz and Sue Wise (1983) *Breaking Out: Feminist Consciousness and Feminist Research*. London: Routledge.
Stewart, John O. (1989) *Drinkers, Drummers, and Decent Folk: Ethnographic Narratives of Village Trinidad*. New York: State University of New York Press.
Strauss, Anselm L. (1987) *Qualitative Analysis for Social Scientists*. Cambridge: Cambridge University Press.
Strauss, Anselm L. (1990) *Basics of Qualitative Research: Grounded Theory Procedures and Techniques*. Newbury Park, CA: Sage.
Sulkunen, Pekka, Pertti Alasuutari, Ritva Nätkin and Merja Kinnunen (1985) *Lähiöravintola* [The Local Tavern]. Helsinki: Otava.
Summa, Hilkka (1989) Hallinnon retoriikka ja politiikkojen synty [The Rhetoric of Administration and the Birth of Politics]. *Politiikka* 31, 159–168.
Summa, Hilkka (1992) The Rhetoric of Efficiency: Applied Social Science as Depoliticization. In Richard Harvey Brown (ed.), *Writing the Social Text: Poetics and Politics in Social Science Discourse*. New York: Aldine de Gruyter, 135–154.
Thompson, E.P. (1968) *The Making of the English Working Class*. Harmondsworth: Penguin Books.
Turner, Bryan S. (1986) Personhood and Citizenship. *Theory, Culture and Society* 3, 1–16.
Vilkko, Anni (1988) Eletty elämä, kerrottu elämä, tarinoitunut elämä – omaelämäkerta ja yhteisymmärrrys [Lived Life, Told Life, Narrated Life – Biography and Mutual Understanding]. *Sosiologia* 25, 81–90.
Webb, Eugene J. Donald T. Campbell, Richard D. Schwartz and Lee Sechrest (1966) *Unobtrusive Measures: Nonreactive Research in the Social Sciences*. Chicago: Rand McNally.
Weber, Max (1978a) *Economy and Society, Vol. 1*, Berkeley, CA: University of California Press.
Weber, Max (1978b) *Economy and Society, Vol. 2*. Berkeley, CA: University of California Press.
Westkott, Marcia (1979) Feminist Criticism of the Social Sciences. *Harvard Educational Review* 49(4), 422–30.

White, Hayden (1975) *Metahistory: The Historical Imagination in Nineteenth-Century Europe*. Baltimore. MD: Johns Hopkins University Press.

White, Hayden (1987) *Tropics of Discourse: Essays in Cultural Criticism*. Baltimore, MD: Johns Hopkins University Press.

Williams, Raymond (1961a) *Culture and Society, 1780–1950*. Harmondsworth: Penguin Books.

Williams, Raymond (1961b) *The Long Revolution*. Harmondsworth: Penguin Books.

Willis, Paul (1977) *Learning to Labour: How Working Class Kids Get Working Class Jobs*. Aldershot: Gower.

Willis, Paul (1978) *Profane Culture*. London: Routledge & Kegan Paul.

Willner-Rönnholm, Margareta (1990) Det 'andra' könet i forskningsprosessen: Forskaren som subjekt och objekt [The 'Other' Gender in the Research Process: Researcher as Subject and Object]. *Naistutkimus Kvinnoforskning* 3, 41–56.

Winch, Peter (1971) *The Idea of a Social Science and Its Relation to Philosophy*. London: Routledge & Kegan Paul.

Wright, Will (1975) *Sixguns and Society: A Structural Study of the Western*. Berkeley, CA: University of California Press.

Index